GILDING THE LILY

AMY STEWART is the author of *The Earth Moved: On the Remarkable Achievements of Earthworms* and *From the Ground Up: The Story of a First Garden*. She lives in California, where she writes for the *New York Times*, the *San Francisco Chronicle*, *Organic Gardening* and others. www.amystewart.com

From the US reviews:

"Engaging and scrupulously reported."

New York Times Book Review

"Eye opening . . . Stewart's journey takes us down many paths, all connected by her own curiosity and highly readable prose . . . [*Gilding the Lily*] helps us grasp our modern world."

Washington Post Book World

"A quirky but entertaining book . . . [Stewart] is the good-natured outsider—occasionally dishing the dirt but usually celebrating the beautiful things that grow in it." *Wall Street Journal*

"The facts are surprising and intriguing. But it is the way nature writer Stewart packages them that makes [*Gilding the Lily*] that rare nonfiction book that keeps you turning pages."

Scientific American

"[A] fascinating examination of the cut-flower industry."

Chicago Tribune

"[Stewart] peeks into many of the world's greenhouses and flower markets with a contagious enthusiasm for discovery."

Miami Herald

"A concise, engaging, sometimes humorous exposé of the world-wide multibillion-dollar cut flower industry."

E/The Environmental Magazine

"This is not your mother's flower garden . . . Stewart is an acute observer and intelligent writer, and [*Gilding the Lily*] is a compelling read." *San Francisco Chronicle*

"Revelatory . . . Informative at every level." *Boston Globe*

"Stewart prompts shoppers to think hard about where their stems come from and how they got to market. The book may just get readers to see bouquets in a whole new light."

Los Angeles Times

"Amy Stewart is, as she puts it, 'a gardener and passionate consumer of flowers.' Add 'fine writer' to that list, too. All three — her gardening knowledge, her passion, and her way with words — come through in [*Gilding the Lily*]." *Richmond Times-Dispatch*

"A glorious little book, informative but fun to read, personal and environmentally conscious but clear-eyed." *Bookslut*

"Fascinating . . . Stewart brings her infectious curiosity to bear on the ins and outs of this $40 billion dollar global industry."

American Gardener

Gilding the Lily

Inside the Cut Flower Industry

AMY STEWART

Portobello
BOOKS

Published by Portobello Books Ltd 2009

Portobello Books Ltd
Twelve Addison Avenue
Holland Park
London
W11 4QR

First published as *Flower Confidential: The Good, the Bad and the Beautiful* in
the United States by Algonquin Books of Chapel Hill in 2007

The author wishes to thank the National Endowment for the Arts for
its generous support.

A CIP catalogue record is available from the British Library

9 8 7 6 5 4 3 2 1

ISBN 978 1 84627 174 8

www.portobellobooks.com

Text designed by Tracy Baldwin
Illustrations by Emma Skurnick

Printed in the UK by CPI William Clowes Beccles NR34 7TL

To PSB

Contents

INTRODUCTION

What's the first thing a person does when you hand them flowers? They smell them. But walk through a flower market today and just try to catch the fragrance of rose or lily. There's nothing there. Modern flowers have all been bred for the industry, selected for color and size, and most of all for durability. One of the things that flowers lose in that trade-off is scent.

Even without the fragrance, a visit to a modern commercial flower market is extraordinary. Hundreds of snapdragons wheel past on a metal hand cart. Thousands of carnations sit in buckets. Roses are bunched just the way they left the farm, with each bud wrapped in a little piece of tissue. There are gardenia corsages. Artificially dyed chrysanthemums. Orchids from Thailand. Tulips from Holland. Lilies from California. Ginger blossoms from Hawaii. Silk magnolias. Dried larkspur. Wreaths, houseplants, vases, baskets, ribbons, greens. It's all here. It's overpowering and bright and gorgeous.

You might not find a flower with a fragrance, but you will find an extraordinary mixture of Wall Street and the garden of Eden. This is the flower market.

I SET OUT to go behind the scenes in the global flower market because I was fascinated with the idea that flowers had a life before they arrived in the flower shop. How did they get from breeder to grower to broker to florist? My curiosity took me from California to Holland, to New York, to Miami, and to Ecuador. I found many parallels between specialty growers in the United States and in Great Britain, and I realized that the challenges and controversy surrounding growers in Latin America were very similar to those in Africa.

What amazed me most about this extraordinarily complex worldwide industry is this: they do it all for something as perishable and ephemeral as a flower. Airplanes fly in from Kenya and trucks drive from Holland and acres of greenhouses get built and billions of dollars change hands. All that for the alstroemerias you pick up at the grocery store as an afterthought. All that for the delphiniums you send to the hospital to cheer up your sister. All that for the violets on a grave, the carnation in your buttonhole.

There's an inherent contradiction in offering flowers up for sale, something I couldn't quite put my finger on, and I hoped that getting close to the action would help explain it. Finally, I realized what it was: flowers are like nothing else that we buy. They don't play by the same rules. For one thing, they are basically free. You can pick a flower by the side of the road. You can grow one in your garden for next to nothing. A flower is as perishable as a piece of fruit, but less practical—you can't eat it, after all. Put a rose in a vase and it'll be dead within a week. That's all you get for your money. In spite of this, the cut flower market is a forty-billion-dollar business worldwide. Breeders pour big money into building a better flower: one that lasts longer in the vase, one that doesn't drop petals or shed pollen, one that meets the peculiar demands of autumn brides or supermarket shoppers.

The floral trade—the business end of our relationship with cut flowers—has ancient origins. Consider this letter:

Roses are not yet in full bloom here—in fact they are scarce —and from all the nurseries and all the garland-weavers we could just barely get together the thousand that we sent you . . . even with picking the ones that ought not to have been picked till tomorrow. We had all the narcissi you wanted, so instead of the two thousand you asked for we sent four thousand.

This ordinary bit of business correspondence could have been written last week, but in fact it was scribbled on papyrus in Roman Egypt and dates to shortly before the birth of Christ. Imagine: flowers were already grown in fields, ordered in bulk, and shipped by the thousands in hopes that they would arrive in time for a party or a holiday. The most modern rose grower can sympathize with the problem of having to pick roses before they are quite ready. This anonymous, ancient tradesman probably worried, just as rose growers do today, that blossoms picked at this stage would never open in the vase and would leave his customers unsatisfied.

The Romans developed a sophisticated flower trade, complete with all the taxation, accounting, and logistical issues that accompany any commercial enterprise. They knew how to force flowers to bloom early by pumping steam or hot water past them. They attempted greenhouses with thin walls of mica and used wheeled carts to move plants in and out of the sun. And as soon as these artificial means of cultivating flowers developed, along came their critics, who saw the floral trade as a bit unnatural, given the way it used technology to stay out of step with the seasons. It makes me uncomfortable to see sunflowers for sale at Christmas, so far from their summer season, and I am not alone. The Roman playwright and philosopher Lucius Annaeus Seneca wrote this in the first century AD: "Do not men live contrary to Nature who crave roses in winter or seek to raise a spring flower like a lily by means of hot-water heaters and artificial changes of temperature?"

The cut flower trade is all about this struggle between what is natural and unspoiled and what is mass produced and commercial. We like being able to buy a summer flower in February—in fact, we've built a holiday around it—but we also distrust fakery. The Victorian writer Charles Manby Smith voiced a complaint in 1853 that florists still hear today. The flowers he bought from a traveling florist in London drooped within a day or two of purchase, owing perhaps to "an overdose of stimulating fluid." That's the trouble with this business: the product is unpredictable, and the customers are fickle. Although the demand for flowers in London was on the increase, Smith warned that "the commerce in blossoming flowers is one of the most uncertain and dangerous speculations in which the small street-traders of London can engage."

So are we being tricked when a scientist engineers a lily that doesn't shed pollen or when a grower forces tulips to bloom in December? Does it matter that a dewy-fresh bouquet of roses traveled halfway around the world and lived without water for several days before it arrived at the supermarket? If the mixed bouquet of red roses and pink chrysanthemums designed by a national wire service at Valentine's Day is indistinguishable from thousands of others delivered that same day all across the country, does that make the message it carries any less significant?

Yes and no. There's no doubt that flowers underwent a complete makeover in the twentieth century. New breeding techniques, advanced greenhouse technology, and global transportation systems saw to that. Thanks to those advances, there are some fantastic flowers on the market, all year long, for a remarkably cheap price. But modern flowers have lost something, too. They're tamer, better behaved, less fickle, and less seasonal. Many have lost their scent, and I wondered if they were also losing their identity, their power, or their passion. We want a flower to be perfect, but we also want it to be unique, extraordinary. We want it to be a revelation, a one-of-a-kind experience. Such a thing gets harder to find every year.

FLORISTS IN THE US look with envy at the United Kingdom, where per-capita consumption is double that of the Americans. Most small shops in the UK buy from brokers or importers who participate in the giant Dutch flower auctions, bringing the most extraordinary flowers from around the world straight to their loading docks. Even supermarket flowers are rumored to be better in the UK: the quality is higher, and sell-by dates, which are almost never seen in the United States, ensure that they are fresher.

In the UK, the debate over the environmental and socioeconomic impact of imported food had already spilled over into flowers. While people in the United States were only beginning to talk about "food miles," flower lovers in England were already debating "flower miles." Does it make more sense to import roses from Kenya or to buy them from an artificially heated and lit Dutch greenhouse and truck them to market? Should one only buy roses when they are available from the English countryside, grown in the fields, even if that means forsaking them at Valentine's Day?

There are no easy answers to these questions. I have spoken to farmers in Kenya and in Latin America who are determined to provide good jobs and to farm in an environmentally sound manner. From their perspective, the path out of poverty must involve selling their goods to wealthier nations where the market is stronger. On the other hand, flower farmers like Jane Lindsey in Scotland and Heather Gorringe in Herefordshire make a strong case for buying fresh, seasonal flowers from local farmers.

Regardless, the market for flowers in the United Kingdom is enormous: in all, imported flowers are a $1.1 billion business in the UK. Holland ships flowers worth $876m to the UK each year, with Kenya supplying about $104m and Colombia in third place with $71m. In terms of per-capita flower consumption, Great Britain ranks fifth in the world, spending 47 euros per person on cut flowers each year.

THE IDEA OF all this floral commerce, rather than crushing my passion for flowers, only fueled it. Flowers are created in laboratories, bred in test tubes, grown in factories, harvested by machines, packed into boxes, sold at auctions, and then flown across oceans and continents. Imagine sixty acres of greenhouses in one place. Nineteen million flowers on the auction floor and people buying, with a wave of the hand, more roses than most of us will purchase in a lifetime. Forty billion dollars changing hands each year, all in the name of flowers. The idea was intoxicating.

Before long, it became clear to me that this global flower traffic was not without consequence. A hundred years ago, for example, almost all of the cut flowers sold in the United States were also grown here; now roughly three-fourths of our flowers are imports, mostly coming from Latin America. The flowers themselves have been forced to change in response. They are now bred more for their suitability as freight than for any of their more refined qualities — delicacy, grace, and fragrance. They may have lost their scent, but they've gained a longer vase life. They've lost their individuality but have gained the ability to travel all the way from Ecuador or Holland to sit on your hall table in the middle of December.

This global shift also affects people, like the growers in California who have left their family farms and gone into the import business or the Main Street florist who sells more cheap cash-and-carry bouquets than artfully designed arrangements. And every year around Valentine's Day, some newspaper is likely to run what I've come to call the "blood and roses" story — the one that warns that behind every Latin American or African rose is an exploited worker and a poisoned river. There's some truth to that story. In Ecuador I watched women dip long-stemmed roses, blossom first, into barrels of fungicide—a spectacle that put me off roses for months.

IT MIGHT BE THAT it's unromantic to call a flower a commodity or a manufactured product, but flowers are all of these things at once. They are ephemeral, emotional, and impractical, but we Americans buy about four billion of them a year. We buy more flowers than we do Big Macs. Flowers are big business. It just happens to be a gorgeous, bewitching, bewildering business.

It would be impossible to tell the story of every flower in every market around the world, but here is a cast of characters who represent, in some way, this quest for perfection: John Mason and his blue rose. Leslie Woodriff and his 'Star Gazer' lily. Lane DeVries, owner of the largest cut flower farm in the United States. Roberto Nevado, a socially conscious rose grower in Ecuador. I've come to realize that they all want the same thing: to produce the ideal flower, the one you can't do without.

I'm not a florist or a hybridizer or a grower. I'm a gardener and a passionate consumer of flowers. The more time I spent around the flower industry, the more I wondered if we were expecting too much from them. Who are we to take a symbol of perfection, purity, and love and try to improve upon it, to spiff it up for the marketplace?

In the fourth act of Shakespeare's *King John,* the Earl of Salisbury counsels the king against a second coronation, calling it "wasteful and ridiculous excess":

To gild refined gold, to paint the lily,
To throw a perfume on the violet

For the last two hundred years, we have abbreviated these words and used the phrase "gild the lily" to describe unnecessary embellishment. To spray glitter or perfume on a flower may seem excessive, but the industry does both of those things. They also artificially extend their lives, engineer brighter colors, and tinker with scent, all in an effort to give us what we want.

Where have our desires led us? Are we, in fact, gilding the lily?

PART **I** *Breeding*

CHAPTER I

The Birds, the Bees, and a Camel Hair Brush

A mong lily breeders, Leslie Woodriff is a horticultural legend, but in my hometown people remember him as the eccentric old guy in the broken-down greenhouse along the highway. I've only seen photographs of him — he died in 1997 — but I think "eccentric" is a fair description. He had a shock of stiff white hair that stood up in every direction, a strong, square face, and wildly uneven teeth that he never tried to hide. In every picture he is smiling broadly, and he is always surrounded by his lilies.

In 1988, a Dutch grower named Piet Koopman came to visit Woodriff and get to know the man who bred the famous 'Star Gazer' lily. If he expected a genteel, tweedy, professorial fellow with a country home and a sparkling conservatory full of wonders, he was in for a rude shock. Woodriff was broke, his health was failing, and his house seemed to be on the verge of collapse. He was never known for keeping a particularly tidy greenhouse, and Koopman was astonished to see his world-class collection of lilies stored haphazardly in a musty, insect-ridden environment. Woodriff appeared unconcerned and was interested in talking with Koopman only about the one subject that held his interest: lily breeding. He had a photographic memory for lilies and knew each species and cultivar by heart. He seemed to dream of a lily before he bred it, grasping in some intuitive way those traits that could be combined to create the lily that lived in his imagination. But Koopman was so distracted by what he saw that he found it hard to concentrate on the conversation.

"I could not believe that this man, who had done so much for the lily industry, was living like this," Koopman told me. "I was shocked about his situation. I had my video camera with me, but I was too embarrassed to even make a video. The Dutch growers made so much money from 'Star Gazer', and I could not believe that he had so little." Koopman didn't stay long. He went back to Holland, surprised and confused, trying to decide if publicizing the famous breeder's plight would help Woodriff or humiliate him.

THIS IS WHERE the quest for the perfect flower begins— in the greenhouse or laboratory of a breeder like Leslie Woodriff who has a vision for a flower that everyone will want. A flower like that doesn't happen by itself. It takes a hybridizer to turn an ordinary garden bloom into the most sought-after designer flower of the season. Woodriff's 'Star Gazer' lily is one of the most remarkable such flowers to come along in a century. Its story has all the elements of the grand sweeping history of flower breeding: risks taken, flowers prized and sought after, fortunes won and lost. Because it came along when it did, the 'Star Gazer' lily stands at a crossroads between old-fashioned plant breeders and modern hybridizers, between small-time florists and global corporations.

What Leslie Woodriff did to his lilies is no different from what a bee or a butterfly would do: he brushed pollen from the stamen of one flower onto the stigma of another. There was no microscope, no gene splicing, not even a sterile environment. Woodriff, and breeders like him, interfered with the sexual activities of plants for one reason: a passion for flowers. He worked tirelessly to create new breeds of lilies because he was wildly in love with the flower and emboldened to push it to its limits, attempting to cross species that everyone else had declared incompatible. He hoped to make a living by breeding and selling lilies, but he was never a businessman. Leslie Woodriff was simply unable to do anything besides breed flowers, and in some ways it didn't matter whether he got paid for it or not.

Today, most hybridizers in the cut flower industry are geneticists working in laboratories, and they may or may not have any interest in flowers at all. A scientist who works for Suntory, a Japanese company that sells liquor as well as cut flowers, told me, "My last assignment was developing yeast for beer. Now it's roses. Under the microscope, it's really all the same to me." I can only imagine what Woodriff would say in response to that. A rose is not a fungus. A lily is not a carrot. Of course two living things are not the same, under a microscope or anywhere else.

LILIES ARE EASY to breed because they are so anatomically simple. From just one lily, you can learn almost everything you need to know about how flowers are made. Its anatomy is right there, out in the open — there's no need to go hunting around between crumpled petals to find a stamen or a stigma the way you might with a rose. Lilies, which occupy the same taxonomic family as tulips and fritillaries, rise on a single, usually leafless, stalk from a soft, fleshy bulb. The bulb produces scales, often in a concentric, spiral pattern originating from the base, which can be teased away to produce new plants. (Breeders call this method of propagation "scaling a lily.")

The flowers themselves, of which there can be one, a half-dozen, or several dozen, connect to the main stem by means of a short stalk called a pedicle. All lilies have six petals, but to be entirely accurate, the three outermost petals are called sepals — the outer coverings that fold back to reveal the flower inside. (On many other flowers, the sepals are not so similar to the petals themselves. Picture the small green sepals at the base of a rose, for instance.) Some lilies sport several blossoms arranged in a series along the stalk—this is called a raceme structure—and others burst out together from a single point on the tip of the stalk, which is called an umbel structure. (Queen Anne's lace is a good example of an umbel—the tiny white blossoms all emerge from the end of the stalk and are connected to it by thin pedicles.) Sometimes a lily's petals curl back and almost touch behind the flower—these are called turkscap lilies—and others open into a gentle saucer shape. Some, including the ubiquitous Easter lily, form a trumpet or funnel shape.

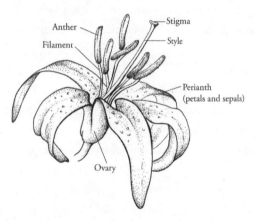

Regardless of the precise shape of the flowers they are all quite similar inside. All lilies have six stamens arranged in a hexagon shape around the center. Each stamen consists of a filament—a thin stalk—and an anther—the yellow or reddish head that discharges pollen. From the center of the flower emerges one single, unique structure called the pistil, which is the female part of the anatomy that includes the stigma, the style, and the ovary. The stigma is the sweet sticky end of the female anatomy that lures butterflies and moths, who slide their long, narrow tongues inside to sip nectar. In the process, they often brush against the anthers and carry pollen from one lily to another. If the pollen is just the right shape and size, it will travel down the style to the ovary, where three hundred to five hundred eggs await fertilization. The stigma will accept the pollen of many different kinds of lilies, so that one seed capsule can produce offspring from any number of fathers. But if for some reason the pollen isn't compatible with the egg, it will not be fertilized. Split a lily's seed capsule open and shake the seeds onto a light table: the fertilized seeds will stand out because the embryo will show up as a dark, curved center inside the seed.

To make a cross, a lily breeder considers more than color and scent. Each parent plant brings with it a set of characteristics that include the shape of the bulb; the number and size of leaves; the color of the pollen; the presence of speckles near the center of the flower; the size and shape of the blossom; susceptibility to frost, dampness, and drought; disease resistance; and hundreds of other characteristics. To get the best results, a breeder will often attempt a reciprocal cross, meaning that if the pollen from the first plant fertilized the second, then pollen from the second plant should also be able to fertilize the first. Sometimes these reciprocal crosses can produce hardier, more fertile offspring, but this is not the only tool lily breeders have available to them: since 1935, it's been known that colchicine, an alkaloid derived from autumn crocus, can be applied to seeds or seedlings to double the number of chromosomes from twenty-four to forty-eight. These superlilies, called tetraploids, are usually stronger and sturdier. While this kind of genetic tinkering sounds pretty technical, many tetraploid lilies have been produced by amateur breeders who dropped crocus bulbs into a blender and made a crude colchicine solution to use in the greenhouse.

There are about a hundred species of lilies and countless crosses have been made from those. The species are broadly grouped into eight categories, and the most popular among those for the cut flower industry are the trumpet lilies, the Asiatic hybrids, and the Oriental hybrids. Oriental lilies are the largest, most flamboyant, and most fragrant of their genus, but they weren't used much in the cut flower trade because the downward-facing flowers had a tendency to snap off the stem during harvesting and packing. They were difficult to work into bouquets as well: in a mixed bunch of upward-facing flowers like roses, daisies, and carnations, the droopy Orientals looked out of place. Asiatics are popular for their bright, bold colors, but they are also smaller and unscented. There are upward-facing Asiatics, including 'Enchantment', which have been on the market since the 1940s. Breeders thought that if only someone could take the upward habit of the Asiatics and work it into the big, bold, fragrant Orientals, it could revolutionize the cut flower trade in lilies. No one could figure out how to do it until Leslie Woodriff, through some combination of idiosyncrasy and instinct, hit upon the right cross.

WOODRIFF WAS PART of the last generation of true, old-fashioned flower breeders. People have enjoyed cut flowers for thousands of years, and over the last few centuries men like Woodriff have made it possible to breed a flower for commercial purposes — to make a flower do what the breeder wants it to do. In the mid-1600s, a physician in England named Nehemiah Grew was the first to suggest that although some of the "outward elegancies of plants" (i.e., the flower itself) might be for man's delight, the "inward ones, which are as precise and varied as the outward," must be for the benefit of the plants, not their admirers. He believed that petals and scents were created by God to delight humans, but he was one of the first to realize that inside the flower lay structures that might enable them to reproduce.

It wasn't until the late 1600s that botanists began to speculate that pollen might be the equivalent of sperm, but even that notion had its detractors, including a scientist in the early eighteenth century named Johann Siegesbeck who believed that "sex in flowers was not only scientifically unconvincing but morally revolting as well." But horticulturalists would not be deterred, and in the early 1760s Joseph Koelreuter, a German botanist, created what may have been the first hybrid by crossing two species of tobacco.

Gradually, during the 1700s and 1800s, botanists came to understand the role of insects in the pollination of flowers, but it was Charles Darwin's work with orchids that proved that plants may adapt themselves to their pollinators. This was an important discovery that shaped much of what we know about flower genetics. Consider the shape of a snapdragon, with its cup-shaped blossom designed to snap open when a bee enters, or the "bee lines" leading to the center of an alstroemeria, or the bull's-eye pattern of contrasting color in the center of a hibiscus. Now we know that some flowers have evolved to change colors after they've been successfully pollinated, often shifting to a hue that their pollinator can't see. (Bees, for instance, can't see red, so a flower like red-hot poker will change from yellow to red after it's been pollinated so the bee will move on.) This may or may not be a desirable feature to a grower who wants to be able to count on flowers staying a stable color at harvest time.

What does it mean, then, when we take what is basically a bouquet of sexual organs and expect them to stop behaving like sexual organs? We require flowers to live a long time after they've been cut; we want them to hold on to their pollen or not produce it at all; and we prefer them to have a scent that is more pleasing to us than it might be to a bee or a hummingbird. The supreme irony of cut flower breeding lies in the fact that we use all the science and technology available to us to make a flower stop acting like a flower. But no one can change the fact that a flower exists for just one purpose: to reproduce and die. Leslie Woodriff understood that, and he saw the magic in it.

WOODRIFF HAD BEEN breeding lilies for decades before he came to Humboldt County under the terms of a business arrangement he made with a grower named Ted Kirsch, who was the first owner of what is now Sun Valley Floral Farms. Several years after Kirsch died, I met his daughter, Laura Dun. She and her husband, David, along with her mother, Eloise, have told me the story of Kirsch and Woodriff in bits and pieces over the years. (Kirsch died in 1996, just before Woodriff.) David remembers driving to Brookings, Oregon, in the early seventies with his future father-in-law. "I guess I was invited in my capacity as the future family lawyer." He was just starting law school at the time. "Ted had this idea that he could make a deal with Leslie to buy his lilies and give the Woodriffs a job on the farm."

Ted Kirsch got his start growing daffodil bulbs in his backyard in Oregon around 1942. He was the high school agriculture teacher; the bulbs supplied a little extra income and gave the students something to do. Pretty soon he'd obtained some financial backing and expanded his operation, making the flower farm a full-time family enterprise. He eventually bought land in Arcata, California, and founded Sun Valley. By the time he and David took their drive up the coast, he was farming in Arcata full time.

Kirsch had known Leslie Woodriff for years. Everybody in the lily business knew him as a kind of crazy lily breeder who came up with wild hybrids that nobody thought were possible. "But the thing is," David told me, "the guy had no business sense. He never did make a dime off his lilies. He lived on this rundown farm with his wife, Ruth, and his daughter Winkey. Kirsch heard that he'd defaulted on a loan from the Small Business Administration and was about to lose his farm.

"So we showed up at the Woodriffs' place, and it was immediately clear to me that this is not going to work. Their place was falling down, everything was a mess—it just looked like a real can of worms to me. But Ted said, 'The lilies are wonderful. If someone could just harness their creativity and take care of the business side, this could really work.'"

David tried to talk him out of doing the deal, but there was no way to change his mind. Kirsch and Woodriff worked out an agreement, and soon the Woodriffs were on their way to Arcata. There's some confusion over how Woodriff's hybrid lily 'Star Gazer' came to be at Sun Valley—everybody I talked to had a different version of this story, each one more like a legend or a fairy tale than the last—but David and Laura remember it this way: When the Woodriffs arrived in Arcata, they brought with them Woodriff's hybridized lilies. Kirsch planted a field of these hybrids—they mostly weren't labeled, so he really had no idea what he'd bought or what they'd look like when they bloomed—but one day he walked out into the field and stood among all those downward-facing lilies, and there was one red Oriental looking straight up at the sky. So he called it 'Star Gazer'. And that changed the lily business forever.

LESLIE WOODRIFF'S SON George and his daughter Betty remember their father as a plainspoken, hardworking man who never wavered in his dedication to his lilies. He was a horticultural genius, they told me, who was ahead of his time. I know they'd shudder if they heard people describe their father or his greenhouse as "a mess," and I can't blame them—when I look at photographs of Woodriff, I see a tough but cheerful man who made his living with his hands. There doesn't seem to be anything particularly messy or crazy about him. Many of his colleagues in the world of lily breeding believed that Woodriff created such extraordinary hybrids mostly because he was fearless. Not crazy, exactly, just not bound by the rules that most lily breeders follow. He'd cross anything, even two lily species that were supposed to be incompatible. He was not methodical, he was not consistent, he was not precise or even sanitary. A grower who worked for him in the early 1980s said, "Part of the reason Leslie's lilies are so hardy and disease resistant is that they had to survive in his greenhouse. I've never seen such a mess. Viruses, bugs, flats of seedlings just piled on top of each other and crowded under benches where they didn't get any light or water—really, it was a situation where only the strong survived."

His lilies may have been tough, but Leslie Woodriff was a man in search of beauty and poetry. George told me that he always carried the image of the perfect lily in his head. He dreamed of a black lily and a blue lily. He was in search of a lily that broke all the rules, one that crossed all the boundaries that had previously held the genus back. An agricultural inspector once told Woodriff that he should not bother with brightly colored lilies because when people thought of lilies, they would always think of the white Easter lily, which was a sign of purity. Woodriff told him that his lilies were for people who were less than pure.

He called radio talk shows and interrupted debates over Vietnam or Watergate to talk about lily breeding. He even sent a photo of a new variety to Jimmy Carter in 1979, along with a letter that explained the bulb's parentage, as if Carter had time—forty-four days into the Iran hostage crisis—to catch up on new developments in lily breeding. "This is the best pot type we have had from near a million seedlings," he told the president, "combining Rubellum, the tiny pink trumpet mountain lily of Japan that blooms in early May, the pink reflex rubrum that flowers in Sept., and the huge bowl-shaped auratum that flowers in early August, in one plant showing intermediate shape, color of rubrum only brighter, size of auratum, and some of the shortness and earliness of rubellum." He asked Carter to help him fund his research and closed his letter with, "Let's make this world a more beautiful place. We are trying." He may have received a form letter from the White House, but the president himself never wrote back.

Woodriff's friends told me that he didn't take many notes about his crosses, and he didn't much care about a lily's parentage, although his letter to Carter shows that he certainly had some idea of where he was going with a cross. It may also be that they just failed to understand his system: his son George remembers him placing a tag on every cross but said that the codes he used to mark the lilies were impossible for anyone else to follow. Most would agree, however, that once Woodriff made a cross, he wasn't all that interested in growing out the new hybrid in enough quantity to sell. As one breeder after another explained to me, what he loved was the process. He was enthralled with the physical act of taking pollen from one lily and brushing it onto the stigma of another. That's it. That's all he wanted to do.

Bert Walker, an agriculture instructor at College of the Redwoods, remembers taking his students to Woodriff's greenhouse. "He had all these little glass bottles, and he'd pour black paint in them and swirl it around so they were completely black inside. Then he'd put the cap back on and poke a hole in the cap with an ice pick, and he'd turn a camel hair brush upside down and put it in that hole. He'd tell my students, 'This little bottle doesn't have anything in it but dried paint — nothing you can get high on — but once you get addicted to it, you can't get over it.'"

Woodriff used these little black bottles — the outside of the bottle, not the inside — to gather pollen. He chose bottles with flat sides so he'd have a good surface to work on. By coating the inside of the bottle with black paint, the outer surface was almost like a mirror. He'd tap on one lily, shake the pollen onto the flat side of the bottle where he could see it, pull out the camel hair brush, and use it to pick up the pollen and fertilize another lily.

"He had those bottles all over," Bert told me. "That was his addiction. He was very straightforward that he was addicted to that moment. And the thing is, he may have known how he got a particular cross, but he didn't have it written down and he didn't do a bunch of meticulous repetition to be sure." Even when Woodriff claimed that he knew the lineage of one of his lilies, Bert wasn't always convinced. The camel hair brushes were never very clean, and there was no way to tell how much pollen, from how many different lilies, they carried from day to day. Besides, he deliberately introduced an element of chaos into the process—he was known to fill a jar with assorted pollen, shake it up, and scatter it across a field of lilies in bloom. One grower told me, "Here was Leslie's own philosophy. This is what he'd tell you: 'You take a deck of cards and throw it in the air. Start picking up the cards, and eventually you'll hit a royal flush.' So he was just scattering the genetics. That's what was so unique about his work. He would try things that people said couldn't be done."

Bert remembers the way Woodriff used to carry photographs of lilies around in his shirt pocket. "No matter where he went—a nursery association meeting, a plant talk, even if you saw him downtown—he'd pull out those pictures and show them to you. He'd say, 'This one's very interesting. Now, if I could just get the upright growth of this one, and if I could just get the fragrance of this one, and I'd like to get this color, and—well, you could make a million dollars.' Just like that. We'd all say, 'Well, that's really great, Les.' But we were thinking, 'Hey, this guy's a dreamer.' And he was. Les was a dreamer. And he never made his million dollars."

THE ONLY SURE WAY a breeder can make money from a hybrid is to patent it, and even that is a fairly new development. Horticulturalist Luther Burbank, breeder of the Shasta daisy and over eight hundred other varieties of plants, wrote in the early 1900s, "A man can patent a mousetrap or copyright a song, but if he gives to the world a new fruit he will be fortunate if he is rewarded by so much as having his name connected with the result." The Plant Patent Act of 1930 came about too late for Burbank, who died in 1926, but it did solve the problem of plant breeders getting no financial reward for their invention. Thomas Edison, a friend of Burbank's, was one of the act's early supporters. "The manufacturer gets protection and the farmer has the same right," he said. "As a rule the plant breeder is a poor man, with no opportunity for material reward. Now he has a grubstake."

The act, as originally written, covered only plants that were asexually propagated, meaning that they could be reproduced by means of grafting, cuttings, and the like. Seeds and tubers were specifically excluded because they were also sold as food and it seemed too difficult to regulate, especially at a time when food was in short supply. The exclusion of seeds also ensured that only the particular cultivar being patented was protected; many hybrids do not grow "true from seed," and patenting the seed might result in the unintentional patenting of parent or grandparent stock as well. Patented plants could either be bred or discovered, but the act would not allow anyone to patent a wild plant that had simply been stumbled across in a field. The plant must have been demonstrably new or improved, and offered for sale for no more than a year prior to the patent application. Patents were granted for a period of seventeen years with the expectation that breeders could realize a return on their investment within that period.

Plant Patent 1 went to Henry F. Bosenberg, who patented an

everblooming variety of climbing rose. There is nothing in Mr. Bosenberg's application to suggest that he was conscious of making history with the first plant patent; his description of his invention was utterly lacking in poetry or excitement. He explained quite simply why it might be desirable to have a climbing rose that bloomed continuously rather than all at once, and wrote, "No claim is made as to novelty in color or other physical characteristics of the individual blossoms, nor as to the foliage or growing habits of this rose other than as described above." He didn't even name it; he just called it a "climbing or trailing rose." The second plant patent was also for a rose; then along came a carnation, a dewberry, and yet another rose. Of the first three hundred patents registered, half were for roses. Although the Great Depression was under way, far more patents were registered for flowers than for food. One reporter lamented that in the first five years after the act passed, "Patented vegetables are conspicuous by their absence, but there is one patented mushroom."

Plant patents were big business: General Electric even got in on it during the early days, registering Plant Patent 165 for 'Regal Lily', which, thanks to a thirty-second X-ray exposure, no longer shed pollen. The bulblets (small offshoots that would grow into full-sized bulbs) produced from the X-rayed lily shared this characteristic, so it met the act's early requirement that the patented plant be propagated by some means other than seed. Other than subjecting the bulb to radiation, there was no real inventing involved—no hybridization, and no trial-and-error with parent stock. But General Electric's lily was one of the earliest applications of modern technology to cut flower breeding.

In 1970 the act was amended to include new varieties produced by seed. By then, 3,320 plant patents had been granted, and the change to the law cleared the way for the patenting of lettuce, beans, wheat, and cotton, among others. In 1995 the patent term was extended to twenty years, making it possible for breeders to collect royalties from their inventions for two solid decades before a plant slipped its bonds and escaped, unfettered and unprotected, into the wilds of the marketplace.

MANY PLANT PATENT applications state the parentage of the new hybrid to help establish that it is, in fact, a new and unique creation. But even today, no one knows the exact parentage of Woodriff's 'Star Gazer'. One lily grower speculated that it might come from *Lilium nobilissimum,* an Oriental that grows wild on the steep cliffs of an island in the southern archipelagos of Japan. Although it has upward-facing flowers, it is prone to diseases, an unpredictable bloomer, susceptible to cold, and in need of stony soil. Still, it appears that Woodriff got hold of *L. nobilissimum* at a national lily show in the early 1950s and saw its potential. 'Star Gazer' probably also contains a little *L. auratum,* a freckled gold and white lily with a red flush running down the center of each petal. *L. speciosum* is almost certainly present as well, lending its strong fragrance and pink to crimson coloring.

What is certain is that when Ted Kirsch walked into his fields at Sun Valley and looked into the ruffled, backward-curving petals of 'Star Gazer', and saw the deep crimson flush edged in white, the carmine freckles, the yellow star-shaped markings at the center, and the lime green filaments supporting bronze pollen, he knew he had something. By the mid-1970s, he was sending 'Star Gazer' to growers in Oregon and Holland, hoping they would grow the lily on a larger scale and under different conditions to evaluate its suitability as a cut flower. In September 1976 Kirsch filed a patent application for 'Star Gazer'. His statement read: "My new variety of lily plant originated as a seedling of unknown parentage and was discovered by me in 1971 among plants grown in a test plot maintained by me at Arcata, Calif., in connection with my endeavors to develop new and improved lily varieties." There was no mention of Leslie Woodriff in the patent application.

That's not to say that Kirsch didn't give Woodriff credit for his work. He and Woodriff both made it known that 'Star Gazer' was a Woodriff hybrid that Kirsch selected. ("Woodriff couldn't choose," David told me. "He loved the hybridizing, but sooner or later you've got to choose one and grow it out.") Bulletins of the North American Lily Society and books on lily breeding have always credited Leslie Woodriff with the hybrid, but Kirsch bought the Woodriff lilies and, with them, the right to make selections and patent them. Kirsch went on to patent twenty-six more lilies, including twenty-five that were similarly described as "seedlings of unknown parentage." I recognize a few names on the list as Woodriff's; he is widely credited, for instance, with 'Le Rêve,' a dreamy, pink, late-blooming Oriental that is registered in Kirsch's name as Plant Patent 5189. His contract with Woodriff also gave Kirsch the right to name the lilies (Plant Patent 4881 is named after his daughter, Laura). Woodriff, on the other hand, registered only two plant patents in his life, and both were for his other passion—begonias. He claimed in a newspaper interview that it was too much work to police a patent and he just didn't have time for it. That decision meant that Kirsch, not Woodriff, was able to patent the lily and collect royalties from it.

It's hard to fault Kirsch for what he did. He was a businessman, by all accounts honest and straightforward, tough but compassionate. He genuinely wanted to help the Woodriffs, and it is clear that they sought him out. Ruth Woodriff originally approached Kirsch about the arrangement when she ran into him at a gas station in Oregon, and Woodriff's friends agreed that he was "always looking for a sugar daddy." (Even after Woodriff's relationship with Sun Valley came to an end, one of his hand-typed lily catalogs included the nursery itself among the list of items for sale, stating that the business had "far outgrown what a family can do so we are looking for a working partner, also investment capital in the formation of a corporation.") Members of the Woodriff family feel to this day that he was forced into the situation as the result of poverty and one bad business deal after another. Still, Kirsch believed that he'd made a fair offer for purchase of the lilies, and his right to patent and name them was clearly spelled out in the agreement. He also felt that he'd been more than generous in giving them jobs.

"It was clear that you couldn't just take the lilies away from the Woodriffs," David told me, "because then what would they do? They were lily-ites. This was their life. Ted sincerely believed that he could clean them up, put them in a regular house, pay them a wage, and the whole thing would be good for them. But I was not the least surprised when Ted called and said they were taking lilies home and hiding them under the bed."

The relationship between Kirsch and Woodriff soured quickly. Kirsch's family remembers thinking that the Woodriffs simply weren't employable. "You just couldn't tell them to show up at eight and work until five and take an hour lunch and go home on the weekends," David said. "They had never operated like that in their lives." On the other hand, Woodriff's son George and daughter Betty told me that their father had agreed to come to Sun Valley with the understanding that he'd work as a scientist, and instead he was put to work as a laborer, building and repairing greenhouses. He had debilitating back injuries dating to his childhood, so he felt that this work was both beneath him as a plant breeder and beyond the scope of what his physical limitations would allow.

To add insult to injury, a lily grower who knew both men told me that Kirsch plowed under a field at Sun Valley that had been planted with many of Woodriff's odd and unusual lily crosses, an act that must have outraged the Woodriff family. In fact, Sun

Valley's 1976 catalog suggests that just such a thing might have happened. It read, in part: "We have discarded hundreds of lilies that have not performed for us. We have purchased lilies from over fifteen hybridizers and have over two thousand different clones at the present time. We are more concerned about you getting a high quality lily than we are about when it was developed and who developed it . . . We are now selecting from twenty-five thousand of our own seedlings. We feel lilies are the flower of the future."

While there may have been a good reason for discarding some of Woodriff's lilies — Kirsch, as a businessman, was probably not interested in devoting precious field and greenhouse space to coddling thousands of unproven, unlabeled hybrids — it is also easy to understand how Woodriff would have felt as though his life's work had been destroyed. If I were Leslie Woodriff, I might have hidden a few bulbs under the bed, too.

It was perhaps inevitable that 'Star Gazer' and all the other lilies Kirsch bought from Woodriff would end up in court. The dispute between the two men must have been heartbreaking on both sides: Woodriff felt that he'd been cheated out of his lilies, and Kirsch felt that in return for his generosity and good faith he'd gotten himself tangled up in an unpleasant legal battle. Both men must have been surprised at how quickly their business relationship fell apart.

The initial contract was dated March 5, 1970. In addition to buying all of Woodriff's lilies (including the right to name and patent them), and employing the Woodriffs at Sun Valley, Kirsch also took title to their land in Brookings with the intention of selling it to recoup his costs. He paid $1,000 for the bulbs, spent $12,000 paying off the Woodriff's debts, and agreed to pay Woodriff $2 an hour and to hire his wife, his son Alan, and his daughter Winkey for $1.65 per hour. They would live in a house at Sun Valley, and

$25 dollars per month would be deducted from each of their paychecks for rent. Woodriff would also get 5 percent of the profits generated through the sale of his lilies. The employment contract was expected to run for seven years unless it was terminated earlier, and the Woodriffs agreed to a three-year noncompete clause after they left Sun Valley's employment.

The Brookings farm continued to operate — Woodriff called his business Fairyland Lily Gardens because he liked to say that rubbing a bit of of pollen into a flower created magic — until October of 1970, when the family moved to Arcata. It was just nine months later that Kirsch issued a formal termination letter to the Woodriffs. They had, he claimed, refused to take instructions from a supervisor; prematurely removed lilies from the premises; and, most mysterious of all, failed to report "the loss of one of the most valuable lily bulbs involved in our project," which disappeared for several months until Woodriff was "pressed for an answer as to its whereabouts." No one remembers exactly what lily went missing, but it is clear that Kirsch had a keen interest in 'Star Gazer' from the beginning, and the loss of this particular lily would certainly have caused him a great deal of worry.

Woodriff filed suit in August, claiming breach of contract. He said that he and his family were perfectly willing to do the work for which they had been hired, that he had not refused to perform any duties that had been assigned to him, and that Kirsch had terminated the contract without cause and kept the lilies. The flowers and the other assets he sold to Kirsch, plus the potential future profits from them, were worth, he claimed, $301,000 — far surpassing the amount for which he had sold them just a year earlier. Kirsch filed a countersuit, claiming that he was out $6,000 for damages and "certain lily bulbs" that Woodriff had failed to deliver. It took two years for the case to go to trial.

The transcripts from the trial have been destroyed, but David remembers those days in court. "Ted didn't need much of a defense," David said. "All you had to do was put Leslie on the stand and let him talk. It was clear to the judge and everyone that this guy was unemployable. The whole thing was pretty sad—nobody wanted to go through this lawsuit—but there we were. So Leslie took the stand and everybody realized that there was no way this guy could carry out the terms of an employment contract."

The Woodriff family remembers few specific details from the case. George, the eldest, who had warned his father not to do the deal with Sun Valley, recalls hearing that his father "couldn't do all the physical labor they wanted him to do. They were really stupid because they had him doing a job that a carpenter could have done. He could have been making them a lot of money hybridizing lilies. But they got crossways right off the bat, and I know they [Sun Valley] didn't live up to their end of the bargain." He suspects that his parents kept the particulars from him because "they were reluctant to share it with me. They knew I didn't like it that they went down there in the first place. But I know it wasn't a good fit for Dad anymore. He was miserable."

In the spring of 1974 the judge awarded five thousand dollars to the Woodriffs in recognition of "personal property transferred" to Sun Valley, along with a few hundred dollars in legal costs, and rejected out of hand the Woodriffs' claim that these lilies had the potential to someday generate far more money than the paltry sums that had changed hands so far. "Future profits may be possible," the judge wrote, "but it is too speculative to assign any present value."

By THE TIME the case concluded, 'Star Gazer' was getting ready for market. One California grower told me, "My prejudice about the Dutch is that they don't feel that a flower is worth a whole lot unless they worked on it in Holland. So they would come over here, take some genetic stock back, play with it for a little while, and make their own hybrids. Of course, these hybrids usually do need work. There's always some refinement. 'Star Gazer' was the first lily to be considered a finished product right off the bat. It worked commercially. It was perfect just as it was." All the Dutch had to do was clone 'Star Gazer' using a process called meristemming, which allows virus-free tissue cultures to grow quickly in the laboratory.

Sun Valley offered 'Star Gazer' for sale in 1976, just after submitting the patent application. In its catalog, the company described it this way: "This acute upright red oriental is something to write home about. A little darker color and bigger flower than 'Journey's End' with even better vigor. This lily has caused more excitement in Holland than any lily since 'Enchantment'. Hybridizers cannot afford to be without this lily. It is sure to be the parent or the granddaddy of many exciting new oriental strains and clones."

Still, the lily was slow to gain acceptance among American florists who thought the fragrance overpowering, the blooms too large, and the color too dramatic. As a North American Lily Society bulletin put it in 1980, "The outstanding feature of 'Star Gazer' was in packing. Its pedicles are nearly vertical and twice as many stems can be put in a shipping box as compared to most Orientals." The benefits of 'Star Gazer', then, had less to do with what customers wanted and more to do with the preferences of growers and wholesalers. Here was a lily that wouldn't snap apart when you handled it. If only the public could be won over, too.

In Holland, 'Star Gazer' had yet another advantage that was important only to the grower: Kirsch never obtained growers' rights in the Netherlands. A handwritten contract between him and his Dutch partner stipulated that in exchange for purchasing up to three thousand bulbs for five dollars apiece in 1976, Kirsch would agree not to apply for growers' rights in Holland. That meant that although the plant would be patented in the United States, Dutch growers were free to propagate and sell it without paying any royalties at all. The larger, showier flowers appealed to their customers, and 'Star Gazer' quickly became the best-selling Oriental in Holland. Eventually, American customers grew to like it, too, perhaps worn down rather than won over. (Many people complain about the overpowering scent of lilies, and whether they realize it or not they are mostly complaining about 'Star Gazer'.) Today it is still the gold standard among Oriental lilies, with about thirty-six million stems sold annually through Dutch auctions alone. Although new hybrids are beginning to edge out 'Star Gazer', many of them can, as Kirsch predicted, claim the famous lily as their parent or granddaddy.

Leslie Woodriff watched with dismay as his lily became a best seller. He never got over the loss of the flower, or of the potential income—he would have certainly had his million dollars if he'd held onto the rights. His friends told me that after 'Star Gazer' was patented and put into production, it was ten years before he had a single bulb of the hybrid lily in his possession again. It must have been maddening to walk into a coffee shop and see a bouquet of 'Star Gazers' at the cash register, or to notice florists delivering them at Mother's Day and Valentine's Day, and to know that it had all slipped through his fingers.

Although it may not have been any comfort to Woodriff, Kirsch didn't get rich from 'Star Gazer', either. It's a sad irony that Woodriff sold all his lilies to Kirsch for just a thousand dollars, and then Kirsch sold 'Star Gazer' to the Dutch for only about fifteen thousand. The lily made millions, but not for its hybridizer or its owner. Kirsch was even relaxed about enforcing his patent in the United States. In 1981 he brought legal action against the Washington Bulb Company for patent infringement; the matter was eventually settled out of court and Washington Bulb agreed to pay royalties of ten cents a stem on every 'Star Gazer' sold. David, by this time the family attorney, sent letters to a few other growers warning them of possible patent infringements, but over-all the royalties Kirsch collected for 'Star Gazer' never amounted to much, and most 'Star Gazer' lilies came into the country from Holland anyway.

By the mid-1980s, Kirsch was ready to retire. He sold Sun Valley to an Oregon company called Melridge, Inc., which was buying up Pacific Northwest flower farms in an attempt to form one giant flower corporation, complete with a splashy initial public offering. Melridge turned out to be a precursor to the dot-com bust of the late nineties: the accountants overvalued the company, the share-holders sued, the owner fled the country, and the farmers, many of whom had sold their farms in exchange for Melridge stock, were left with nothing. Ted Kirsch knew better than to take the stock as payment for his farm—he was one of the few who insisted on being paid in cash. When he sold the farm, the 'Star Gazer' patent went along with it. Kirsch was still living in Arcata at the time, and as much as it pained Woodriff to watch the success of 'Star Gazer', it also hurt Kirsch to watch Sun Valley's sudden failure. Fortunately, he lived long enough to see Lane DeVries, then an employee of Melridge, join with some Dutch partners to buy the assets—including the 'Star Gazer' patent—out of bankruptcy. David told me, "Ted always used to say that he should have just handed the company to Lane DeVries the minute he met him and saved all that heartache." Today 'Star Gazer' is still Sun Valley's signature lily.

THE DUTCH GROWERS never forgot Leslie Woodriff's contributions. 'Star Gazer' was not his only accomplishment; he is also known for the dramatic 'Black Beauty', a five- to eight-foot dark red lily edged in silver, and for 'White Henryi', a gorgeous white lily with a butterscotch blush and appealing cinnamon-colored freckles. (Woodriff once climbed aboard a commuter plane with a six-foot-tall stalk of 'Black Beauty' over his shoulder; although the pilot made him toss most of the plant off the plane, the remaining blooms still won an award at that year's North American Lily Society show.) It was because of these accomplishments that Piet Koopman traveled to Arcata to meet him in 1988. I can picture Woodriff as his friends described him in those days: almost wheelchair-bound, usually sitting out in the greenhouse in an old chair that looked like it had been ripped out of a van. He carried a radio on a string around his neck, and whenever anyone new came to the greenhouse in search of his legendary lilies, he pulled one of his black bottles out of his shirt pocket and shook it at them, shouting, "I'm hooked on the bottle!"

After thinking over Woodriff's plight, Koopman did decide to publicize the man's situation and raise some funds for him. "I'm the son of a hybridizer and I know how much money is involved," he said. "It was the only thing I could do for him." Koopman wrote an article for a trade journal and raised about forty-five thousand dollars, enough to send Woodriff a small check every month for the rest of his life. A group of Dutch growers introduced a soft pink Oriental called 'Woodriff's Memory' whose royalties would benefit the famous breeder. Looking back, Koopman said of Woodriff, "He was a nice but a naïve man — too good of trust and too good for this world."

Another Dutch group came to California in the early nineties to bestow upon Woodriff the Royal Dutch Bulb Growers Association's prestigious Dix Medal. His wife, Ruth, didn't get to see him win this award — she died in 1990, and he followed in 1997. Both died of cancer, as did one of their daughters. Woodriff's daughter Betty suspects that all three deaths may be attributed to the pesticides they used in the greenhouse, usually without any protection at all—a high price to pay for their devotion to lilies. One of his colleagues in the industry told me, " 'Star Gazer' was the most popular lily of all time. It was a success story, but not for the man who bred it. I would not call him a genius, but he was an optimist. Leslie Woodriff had a dream that no one else had."

CHAPTER 2

Engineered to Perfection

Walk into a grocery store and you'll see the old and the new ways of cut flower breeding side by side in the floral department. Sun Valley's 'Star Gazer' will be there, offered in bouquets of a half-dozen stems, the pale pink buds mostly closed and giving little hint of what is inside. Knowing its story, I see it as a flower of missed opportunities, of rags and riches, of old men who don't have a place in the cut flower industry anymore. It is a flower of the past, a flower that came into being without the involvement of a business plan or a corporate strategy.

Right next to it, wrapped in a clear cellophane sleeve, you might find a bunch of dark purple carnations. When I was a kid, my mother's drink was Crown Royal whiskey; she saved the purple felt bags the bottles came in, and I can think of no other way to describe the color of these carnations except to say that they are the precise hue of those Crown Royal bags. You'll probably find a sticker on the bouquet's sleeve that reads FLORIGENE MOONVISTA. These are John Mason's carnations.

Mason is the research manager for Florigene, an Australian company that makes no secret of the fact that it is racing toward the goal of developing a blue rose. Not lilac, not lavender, not dark purple bordering on blackish blue, but true blue. Delphinium blue. Forget-me-not blue. Some would call it the holy grail of rose breeding; others consider it an abomination. I won't judge the thing until I've seen it—and since it does not exist, I may have to wait a while—but it's hard to imagine a blue rose I would like. When I see white roses that have been stem-dyed or sprayed with glittery blue paint, I just shudder and look away. These are phonies, clearly artificial, entirely unnatural. But what about engineering it in a laboratory?

The quest for a blue rose is nothing new. The mere fact that it doesn't exist, that it can't exist in nature, seems to inspire all kinds of ludicrous attempts to force it into being. Roses are utterly lacking in delphinidin, the pigment that produces blue petal colors. No amount of crossbreeding can change that. Still, the history of rose hybridizing is filled with tall tales: a twelfth-century gardener claimed to have a blue rose, until someone proved that he'd been mixing indigo dye into his irrigation water, a famous fourth-generation Irish rose breeder claimed that he had bred a blue rose, but his father destroyed it because he feared it would "corrupt the public's taste," and Peter Henderson, author of *Practical Floriculture* and a number of other late-nineteenth and early-twentieth-century books for florists, loved to expose charlatans who fraudulently sold young rose plants that were purported to be blue but instead bloomed in ordinary shades of yellow, red, pink, and white.

The only way to breed a blue rose is to bypass Leslie Woodriff's clumsy, old-fashioned tools—his camel hair brush and glass bottle—and to splice in a gene from another species. It hasn't entirely worked yet, however, at least not for roses. It turns out that it's easier to get purple than blue, and it's easier to do anything at all with a carnation than a rose—which is why Florigene's purple carnations are selling at Safeway while the blue rose is still on the drafting table.

When Florigene released its "Moon Series" carnations, it became the first company to offer transgenic flowers for sale. To get the blue gene the company's scientists turned to petunias, which serve as a sort of lab rat for flower breeders. "In terms of flower color, the petunia is one of the most studied flowers around," John Mason told me. "A large number of mutants have been identified in petunias, so there's a lot of genetics out there to work with. The other reason is that petunias are relatively easy to manipulate using genetic engineering. Put those two things together and you end up with a good test plant. They're also easy to grow, they produce a lot of seed, and they've been studied for a long time."

But getting any flower to turn blue, whether it's a carnation or a rose, is not as simple as implanting the gene and letting it multiply. Mason and his colleagues have had to grapple with the fact that there is more to a petal's color than the presence or lack of a particular gene. It's not as simple as mixing paint colors on a palette.

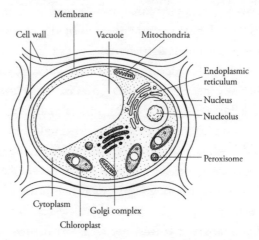

To get a very rough idea of what a plant cell looks like, imagine a cross-section of a hard-boiled egg. The eggshell is the cell wall. The egg white is actually a very busy and crowded place that is made up of a jellylike material called cytoplasm, and it holds the cell's nucleus and any number of small bodies called organelles that carry out various plant functions. Some of those organelles are called chloroplasts. They hold chlorophyll, the plant pigment that is responsible for the color green. You'll find fewer chloroplasts in roots and in petals where the green color isn't present, and more in leaves and stems. There are other organelles called chromoplasts that contain different pigments, most often carotenoids, which are responsible for some yellow and orange colors. Picture a leaf on a tree turning from green to yellow in autumn. The tree has slowed down its production of green chlorophyll, unmasking the yellow carotenoid pigment that is always present in the leaf.

Now think about the yolk of this egg as the vacuole, a cavity inside the cell that holds water, food, and metabolic waste, along with substances called flavonoids. This is where you'll find the pigments that John Mason is after. Flavonoids carry out a variety of functions, but some of them include the plant pigments responsible for colors ranging from blue to pink to purple to red. They are found only inside this fluid-filled vacuole. In particular, the group of flavonoids that control petal color are called anthocyanins, and they include a red or pink pigment called cyanidin, a scarlet or brick red pigment called pelargonidin, and the true blue delphinidin. Anytime you see a flower with streaks of red, purple, or pink against a white background, it has come about because the vacuoles of some cells have been emptied of their anthocyanin pigments, making just those parts of the plant look white.

So Florigene set about extracting the genes for delphinidin from the vacuoles of petunias and feeding them to a particular species of bacteria, which then penetrate the walls of rose cells and implant the delphinidin gene. This process was simple enough, by a geneticist's standards, but it got more complicated from there.

"If you were to extract all the pigment from a petal and have it in a test tube," John told me, "you'll find your color compound—let's say it's 100 percent delphinidin—but in that chemical soup there are these other compounds, these copigments, some of which are known and some of which are still unknown. They are very similar to the pigments themselves in chemical structure, but they are colorless. They work with the pigments and affect the brightness and brilliance of the color, and they vary a great deal from flower to flower." Knowing how the copigments will react with the delphinidin is a major obstacle, and it's one of the reasons that scientists work with a wide variety of roses to find one that will have an easier time accepting the blue pigment.

"Now, having said that," John continued, "there are other factors that are known to impart color, and I daresay there are some that we don't even know about yet, which makes it all the more intriguing. One of the factors we do know about is pH, or the acidity level where these pigments are stored. For instance, if you were to mash up some of our purple carnations and get a sort of solution in a test tube, and then if you raised the pH slightly to make it more alkaline, they'll go blue. The delphinidin pigments are actually quite a good indicator of pH, and that's one of the reasons you don't see so many true blue flowers out there. There appears to be a natural limit to the pH you can get in the vacuoles where the pigments are stored."

I asked him about hydrangeas, whose flowers turn more blue in an acid, not alkaline, soil. "That's related to pH, but in a different way," he said. "In a more acid soil, you get uptake of aluminum ions, which are toxic to most plants. So the plant wants to put the aluminum ions away in a place where they can't hurt anything, and these vacuoles are a good place to put them. They interact with the pigments and make them look blue. When you talk about copigments, metal ions are important. Think of cornflowers or Himalayan poppies, both of which are beautiful blue colors. They are actually red pigmented flowers. In the case of cornflowers, it's the interaction with metal ions—magnesium, I think—that causes the shift to blue. Nobody's done much work on this, including us, so it's one of the less understood factors that affects color. It may be that some of the Old World roses have more metal ions in their vacuoles which brings about the mauve or purple colors—I don't know, but it's an interesting question."

That's not all—even the petal surface impacts color. Under a microscope, many flower petals are actually quite bumpy. Some are covered in conical shapes and others in gentle mounds. Those shapes impact how light is reflected and how the pigment appears to the eye. Add to that the fact that once John makes the genetic modifications to a flower, he has a long wait ahead of him before the plant blooms and he can see the results. A carnation raised in a laboratory might take nine months from test tube to first flower, and a rose takes over a year, even when a bit of tissue is grafted onto an already mature plant. Florigene has a greenhouse near the laboratory; once every week or two, John and his colleagues stroll through the rows of flowers and look for signs that their experiments have borne fruit. But so far, a true blue rose hasn't bloomed in Florigene's greenhouse. He's still waiting for the day when the phone rings and the greenhouse manager says, "John, you'd better get down here."

THERE'S A STRANGE paradox inherent in this quest for the blue rose. Breeders have been fascinated with the idea for centuries, and Florigene is putting considerable resources into engineering in a laboratory what nature refuses to do on its own, but I have yet to meet anyone who actually wants a blue rose. When I talk to consumers—friends, family, fellow gardeners, other flower lovers—they all wrinkle their noses and tell me that they can't imagine why anyone would buy such a thing. Retail florists seem fairly hesitant, too, mostly because they're unsure they could convince their customers to try it. Even wholesalers won't admit to personally wanting a blue rose to exist, but at least they will tell me that it might be a moneymaker. "It's unusual," one wholesaler told me. "It's a novelty. Besides, look at those dyed blue roses. Somebody's buying those." It's true, somebody must be buying them. The trouble is, I can't figure out who.

John Mason told me that Florigene held focus groups about this question many years ago. "It turns out that a lot of people associate different colored roses with different occasions," he said. "You know, red roses on Valentine's Day, yellow roses for friendship, white roses at a funeral, that sort of thing. That was one of the biggest blocks people had when they thought about a blue rose—what would it stand for? A lot of their comments were quite negative, really."

This may be the biggest challenge that breeders of a blue rose face. Roses, more than any other flower, are laden with symbolism. In Greek mythology, one account of Adonis's death has the first rose springing from the dying man's blood. In another version, his lover, Aphrodite, is pricked by a thorn as she stumbles around in her grief over his death, and her blood turns white roses red. Red roses became the flower of undying passion, enduring love. The eighteenth-century poet Robert Burns wrote, "O my Luve's like a red, red rose" and pledged his love "Till a' the seas gang dry, my dear / And the rocks melt wi' the sun."

The white rose has long been a symbol of purity, innocence, and faith; it has been associated with the Virgin Mary, and church reformer Martin Luther adopted it as his symbol. During the fifteenth-century Wars of the Roses, the white rose stood for the House of York; the rival House of Lancaster adopted the red rose, and when Henry Tudor took the throne and ended the conflict, he created the red and white Tudor Rose insignia to symbolize the union. In World War II, the German White Rose Society stood in opposition to the Nazi regime.

But a blue rose has no history, no mythology, and therefore no meaning. Victorians suggested that a blue rose, which was to them an impossible creation, would stand for mystery. Given the color's association with the sky, the heavens, and the vast unknowable sea, that may be appropriate. But what message does "mystery" impart to the recipient?

This is a problem that florists will have to solve. John Mason sounded confident that the public would be won over once they saw the real thing. "If you doctor a picture of a blue rose on a computer and show it to somebody," he said, "most people would say, 'Well, that's artificial.' But if you had the flower in your hand and it was blue, and a normal pigment was used to make it blue—well, it will be interesting to see what the response is."

So I asked John if he, personally, wanted there to be a blue rose. "I mean, do you look around your garden and say, 'What this place needs is a blue rose'?" I asked. "Would you send a bouquet of blue roses to your wife? And what would you be saying to her if you did?"

He paused and laughed. "Um . . . yeah," he said. "That's a tricky one. I know people will say, 'Oh, that'll be horrible and unnatural.' But I'm really intrigued as to how it would look. I love the color blue. One of my favorite flowers is the Himalayan poppy, a beautiful blue. And I think, well, it would be very nice to have a rose that color, but . . . well . . ." He faltered, then said, "It will be interesting to see how it looks."

As with any genetically modified product, there are larger issues at stake than how the flower looks. Because carnations don't go freely to seed, Florigene's carnations are not likely to escape into the wild, so there's less concern about this transgenic crop than there might be for, say, a bioengineered variety of corn whose pollen could drift into a neighboring field of organic corn. Still, when Florigene filed a public notification in the Netherlands regarding the sale of their carnations, the company had to provide quite a bit of information about the potential, or lack of potential, for the carnation's pollen to somehow find its way to another carnation growing in a garden. This is quite unlikely, the company emphasized in its notice, and besides, "Carnation is not a weed in Europe and despite hundreds of years of cultivation and plantings in parks and gardens, it has not become a weed, or escaped from cultivation, anywhere in the world." It also stressed that the flower won't — or shouldn't — be eaten by humans: "Carnation is not used as a food but there is a slight possibility that some home consumers may decide to eat flower petals, or garnish foods with flower petals. In the event that this did occur we do not believe the transgenic carnation poses any health risk . . ." Finally, the notice pointed out, "Imported carnation flowers will not survive more than 3 weeks in the hands of the consumer. During this time seed set is impossible. Discarded carnations have no vegetative propagation ability."

Florigene's carnations are not yet grown in the United States. The company has contracted with growers in Latin America to grow the carnations and sell them back to Florigene, which acts as a wholesaler and sells them into the U.S. cut flower market. I asked Jane Rissler, a scientist at the Union of Concerned Scientists, if GMO cut flowers posed much of a concern to American consumers. "Well, for any genetically modified organism, we look at risks versus benefits. Now, we're skeptical of the benefits and more concerned with risks. But we're not opposed to all genetically modified organisms. If the flowers are brought in as cut flowers, and they're not being eaten, there are very few consumer concerns. You might also ask whether the genetic engineering introduces any substance that might be an allergen for flower workers. But I don't think that's likely. So these would not fall into the same category as, say, corn, where there's a concern about pollen drift. Now, wherever they are being grown, one should look at environmental issues, wild relatives, and so forth. For example, could the carnation's new characteristics enhance its weediness? Those are the kinds of questions you'd need to ask. But there is a big difference between cut flowers and food. It certainly wouldn't be high on the list of things we worry about as a genetically engineered product."

When I asked John Mason whether Florigene encountered any resistance when it rolled out the first genetically modified cut flower, he said, "We've actually taken very little flack. Most of it has been along the lines of 'What a waste of human effort to do this with flowers. Aren't you trivial people, why don't you do something worthwhile like cure cancer,' and so forth. Which is good news to us, I suppose, that people don't see them as dangerous."

ABOUT A YEAR after I spoke to John Mason for the first time, I opened the newspaper and there it was: an announcement that the world's first blue rose was about to be introduced. Suntory, a Japanese liquor and food company that had recently acquired Florigene, announced that it had developed a rose whose pigment came almost entirely from delphinidin.

I sat for a long time and stared at the photograph that accompanied the story. The precise reproduction of flower colors is challenging for the best photographers, and newspaper images are particularly tricky. Still, I was pretty sure that the rose in the photograph wasn't blue. It looked purple to me.

Finally I went upstairs and called John. "So," I said. "Tell me about this blue rose."

There was silence on the other end of the line, and then he laughed. "Um, well, first of all, it's not blue," he said. "We refer to Royal Horticultural Society color charts—most breeders do that—and I think the colors that we've got are in the violet group, more like our carnations. The point for us is that the color is clearly a new color. But the marketing people will tend to use the word 'blue' whenever they can." The announcement was probably also driven by more pragmatic needs—after buying up 98.5 percent of Florigene's shares, Suntory was eager to announce some results to the public and to its own investors. But how long would it be before Florigene managed to deliver the true blue rose it had been seeking?

"Yeah, that's a good question," John said. "Traditionally we say three to five years, but we've been saying that for ten years, haven't we?"

THE ROSE FLORIGENE chose as breeding stock for its new blue-rose-that's-actually-violet is 'Lavande', a gorgeous lavender rose that's well known in the cut flower trade for its heady perfume. Brides in particular request this rose when they want a flower with a fragrance and they don't mind the fact that it will be short-lived. And as Mason explained, this is one of the key trade-offs that breeders make when they try to engineer a flower that will meet the market's needs—scent uses up a great deal of a flower's resources, thus shortening its life. This is the newest paradox with which cut flower breeders must grapple: if you want a rose that smells like a rose, it will die within a few days. Knowing that, are you still willing to pay five dollars a stem? Florists aren't so sure.

Scent, like taste, can't be recorded on film or captured on canvas. If I showed you a photograph of a 'Sterling' rose from my garden, you would have a pretty good idea what it looked like: deep purple buds that unfurl into a small but luscious lavender bloom and fade eventually to white. But no matter how hard I tried to describe its musky, old rose scent, you wouldn't really know it until you inhaled the fragrance yourself. Maybe that's why so many flowers are described in the vocabulary of an equally elusive sense—taste. A sweet pea smells like honey; a rose smells like apple; a dianthus is sweet as cotton candy; and a geranium, when crushed, gives off the unmistakable essence of cinnamon and nutmeg.

The connection between food and scent is no surprise: when a muscat wine is described as having "notes of jasmine," a chemical analysis can confirm that in fact both muscat and jasmine blossoms contain a compound called linalool, which is also found in other flowers and plants like lavender, rosemary, and sage. In fact, most flavors we experience are not actually tastes at all. The tongue is capable of sensing only saltiness, sweetness, sourness, and bitterness. (The presence of a fifth sense, umami, is still under debate. It is believed to correspond to savory, meaty flavors.) Other flavors in food are actually scents—in many cases, these volatile oils produced by plants—that we experience through olfactory receptor cells located just behind the bridge of the nose. This is why when you have a cold it is just as difficult to taste food as it is to smell it.

A single flower creates dozens of these scent compounds over its short lifespan. Their chief purpose is not to add flavor to our food or create a heady bouquet of perfume but rather to communicate to the pollinators they rely upon for reproduction. Scents tell insects where they can find nectar, where they can lay their eggs, where there might be pollen to gather. The flower relies on the scent glands of insects to interpret its messages so that its wishes can be carried out.

Those complex messages are nothing but perfume and spice to us; the signals blend into a symphony whose individual notes are difficult, if not impossible, to discern. When we press our face into a bouquet of roses or lilies, we have no idea what kind of communication network we've blundered into. The sharp perfume we inhale might smell exactly like the sex hormones of a butterfly. A sickly sweet scent can signal that a blossom has mated satisfactorily and is closing its petals to further amorous visitors. The scent of a flower tells a story; in it we can pick up the thread of all-too-familiar human dramas: desire and hunger, birth and death. Even deceit and mimicry run like a narrative thread through the petals of a flower: some bees release a scent that imitates their favorite blossom, for instance, in the hopes that the scent will draw prospective mates near. A wildly fragrant garden announces its lust and hunger, shelter and satiety.

It is no surprise, then, that we clothe ourselves in the scent of flowers to send out our own messages. A single ounce of Joy perfume contains oils from about ten thousand jasmine flowers and over three hundred roses. Most perfumes include a top note, a bright scent like lilac or orange blossom; a middle note like geranium or lavender that emerges after the wearer's skin has warmed the scent; and a bottom note, a musky animal smell that sends out the frank signal of sex. For that reason, in areas where Africanized bees are a threat, people are warned to avoid perfume. The signal it sends to a bee would be irresistible: it would suggest the presence of a garden in which every flower it loves is in bloom at once.

DR. NATALIA DUDAREVA, a professor at Purdue University, studies these signals that flowers transmit to insects. As a molecular biologist interested in the biochemistry of floral scent production, she began investigating the genetic origins of volatile compounds like linalool and what they communicate to pollinators. At first, she was less concerned about the implications for the cut flower industry and more interested in finding ways that scent could be engineered to lure more bees and increase yields. A watermelon might need twelve visits from pollinators to produce good-sized fruit, and a strawberry could benefit from as many as twenty-five visitors. But many flowers shut down scent production after they've been pollinated once, resulting in a smaller fruit that meets the plant's reproductive needs but doesn't satisfy the farmer. Amplifying an apple tree's scent, then, might be a quick and efficient way to feed more people.

It didn't take long, however, to realize the implications for the cut flower industry. "If we can know how these chemicals are regulated, then we can understand why scent is gone from most commercial varieties," she told me. "A lot of cut flowers were bred for shelf life, shipping characteristics, color and shape. They were never bred for floral scent, and it actually disappeared."

By studying clarkias, petunias, and snapdragons, she realized that the same biochemical pathways are used to produce scents in a wide variety of flowers, which may make it easier for scientists to alter scent production. The base material that is used to produce the essential oils, which is called substrate, is also the same.

She also made surprising discoveries about the timing of scent production. It's been known for a long time that flowers produce scent when they are ready to be pollinated and that they release the scent at the time of day when their particular pollinators are active—a datura, for instance, releases its scent at night when moths are flying. "After a visit from a pollinator," she said, "flowers don't need any scent. But for twenty-four or thirty-six hours afterward, the scent doesn't go down. It turns out that the signal for the plant to shut down scent production comes after fertilization has actually taken place. This means that the plant wants to be sure before it stops attracting pollinators."

What are the implications for cut flowers? If the precise signal that a plant sends to stop scent production is better understood, perhaps it could be turned on or off at will. Natalia is quick to point out the benefits: scent production could be timed to coincide with shipping schedules, for instance, so that flowers are more fragrant when they reach their final destination. Or flowers could be engineered to release scent in the evening, when people come home from work. Most important, a flower could have its original scent bred back into it, or perhaps a new scent could be introduced all together. Just imagine: a tulip that smells like jasmine, a chrysanthemum with the essence of lilac, a chocolate-scented rose. Perfumes are made of natural and synthesized floral scents; is it only a matter of time before a lily is bred to smell like Calvin Klein cologne?

AT THIS POINT, however, there's no getting around the fact that scent is costly for a plant to produce. A cut flower has limited resources available to it—mainly stored carbohydrates and the sugars found in flower food—which has to sustain the flower during its short life in the vase. Now it appears that scent may also be connected to the production of ethylene, an invisible, almost odorless gas that hastens the demise of flowers and the ripening of fruit.

Put a green banana or a rock-hard avocado in a paper bag along with an apple and you'll find out about ethylene. Some plants produce more of the gas than others, but apples in particular are known to pump it out. Ethylene will accelerate the ripening of a green banana, cause a peach placed next to it in a fruit bowl to turn to mush, and it will make flowers wilt. And that makes it an enemy of the cut flower industry.

The role of ethylene is not completely understood, but we do know that it is a gaseous hormone that is involved in every stage of plant growth, from seed formation to fruit ripening to death. In particular, ethylene is responsible for two natural plant functions that florists could do without: abscission and senescence. Abscission is the deliberate separation of part of a plant from its main body, such as a leaf dropping from a tree or a petal falling off a rose. Senescence is simply a polite term for aging and all the processes that go along with it—drooping leaves, withering blossoms, and fading petals.

To forestall this inevitable decline, florists do everything they can to minimize ethylene. One of the first rules of operating a flower shop is to never, ever store a sack lunch in the cooler, out of fear that a piece of fruit could ruin the roses. (Retail florists just roll their eyes at supermarkets that place bouquets near the produce section. It's a sure way to kill the merchandise.) Segregating flowers according to ethylene sensitivity may help, too — for instance, Christmas greens produce the gas in slightly higher quantities and are usually kept away from more sensitive flowers like delphinium, alstroemeria, and baby's breath. Florists change the water in flower buckets as often as possible and sweep away any cut or damaged leaves and stems, because bruised plant material starts to give off ethylene quickly. Keeping flowers cold also helps: a flower is a thousand times more sensitive to ethylene at sixty-five degrees than it is at thirty-five degrees. Larger coolers can even be fitted with special ethylene scrubbers to remove the gas from the air as quickly as it is produced. Exhaust fumes release ethylene, so florists try to keep flowers away from idling cars and trucks, which is not always easy during shipping and home deliveries, and to avoid placing buckets of flowers in a doorway that leads to a busy street or parking lot.

There are chemical treatments available as well: some growers and wholesalers treat flowers by giving them a long drink in a bucket of water mixed with silver thiosulfate. However, the toxicity of this product (which is also used in photo processing) means that its use is closely regulated and disposal requirements are quite strict. Floralife, the company that makes the most popular brand of flower food, has introduced a product called EthylBloc, a powder that when mixed with water releases a gas that blocks ethylene. Coming up with new ways to deal with this problem is serious business: up to 30 percent of floriculture crop losses are due to ethylene damage.

Because of this, a number of scientists around the world are working on ways to cut ethylene production and make flowers less sensitive to the gas. One researcher at the University of Florida, Dr. David Clark, figured out how to accomplish this in that familiar floral lab rat, the petunia. "We were able to knock out the function of the ethylene receptor so the plants could produce longer-lasting flowers," he said. "We made the flowers insensitive to ethylene gas." While this experiment was a tremendous success, there was another surprise in store for him: once the petunias became immune to the effects of ethylene, they stopped producing scent. Some of the genes involved in releasing fragrance, he realized, were regulated by ethylene. He proved in the laboratory what traditional plant breeders have known for a century or more: when you breed a flower for longer vase life, you give up scent.

BREEDING THE PERFECT flower is a balancing act, a compromise between longevity and scent, color and shape, between what the geneticist can imagine and what the flower will allow. But breeders can only do so much. Eventually a flower has to leave the laboratory and enter a world where farmers, truckers, wholesalers, and florists will usher it to market. It's a short, frantic journey to an unnatural ending. The flower, rather than being allowed to reproduce and set seed, finds itself on an airplane, in a retail shop, in a vase.

You can tell a lot about a flower's life from its fragrance, and you can even predict its death. Walk into a flower shop, and what do you smell? A few natural scents, and a few florists' tricks. There are aerosol sprays that impart artificial rose fragrance to unscented roses, and floral preservatives that will release scent from the water the flowers are sitting in. I can understand why these artificial methods are so popular. The temptation to put one's face into a bouquet of flowers and inhale is too great to resist. I still find myself sniffing flowers that I know have no scent at all. But all too often the only odor I can detect is that distinctive scent that hangs around flower shops and their flowers. It's not an unpleasant odor, but it's not entirely floral, either. It's like new car smell — generic, ubiquitous, and immediately recognizable.

Most florists pretend not to know what I mean when I ask them about this scent, but finally one fessed up and explained it to me. "I know the smell you mean," he told me. "It's on my clothes every day when I come home from work." He told me that it comes from a combination of the few flowers that have a scent, like lilies and stock, mingled with the strong, clean odor of eucalyptus, which is used as bouquet filler, and dominated by the scent of decay. "Every time you cut a stem or strip the leaves off a rose," he said, "you get that smell. It's not too different from cut grass. It's the scent of a wounded plant — the bacteria that form around the cut. It's something that florists can't stand — the smell of the flower beginning to die."

PART **2** *Growing*

CHAPTER 3

Italian Violets and
Japanese Chrysanthemums

A hundred years ago, growers grew the plants that had been handed down through their families and did what they could to get them ready for market. Don Garibaldi, a third-generation violet grower, still farms like this. His family has been growing sweet violets on the California coast for a century; he has farmed his particular plot of land for thirty-five years. There, in those muddy violet fields on the coast, you can actually capture the essence of a flower farm before the invention of greenhouses and refrigerated trucks.

To get to his farm, Año Nuevo Flower Growers, you drive down the Pacific Coast Highway from San Francisco. The curvy, two-lane road hugs the shore, winding around hills and climbing up cliffs that get a constant pounding from the surf. There's always mist in the air, and in the winter, when it rains, the hills are a deep green. Sometimes, in a sunny flat field opposite the beach, you'll see the silvery leaves of artichokes or, in fall, orange pumpkins waiting to be harvested. The flower farms are usually hidden behind rows of eucalyptus trees that shield the flowers from the salty breeze and discourage drivers from letting their eyes stray from the road to the sight of a field of delphiniums or sunflowers in full bloom.

Año Nuevo is a state park about an hour and a half south of San Francisco, just north of Santa Cruz. It's famous for the herd of elephant seals that arrives every year to breed on its protected beaches. This flower farm is adjacent to the state park, and it's easy to miss: there's a hand-painted sign, a dirt driveway, and a small trailer where Don keeps an office. Beyond that is a field of flowers too small to even notice at highway speeds. Those are the violets.

A century ago, violets were still one of the most popular cut flowers in the country, ranking just behind roses, carnations, and chrysanthemums. I'm not talking about pansies or African violets—I mean *Viola odorata,* the real, old-fashioned sweet violets with a fragrance that is straight out of another era. The small, woodland flowers bloom early in the spring before the leaves are on the trees; it is for this reason that Napoleon Bonaparte promised, upon being sent to exile, that he would "return with the violets in the spring." His wife, Josephine, loved the flowers so much that he sent her a bunch every year for their wedding anniversary. She died while he was in exile, but immediately after he returned he collected violets from her garden and wore them in a locket until his own death.

Sweet violets belong to the large and wide-ranging Violaceae family. Its members make their home in North America, in Europe, and even in Siberia. Among the five hundred or so species around the world, a few unscented pansies and violas were popular florists' flowers in the early nineteenth century because of their larger size and the interesting markings in the center of the flowers that give them their "face." Breeders in those days found that they could breed *V. odorata* with other, larger violas and get pink and pale blue flowers that had that famous violet scent, but the varieties that were most popular as cut flowers were simply larger and more vigorous versions of the deep purple *odorata* blossoms that grew wild throughout much of Europe.

A violet is a short-lived flower, surviving at most four days from the day it's picked, but that didn't bother Victorian customers who knew no other options besides fragile garden flowers for their corsages and posies. Violets were often grown just outside large cities; for instance, a grower brought the plant to Rhinebeck, New York, in the 1890s, and the town quickly became known as the violet capital of the country. Over 150 families grew violets for sale, some in their backyards and some in elaborate greenhouses, because they were a profitable and fairly easy crop to grow. (I say "fairly easy" because the plants are hardy and produce reliably in winter months, but that doesn't mean they are easy to harvest. Each individual bloom has to be plucked gingerly from the plant; workers would often lay on their bellies, supported only by planks of wood, to harvest the flowers.)

From the late 1890s until the beginning of World War I, Rhinebeck produced as many as thirty-five million blossoms a year, most of them traveling by rail to Manhattan and other big cities, where they were a fashionable flower to wear to the opera or the theater. In those days a bunch of violets, usually with their stems wrapped tightly in ribbon, sold for less than a dollar. Sometimes a gardenia, some sweet peas, or a few lilies of the valley would be included as well, which would have made for an overpowering corsage.

The flowers were a little luxury, a mysterious delight. One *New York Times* account of the floral trade, written in January 1877, includes this tantalizing news:

> Violets are in, not yet in abundance, but becoming more plenty daily. Just now they are worth a cent each at retail. By the way, a great many ladies have developed a passion for chewing violets. They impart a delicious fragrance to the breath, and even at a cent apiece are cheap for this purpose, by comparison with the candied ones imported from France,

and sold at the rate of about $16 a pound. It is interesting to know that many belles have a fancy for thrusting bunches of fresh violets in mysterious places about their corsets, professing to believe that the crushed flowers exhale a more delicately delicious perfume than any of the myriad scented stuffs that they can buy in bottles. And the florists encourage the fashion enthusiastically.

Violets themselves may be dainty, pretty little flowers in their own right, but their appeal lies almost entirely in their scent. Mark Griffiths, writing for the Royal Horticultural Society's magazine the *Garden,* cites a British newspaper article in the late 1800s that reported that "the perfume crept out of our railway parcel office to the astonishment of strangers" when violets arrived by rail in major cities, where "thousands of City clerks appear at the office every morning with a fresh bunch of violets in their buttonholes." Anyone who has ever worn a violet in a buttonhole knows that the little blossom plays a trick on the nose. The essential oils that make up its fragrance contain a compound called ionone, which interferes with scent receptors in the nose and actually makes it impossible to detect the fragrance after just a few whiffs. The nose grows tired of the scent; it becomes temporarily blinded to it. The fleeting sweetness of the violet's perfume caused it to be associated with youth and innocence: in his book *The Foul and the Fragrant,* Alain Corbin wrote that to young girls violets "became secret confidantes, recipients, like the piano, of the impatient sighs of first emotions."

ITALIAN IMMIGRANTS COMING to the West Coast saw a business opportunity in all those impatient sighs. One of the first California violet growers was Don Garibaldi's grandfather Dominik, who arrived in San Francisco from Genoa in 1892 with a box of sweet violet plants under his arm. At the time, if San Francisco wanted the fragrant little flowers, they sent for them by train from Rhinebeck and other eastern farmers. Given the short life span of the flower and the considerable cost of transportation, Garibaldi thought there would be a ready market for fresh violets in the city. He quickly discovered another advantage: northern California's winter climate was perfect for growing violets outdoors. No greenhouses were needed to protect the flowers from snow during the holiday season.

He got a job growing vegetables near Playland, an old-fashioned amusement park that once stood at San Francisco's Ocean Beach. Don, a good-looking, silver-haired man with a strong, sturdy build and twinkling blue eyes, told me, "My grandpa's boss said, 'You can have this piece of land to grow your violets, but you also have to take care of my crops, too, because that's why I brought you here.'" In 1900 Dominik moved to Colma, just south of the city. "If you go back to Genoa," Don said, "it looks just like Colma. Same type of soil. A lot of Genovese ended up in that area." Violet growers in Colma were so successful that before long, they were shipping their flowers east during the winter. Refrigerated cars made it easier to ship flowers and produce across the country. By the early twentieth century, California was already becoming a dominant player in the cut flower industry, and its temperate climate allowed growers to feed the demand for out-of-season flowers.

Dominik Garibaldi did well as a violet grower, but it wasn't always easy. He learned what was perhaps one of the first lessons about the fickle nature of California real estate: he built a house in Colma in 1906 and finished it just two months before the earthquake that destroyed San Francisco. "But he kept going," Don told me, "building greenhouses and growing maidenhair ferns and vegetables and always the violets. In those days, there were probably forty or fifty families who tried violets at one time or another. But now, as far as I know, we're the only ones still growing them."

Don continues to grow the very same violets his grandfather brought from Italy. Unlike most other florists' flowers, they have not been improved upon, genetically modified, or coaxed into growing taller or living longer. There has been no perfume thrown on these violets.

Now his crops include other field flowers like iris, larkspur, and yarrow. "Every year we dig my grandfather's plants up and split them and plant them again," Don said. "I remember him telling us, 'Don't you stop growing the violets. I went through heck to get them here.' So I tell my son and daughter, 'If you want to quit doing this, fine. But as long as you're in the business, never stop growing violets.'"

Today, the violets are in demand as a specialty flower: in his office he showed me magazine articles in which they were used to make luscious, heart-shaped wreaths at Valentine's Day, placed in tiny glass vases as place-card holders at parties, and woven into corsages and hairpieces at weddings. I'd seen bunches of his violets for sale in flower stands around Union Square in San Francisco, where they looked like the perfect indulgence for tourists: short-lived, rare, and unforgettable. For a few dollars, you could buy a bouquet and carry it around with you until dinnertime. Why not? It's a vacation. If you want an experience that will elevate you above the bother and noise of your everyday life, violets can do that.

WHAT MAKES THESE flowers so special is the fact that they are grown on a family farm, handled with extraordinary care, and that they are nearly impossible to find outside of a hundred-mile radius from the farm itself. Before the beginning of the twentieth century, most flower growers operated about like

Don Garibaldi does. They grew their flowers in fields, trucked them to nearby markets, and built their business around a few varieties that grew well in their climate and kept money coming in for as much of the year as possible.

One of the most compelling records of early American flori-culture comes from a man named Michael Floy Jr. He left behind a diary of four years in the 1830s that he spent working for his father's business as a florist, a term that in those days referred to someone who grew as well as sold flowers. (As far back as 1782, James Barclay's *Complete and Universal English Dictionary* defined a florist as "a person curious and skilled in the names, nature, and culture of flowers.") Floy farmed his flowers on a tract of land that extended from 125th to 127th streets between Fourth and Fifth avenues on the island of Manhattan. The diary begins when he was just twenty-five and more interested in reading and collecting books than growing flowers. After a day of paperwork for the fam-ily business, he wrote, "Made out a number of bills, which Father takes and collects and keeps although it is Michl. Floy & Son; but money can do me no good. Only, if father would say, 'Mike, you are very fond of books, and if you want some to purchase for yourself and brother, you can have it,' this would look well." But even though the family business seemed to be a burden to him, he could not help but fall under the spell of the flowers themselves. The camellia in bloom, he wrote, "fairly ravishes me to look at it, the flower as white as the driven snow, every petal put so even as to defy all art to imitate it . . . [The petals] are fringed like a valen-tine, and are as neatly cut as if done with a pair of scissors by the delicate hand of a lady."

Floy, like most florists of his day, grew flowers and sold at least some of them directly to the public — in fact, a common com-plaint at that time was that women had to drag their long skirts through the mud when they came to the greenhouse to buy flowers.

In larger cities like New York, there were also shops selling locally grown flowers, seeds and garden plants, baskets and pots, and a few novelties like birdcages or goldfish in bowls. Manhattan was already known for its floral extravagances: Floy writes of a florist who did a brisk business in his camellias and reported that "a lady (a foolish one) wore a bouquet which cost $50." (By way of comparison, his father purchased a horse that year for $62.) Although retail flower shops were becoming more common in the big cities, most growers continued to sell directly to the public into the early 1900s, and it was not at all unusual for customers to buy their flowers from the person who grew them.

Charles Barnard, writing later in the nineteenth century, created a detailed portrait of the life of a flower grower in *My Ten-Rod Farm; or, How I Became a Florist*. The book is a fictional memoir of a widow named Maria Gilman who turns to flower farming after her husband dies. Although it's fiction, it's full of details about the inner workings of the flower industry. The newly widowed Maria knows nothing about gardening, but a neighbor asks if she can buy some flowers from her late husband's garden, and Maria, who doesn't have any way to support her family, agrees. She's surprised at how much the woman is willing to pay—five dollars for a basket of mignonette (a tall, spiky African flower that has entirely slipped out of vogue among florists today), geraniums, and other blossoms—that she gets up her nerve and takes a box of flowers into town. A retail florist pays her a couple of dollars for her harvest, enough to put food on the table. Each day she cuts more, selling roses, heliotropes, lilies, violets, and carnations. Along the way she encounters a couple of men—perhaps thinly disguised versions of Barnard—who give her friendly advice about her business venture. "I have long had an idea that women could become florists, as well as men," one fellow grower tells her. "Doubtless you can soon learn . . . May I venture to tell you what to do first?"

Maria's sister discovers that she proposes to support her family by growing and selling flowers, and she reacts with shock, exclaiming, "Sell the flowers! How horrid! I'm ashamed of you, Maria," but one of the florists she has befriended defends her by saying, "Are you, madam? Some people think it an honorable employment." Maria learns to handle the bookkeeping, hires extra help to do the heavy lifting, and plants the flowers that are most in demand at the shops around town.

When Barnard isn't expounding on the notion that widows can support themselves in the floral industry, he gives a practical and comprehensive view of how flowers were grown for the trade in the late 1800s. Shops purchased flowers from "private houses," residences with extensive flower gardens that produced more than the owners could use, and "commercial houses," which were owned by people who grew flowers solely as a business. Because the shops depended almost exclusively on local growers, they tried to influence what flowers were offered to them for sale by stocking the seeds and bulbs of the flowers they preferred to carry. Tuberose, jasmine, and mignonette were always in demand for their scent, and fetched a few cents a stem. In cool weather, when flowers got scarcer, the prices went up, and a grower could get a dollar for a dozen roses and a quarter for a stem of heliotrope. (It's surprising how little prices have changed in over a century. The rule of thumb in the industry is that a grower gets one-tenth of what the customer pays for a flower, so if a grower got a dollar for a dozen roses, that means that the roses were probably selling at retail for ten or twelve dollars a bunch. In fact, very high-end roses did sell for a dollar a stem in the late 1800s; today roses are available at the grocery store for that same price. Although one would have been considered a premium florist's rose and the other a discounted, everyday rose, the similarity in prices is astonishing.)

In the winter, a florist with a greenhouse could pay the bills by growing azaleas, heathers, astilbe, and fuchsia under glass. Greenhouses in those days were still quite primitive. To control the temperature, you might crank open a window or light a coal stove. To irrigate the crops, the more ingenious growers rigged up a rubber hose to a tank of rainwater so they wouldn't have to drag watering cans into the greenhouse. But even with a greenhouse, it was impossible to deliver a consistent crop to market, week in and week out. Plant science had not yet evolved enough to explain the origins of plant diseases or mysteries of how day length and temperature influenced flowering, so growers were still at the mercy of the bugs and the weather. There was no refrigeration to keep the flowers fresh after they'd been picked, and they had to endure a rough and dusty journey from the farm to the shop by buggy or streetcar. So florists grew their flowers in or near big cities by necessity: there was no way that orange blossoms, sweet peas, or violets would survive a very long journey. It was not until the late 1800s, when the transcontinental railroad became a viable mode of transportation, that growers even began to consider a flower's suitability as freight. Before then, even the most perfect flower was picked fresh, enjoyed immediately, and gone within a few days.

THE IDEA OF a farm-fresh country bouquet is starting to take hold again in the UK, according to Heather Gorringe, owner of a company called Wiggly Wigglers in Herefordshire. She founded the mail order business in 1990 with the idea of selling plants, seeds, and supplies for country living: compost bins, bird feeders, gardening tools, and the like. A few years ago, she decided to start selling locally-grown flowers by post as well.

"At first, I wasn't sure that flowers fit with what we were doing," she said. "There had to be something important about flowers to make me want to do it." Most of the products she sells are in support of something — local agriculture, wildlife, the environment. Flowers are a luxury, so why bother with them?

"But then I began to think about the things that I hate about a florist's shop," she said. "You go in, there's loads of plastic flowers, those gifts like teddy bears in yellow and pink — it's all very odd. And the flowers themselves have no smell and no joy. I wasn't even enjoying the experience of the shop."

Then she looked at what had happened to English flower farmers. Many couldn't compete with inexpensive imports from Kenya. Those who were continuing to grow flowers in the UK shipped them to one of the giant flower auctions in Holland rather than sell them locally, because local florists simply weren't set up to buy individual lots of flowers from smaller, nearby growers. Everyone worked through an international distributor or broker. "This is mad!" she said. "I thought our customers would be interested in flowers that were grown locally." There was just one problem: the flowers still had to be shipped from the farm to customers around the country. She wasn't sure if they would arrive fresh, and she wondered if she really would be reducing the carbon footprint of flowers if they had to be shipped by courier.

"Is this a good thing to do?" she asked. "We decided that, bearing in mind the size of our country, a few hundred miles was different than many thousands of miles. This is completely arguable, and if you've got somebody within a ten-mile radius supplying flowers that's even better, but we also felt that our profile could raise awareness about local farming as well."

On an average day, fifty bouquets are boxed up and shipped from Wiggly Wigglers' barn at Lower Blakemere Farm. (Heather's husband Phil operates the farm, mostly growing seed crops, and Heather runs the Wiggly Wigglers business out of an office and a few outbuildings on the farm.) Around Mother's Day, they might ship 650 bouquets in a single day. All of them come from English farmers, and they are highly seasonal. Most are grown nearby, but some come from a wholesaler who sources flowers from elsewhere in England at their request. Christmas bouquets are filled with holly, ivy, and crinkly willow, and summer bouquets hold delphinium, peonies, and sweet William. Wiggly customers know when they place their order that they cannot specify any particular flower. They'll get whatever is coming out of the fields. "We don't do color-coordinated bouquets," she said, laughing. "I don't think nature's color-coordinated."

I visited the so-called "cutting patch" on Lower Blakemere Farm one August to see just a few of the blossoms that go into Wiggly bouquets. It was exactly what you'd expect from an old-fashioned flower farm: rows of larkspur in shades of blue and pink in white, cheerful cosmos, and small patches of experimental flowers like flowering tobacco or poppy, just a dozen or two dozen at a time, to see how they'd do on a larger scale. It looked like a slightly better tended version of my own garden. In fact, when I asked Heather whether anyone ever complained about her natural, unfussy bouquets, she said, "We rarely have any complaints because we tell people up front exactly what they'll get. Once in a while someone will say, "'I've got these in my garden,' but I can count on one hand the number of times that's happened. Because most people don't have those kinds of gardens anymore. People tell us that the flowers remind them of the garden that their mother or their grandmother had, and that's exactly what they wanted."

The desire for more authentic flowers led Jane Lindsey of Snapdragon, recently chosen as one of the UK's top fifty florists by the *Independent*, to leave her job as an art gallery curator at the University of Glasgow for a career as a flower farmer. She cultivates an acre near Drymen, in central Scotland, selling seasonal flowers at farmers' markets. In the summer she supplies flowers for one wedding each weekend, turning down as many as twenty brides every year because she simply doesn't have time to do more. In the winter, she offers handmade gifts like sachets and embroidered egg cozies. She's just recently started selling her flowers online, but apart from that modern approach, her business also runs much like the florists of a century ago.

"This is not a field of tractor rows," she said. "It's much more domestic than that, more like a Victorian cutting garden. Every bit of ground is full all the time." Although her growing season only runs from May through September, she tries to expand the season by convincing people that in the winter they can send someone bulbs growing in a pot instead of cut flowers. "In February you can get forced snake's head fritillaries, and they look fantastic in a pot," she said. "And when you're through with them, you can plant them in the garden." She favors interesting and unusual flowers like black hellebore, orange parrot tulips, ornamental grasses, and fragrant blossoms like sweet peas. "If you go around to the flower shops, everybody has the same flowers," she said. "I'm not in that at all. These are not the flowers that come off the refrigerated Dutch van."

Garden writer and broadcaster Sarah Raven is an outspoken advocate for home-grown flowers as well. "The supermarkets demand such unrealistic prices for something that's quite labor intensive," she said. "That, of course, predisposes the market to the huge, monocultural, highly chemical glasshouse regimes, and also really favors the Dutch, because they have much more of the massive glasshouse systems, and also much more governmental support." She's been campaigning for people to think about not just where their food comes from, but where their flowers come from as well. She meets with florists to encourage them to buy their flowers from growers in the UK, and she tries to persuade consumers to favor those flowers that are local, seasonal, and don't require a pampered, energy-intensive greenhouse environment.

"If you've got a garden, grow it yourself," she said. "It's incredibly easy." At Christmas, she encourages people to buy amaryllis, narcissi, and other bulbs that can easily be forced in a pot. At Valentine's Day, she prefers freesia and other fragrant bulbs to roses, which must be grown in greenhouses or imported at that time of year. "I try to convince people that you don't need something imported and sort of glossy for it to be beautiful," she said. "You don't need to use ridiculous, out-of-season stuff to make something that's quite glamorous and sumptuous."

DON GARIBALDI'S FLOWER farm in California has much in common with small-scale UK growers. He doesn't grow a single flower under glass, so he's at the mercy of the weather. He and his family live on the farm, alongside the employees, and he's put in plenty of time working alongside them, too. He sells a gorgeous old flower that he believes in passionately.

One day just after Christmas, I walked with Don through his fields. Of his 150 acres, he has only about an acre and a half planted in violets, and from that he produces about fifteen thousand bunches a year. Each bunch holds twenty-five or thirty-five blossoms with about a dozen leaves tucked around the edges. They start blooming in November and continue through Easter, making them a good winter crop. By May the season is over and it's time to divide the plants and start tending to the summer-blooming annuals.

Don and I stood in the rain, looking out over the field. It was too cold to catch much of a scent from the violets, but we both bent down and peered at them anyway. The plants grew in soft mounds and already I could see young offshoots emerging from the edges of the plant, ready to be pulled apart from the center and replanted in May. Don bent over, tugged gently on a stem, and held the flower up for a photograph. On such a gray day, that damp, crumpled violet looked like the brightest thing I'd ever seen.

DON GARIBALDI'S STORY is part of a larger story of migration — both of the flower industry's migration across the country, and of the immigrant families who pioneered new varieties and techniques. Flower farming has its roots on the East Coast, but with the expansion of the railroad in the late nineteenth century, it became clear that the West offered plenty of opportunity. The carnation industry settled around Denver in the early 1900s, where the high altitude provided the intense sunlight the flowers require and allowed growers to increase their yields by a third over what they got back east. Fern pickers fanned out across the country, paying property owners in Michigan and Wisconsin to let them pick on their land. Oregon and Washington became prime bulb-growing territories, in spite of the misgivings expressed by the Dutch who shipped the first bulbs to the region. (One wrote that he had grave doubts about the ability of a man "who had not been familiarized with the industry from childhood" to succeed in establishing a new bulb-growing region.) Today Washington State's bulb fields attract tourists from around the world who come to see the wild stripes of tulips planted, Holland-style, in the fertile Skagit Valley. This discovery — that bulbs could grow as well in the Pacific Northwest as they could in Holland — meant that bulb crops like lilies, tulips, and daffodils could be grown on the West Coast and shipped across the country in mass quantity, at a time when it was still nearly impossible to get fresh flowers from Holland.

But California attracted more flower growers than any other state. Japanese immigrants who came to San Francisco in the late

1800s intended to pursue urban professions like engineering and teaching as they had in their native country, but they encountered so much discrimination that they turned to agriculture. Several Japanese businessmen noted the high price of cut flowers in San Francisco as compared with the East Coast prices and saw an opportunity. They pioneered many growing techniques that are now considered standard in the industry, including a method for growing what the trade calls pompom chrysanthemums, a kind of mum that has been allowed to produce several flowers on one stalk, as opposed to the standard chrysanthemums that are pinched back to encourage just one large bloom. Many Japanese families settled around Richmond in San Francisco's East Bay, where they were best known for their mums and roses. One particularly well-known grower, Kanetaro Domoto, planted a nursery in Oakland and sold over two hundred varieties of chrysanthemums and fifty different roses.

Italian immigrants like Dominik Garibaldi saw an opportunity to produce field-grown cut flowers like violets, snapdragons, and daisies; he and many other Italian immigrants settled just south of San Francisco along the coast. Chinese growers along the peninsula favored asters, sweet peas, and spray carnations. A similar trend took place in southern California, where Japanese, Chinese, and Korean immigrants found niches for themselves growing cut flowers in Los Angeles and San Diego. Soon each group began forming its own market to sell flowers to the trade.

Although cut flower markets began as informal meeting places where it was convenient for growers to bring their goods (one market sprang up around Lotta's Fountain in downtown San Francisco—the fountain still stands at Kearny and Market—because growers liked the easy access to water), it soon became clear that the different groups had to cooperate and come together under one

roof. The Italian market, called the San Francisco Flower Growers Association, incorporated in 1923. Japanese and Chinese growers were reluctant to join forces with them at first—each group
wanted its autonomy—but California's Alien Land Law of 1913
made it illegal for "aliens not eligible for citizenship" (meaning
Asian immigrants) to own land. Every few years, the restrictions
got tougher and it became easier for the state to seize property.
While Italian immigrants faced plenty of disadvantages, they
tended to have more access to capital through the Bank of Italy,
which later became Bank of America, and faced less difficulty in
navigating real estate transactions and legal proceedings than did
Asian immigrants. Eventually, Japanese and Chinese growers had
to admit that a partnership with Italian growers might offer them
some protection and stability.

The Chinese growers, organized under the name Peninsula
Flower Growers Association, and the Japanese growers, who had
formed the California Flower Growers Association, moved with the
Italians into the California Flower Market at Fifth and Howard
in the 1920s. The building provided twenty-two thousand square
feet of floor space, but each organization operated separately under
that one roof. They made various changes over the years, introducing a bidding system for a few years and then dropping it in favor
of allowing the growers to set their own prices, and relocating
once again when their old facility could no longer hold all the
growers.

Asian growers were forced to get creative in their business dealings;
many transferred the ownership of their land to their U.S.-born
children or created family corporations in which only citizens
held stock. The flower market itself was in jeopardy because of
the Alien Land Laws, and as war with the Japanese became more
likely Japanese board members transferred all their stock to the
American-born Nisei generation. Although FBI agents did seize

control of the California Flower Market for a few days, they returned it after they examined the records and found it to be owned by American citizens.

Still, there was little that Japanese growers could do to protect their land when, in 1942, they were forced to leave their homes. The internment of Japanese families during World War II dealt a devastating blow not just to the families but to the entire industry. Some were able to leave their fields and greenhouses in the hands of employees or trusted colleagues, hoping that they would keep the operation going and pay the taxes on the land, but others had to simply abandon their business altogether. Bill Sakai, whose grandfather started growing roses in the Richmond area in 1927, remembers how the war hurt their business, which was primarily run by Bill's father and brothers at that time. "We left it in the hands of some German employees," he told me, without a trace of irony in his voice. "We were fortunate that we had someone we could trust so that we'd have a nursery to come back to."

The greatest losses were felt among families who had been leasing land and would not be able to return to it, and growers who had devoted considerable resources to creating new hybrids and then had to abandon them. The lack of Japanese-grown flowers during the war was impossible to miss: certain varieties of chrysanthemums, for which Japanese growers were so well known, simply vanished from the market in 1942. When families did return to their farms, they depended more than ever on their American-born children to get their businesses back on sound footing. Before long, Japanese growers were once again growing tokens of love and fidelity for the country that had imprisoned them.

THOSE DAYS ARE A distant memory to most third-generation growers in California. The impact of foreign imports is impossible to ignore, except if you grow a crop that no one has figured out how to mass-produce in another country. Don Garibaldi couldn't compete if he grew roses or carnations. But as long as people want sweet violets and other field crops, he'll keep going.

Don drove me around the farm in his old truck. We couldn't go too far down the road for fear of getting stuck in the mud. He leaned over the steering wheel and pointed through the rain-streaked windshield at each field. This time of year, most of the fields are planted in cover crops, an inexpensive and time-tested way to stop erosion and put nitrogen back into the soil during winter. "We plant vetch, oats, and barley, and they grow five to six feet tall," he told me. "When we turn it under, that's a lot of good stuff going back into the ground. Earthworms? You should see the earthworms we've got. This is some good dirt."

He parked up on a hill and looked out over his fields that stretch down to the sea. Silicon Valley is an hour away. A lot of people would put up with that kind of a commute to get a view like this. He must have had some idea of what I was thinking because he said, "You know, the land values are high around here and everybody wants to build houses. But . . ." And he just shook his head as if to brush off the idea.

"Over here is delphinium," he continued, "and down below is belladonna and then stock. On that side are our bulbs — daffodil, iris, narcissus. And we grow some hydrangeas down here. You should see it in the summer. All the different colors."

I thought about Michael Floy and how he was always bewitched by his camellias, even though he was surrounded by them every day. The impact of a field of flowers in bloom is just something you never get over.

"You know," Garibaldi said as he steered the truck back toward the office, "people come here and I put a bouquet of flowers in their hand, and the response is tremendous. Like nothing else. Whiskey—that's fine. Candies are all right. But flowers? That's something different, I gotta tell you."

CHAPTER 4

Acres under Glass

The first time I went to Sun Valley Floral Farms, it was during one of the open house celebrations that they hold each July. I didn't know anything about this big farm on the outskirts of town, and if I went with any preconceived idea of what a flower farm looked like I probably pictured an operation like Don Garibaldi's. A field of yellow sunflowers, all turned to face the sun. Stripes of brilliant blue delphiniums. Acres of cosmos in cheerful pinks and reds. Maybe a barn off to the side where they kept the scissors and the buckets. It's silly, I know, but that's what I expected.

Sun Valley is nothing like that. If you pulled into their parking lot, you wouldn't know at first whether you'd arrived at a company that produces flowers, televisions, or shoes. Eventually you'd look beyond the loading dock and the warehouse and you'd get your first clue—greenhouses stretching into the distance and open fields beyond that—but initially you'd just see a dusty parking lot, a guard at the gate, and some generic-looking processing facilities. You could be anywhere. The realization that this company ships out about a hundred million stems a year sinks in slowly, as you walk through one greenhouse after another, each with a few hundred thousand lilies or tulips in various stages of bud and bloom.

For the first time, I would see flowers as the factory-produced merchandise they have become. This is business, big business. I could pretend that the flowers I buy to cheer myself up or congratulate a friend on her new baby are somehow unique, fragile, and connected to nature and gardens and plant life, but here there is no denying that each blossom is a unit of profit. What I do with it, what meanings I impose upon it, is my own business. But while it's in the greenhouse, it's a product, pure and simple.

Sun Valley is the largest producer of cut flowers in the nation. The company has 4 million square feet under production (that's how growers like to rank themselves so they don't have to give away company secrets like volume or sales figures), and the next-highest-ranking flower grower in the country has only 1.5 million square feet. Even when you include Sun Valley on a list of other greenhouse growers who produce floriculture and nursery crops like bedding plants, houseplants, seedlings, and so forth, the company still ranks in the top ten, and about 12 percent of all the cut flowers grown in this country come from one of Sun Valley's four farms in northern and southern California. For such a large operation, it somehow manages to keep a low profile. I live in a small town where everybody knows everybody, but I bet if I asked a dozen people to name the largest producer of cut flowers in the nation, not one of them would think to mention Sun Valley Floral Farms, the company just up the road that gives farm tours once a year, complete with a flower-arranging contest, hayrides through the fields, and a Jolly Jumps for the kids.

CUT FLOWER GROWERS in the United States are an endangered species. Over the last decade, the number of large growers—those with over a hundred thousand dollars in annual sales—have been cut nearly in half. The total stems produced in the United States has actually increased, but it has not kept pace with the rising level of imports, which now make up nearly 80 percent of all flowers purchased nationwide. Some flowers are hardly produced at all in this country: in 1995, there were a hundred carnation growers, and in 2005 there were just twenty-four, and they produced a paltry nine million stems while foreign growers provided almost six hundred million. Rose production has declined by a staggering 72 percent in the last ten years, with only fifty-nine large rose growers left, enough to produce less than 10 percent of the roses sold in the United States. California dominates the domestic cut flower market, growing about 68 percent of the flowers grown in the United States. Washington, known for its glorious bulb fields, comes in second with less than 5 percent. Sun Valley is one of the few companies that has managed to survive and even grow in this climate, which is remarkable considering its rocky history.

When Sun Valley president and CEO Lane DeVries was twenty-three, he saw an ad in a Dutch horticultural trade journal for a lily grower. He'd been working for his father—Lane is a fourth-generation Dutch flower farmer—but they'd had to move from their farm and were in search of another piece of land when this job came up. "I'd never done much with lilies before," Lane told me. "We were mostly in tulips. But here was this chance to go to America and try something new, work on my English, so I thought, Why not?"

George Heublein, the Oregon businessman who'd placed the ad, came to Holland to interview Lane. By all accounts, Heublein was a slick guy: stylish clothes, immaculately groomed, perfect hair. A ladies' man. A player. "That was the first American I ever met," Lane told me. "George Heublein was my introduction to the United States. Slick? This guy was all charisma. Fascinating guy. And here I am, this kid right off the farm. What did I know?"

He took the job and went to Oregon where Heublein's company, Melridge, Inc., had purchased another farm called Oregon

Bulb Farms. He was charged with the task of starting a lily-forcing program. "I'd only been there a month," Lane said, "when I started hearing talk about Sun Valley, this place in California where they grow some daffodils and irises and a few lilies."

Lane pulled some data together comparing Oregon's Willamette Valley with Sun Valley's location in Arcata. He looked at temperature, rainfall, day length, and light intensity for both areas and told Heublein, "Here are all the advantages of doing lilies in Arcata instead of Oregon. Building a greenhouse in California makes way more sense than doing it here." Heublein liked the idea, and within a few months, Lane was on a plane for Arcata.

"Three of us went down there," he told me. "We thought we were going to check it out, you know. To write a field report to take back to the boss. What we didn't know is that Heublein had already talked to Ted Kirsch about a deal. The real reason we were going down there was so that Ted could decide which one of us he wanted running the farm."

By this time—around 1983—Kirsch had ended his relationship with Leslie Woodriff, and he was ready to retire. When Heublein called, Kirsch was interested but wary. The men talked by phone a few times, and eventually Kirsch agreed to let Heublein send his staff down to take a look.

Lane and his two coworkers were in town for three days. Each night, a different one of them was invited to dinner with the Kirsch family. "We couldn't figure out why we had to go by ourselves," Lane told me. "Why couldn't we all come to dinner together?" What he didn't realize was that the dinner was a job interview, and Lane got the job.

Kirsch sold Sun Valley to Heublein, and Lane ran the farm for a few years as a Melridge subsidiary. The corporation sold over forty million dollars in stocks and bonds during that time, all based on the value their accountants placed on the flower farms

Heublein had purchased. (Some of the growers in town remember the Melridge accountants coming to town to appraise Sun Valley. "They stood at the edge of a field and tried to assign a value to every bulb in the ground," one grower told me. "We compost those bulbs at the end of the season. Only the flower is worth any money. They didn't know anything about our business.") Eventually the scheme collapsed. The company filed for bankruptcy; the shareholders sued and won; and Heublein was indicted for fraud, later arrested as a fugitive, and finally sentenced to five years in prison in 1997.

Sun Valley wasn't involved in much of the fallout from the Melridge debacle. When the corporation went bankrupt in the late 1980s, a venture capital company bought Sun Valley and a few of Heublein's other assets. That should have come as good news, but Lane remembers those years as the worst the company ever faced. "That time—almost two years—was absolute hell," he said. "We were one of the few subsidiaries that made money, but we were hooked up to this huge suction hose—this big company that was trying to pay off an impossible amount of debt. Finally, they also filed for Chapter 11." After running as a modest, but profitable, family business for decades, Sun Valley was now in its second bankruptcy proceeding in just three years.

Lane remembers the day he tried to convince the bank's lawyers to release enough money to let him pay his employees. He was only thirty years old by the time the company had reached this point, and he had dozens of employees depending on him for their paychecks. "They had frozen all our accounts," he told me. "It was early February, just before Valentine's Day. I kept trying to tell them, you can't do this. We've got to treat our people well. If we don't pay the workers, we don't get the flowers cut in time, and then we're really in trouble. Finally I told them, 'You know, you guys are up there in your nice office on the twentieth floor in downtown Portland and you think you can just deny these people their paychecks. But they had nothing to do with this. At four o'clock, you're going to have a hundred people wondering where their paychecks are. And at the end of the day, I can't guarantee what will happen to your assets if they don't get paid. What you own down here is four hundred thousand square feet of glass. Do you understand this? These are glass houses. I can't promise that at the end of the day these glass houses will still have glass in them.'"

After a long silence, the lawyers agreed to release the money, and that evening Lane handed out the paychecks. "In those days, the banks were still open on Saturday morning," Lane said. "So we gave the whole farm some time off to run and cash those checks. And I called the workers together and told them that we were facing some of the shakiest weeks of our company. I told them I didn't know if we'd even still be standing here next week. Only time would tell."

He worked out a deal with two prominent Dutch bulb growers to partner with him and buy the company out of bankruptcy. Slowly Lane and his staff grew the company out of its financial troubles. Today Sun Valley is a vastly more complex operation, with farms in four locations around California, hundreds of employees, and millions of stems leaving its loading docks every month. But it still comprises the same basic elements: flowers, people, land, and glass houses. And Lane is as fiercely loyal to them as he ever was.

As Sun Valley changed hands and fell in and out of bankruptcy, technology was revolutionizing the industry. When Lane described to me how he pored over climate data to pick the best location to grow lilies, he was pretty casual about the whole thing, as if this is something that anyone with a little common sense could figure out. But the fact is that putting the growing needs of a lily together with temperature, rainfall, and light intensity data is a major step forward for the industry and quite a bit more complicated than it sounds. During the twentieth century, while Don Garibaldi was tending his violets and Leslie Woodriff was sprinkling pollen on his lilies, botanical science took an enormous leap forward and made it possible for a young Dutch guy to land in Oregon, scour weather data, and pinpoint the best location for a lily farm before he ever set foot in California. Thanks to improved air freight systems, people like Lane and his boss could take that knowledge and scout out locations around the globe where flowers could be grown cheaply and reliably, without having to be concerned about whether there was a market nearby for the flowers.

It's surprising, really, how much of the information that growers rely upon has emerged in the last century. The notion of a gene, and the idea of dominant and recessive traits, was not fully understood until the early 1900s. Breeders would slowly figure out how to solve problems for growers by breeding in resistance to disease and pests; the ability to withstand a wider variety of growing conditions; and, as in the case of 'Star Gazer', any number of qualities that would make the flower easier to harvest, pack, and ship. But growers themselves were also innovators, introducing new technologies that made it possible to grow flowers with taller, straighter stems, flowers that bloomed out of season, and flowers that made it to the florist without so much as a blotch on their leaves or a blemish on their petals.

Two of the most popular cut flowers, carnations and chrysanthemums, became so ubiquitous not necessarily because the public loved these particular flowers but instead because growers figured out a way to raise them year-round. Once a steady supply was available to florists, week in and week out, they started finding their way into every kind of floral arrangement, from Valentine's

Day bouquets to fall centerpieces. What made the difference was the discovery, in 1920, of photoperiod.

Two scientists from the U.S. Department of Agriculture (USDA), Wightman Wells Garner and Henry Allard, were trying to cross-pollinate a winter-flowering tobacco with a summer-flowering tobacco, but they couldn't figure out how to get the plants to bloom at the same time so that they could carry out their experiments. They brought both plants into the greenhouse in the summer and tried growing them at different temperatures, hoping to reproduce winter or summer conditions and bring each flower into bloom simultaneously, but nothing worked. Finally they wondered if the development of flowers could be related to the number of daylight hours the plant experienced. It didn't seem logical that a plant could be made to bloom by shortening, not lengthening, its daylight hours, but this mimicked winter conditions so it seemed worth a try. Sure enough, once they put a tent over the winter-flowering tobacco to mimic a day with only eight hours of light, the plant came into bloom. They called this concept "photoperiod," and over time their work contributed to a widely used classification system that divides plants into short-day, long-day, and day-neutral varieties. A short-day plant like chrysanthemum will bloom only when day lengths are shorter than about thirteen hours. A long-day plant like baby's breath will flower when day lengths are longer than fourteen hours. And day-neutral flowers, including some sunflowers and asters, are not specifically influenced by day length at all.

Scientists working after Garner and Allard made another startling discovery: flowering was not actually affected by day length as much as it was by night length. In other words, it is the period of darkness that actually regulates flowering. Experiments proved this by creating artificial "days" of twenty or thirty hours in length, as opposed to a standard twenty-four hour day. If a plant requires sixteen hours of light, therefore getting eight hours of darkness in a normal day, it simply will not flower if it gets, for instance, sixteen hours of light with only four hours of darkness in between. So regardless of the number of hours of light provided, a plant will not bloom unless its requirements for darkness are met.

In spite of this discovery, growers still refer to "day length," mostly because it is more convenient to talk about the length of a day than the length of a night. But this understanding of the importance of darkness did provide growers with a useful tool. Once they knew that nighttime was critical to flower formation, they realized that they could, for example, temporarily shade greenhouses in the summertime when chrysanthemums were at risk of coming into flower too soon to meet the orders they'd taken for a fall holiday. Pulling black cloth across the glass for just a few hours a day was enough to hold them back. In the winter, when growers needed to convince long-day flowers that they were experiencing longer days and shorter nights, they could disturb the plants' sleep by setting the lights in the greenhouse to turn on for five or ten minutes an hour during the night. This brief interruption of the darkness was enough to fool the plants into thinking they were experiencing the shorter nights they need to bloom.

The understanding of photoperiod paved the way for any number of other discoveries about why plants bloom when they do. Growers already knew that some flowers, such as tulips, require a cold winter in order to bloom. But this process, known as vernalization, was imperfectly understood until scientists began carefully controlled studies in greenhouses. By the mid-1950s, growers were compiling lists of flowers and the precise chill requirements of each. The Dutch got it down to a science, designing precise, automated temperature controls that would bring flowers into bloom at exactly the right moment.

Another critical discovery took place in the mid-1980s, when a university researcher named John Erwin grew lilies under a variety of daytime and nighttime temperatures to see what combination would induce flowering first. Once the plants bloomed, he grouped them together to take photographs of them. Seeing them lined up together like that made him realize that the plants that had been exposed to the same difference in night and day temperatures were all the same height when they bloomed. In other words, it did not matter precisely what temperature the plants were exposed to, but the difference in the number of degrees between night and day temperatures did impact stem length and some other factors. This concept is called DIF (short for "difference") and is expressed by subtracting the nighttime temperature from the daytime temperature. A growing environment is described as "DIF-positive" if the DIF is a positive number, meaning that the temperature is higher during the day than at night, or "DIF-negative" if the nighttime temperature is higher. The advantage to a DIF-negative environment is that the flowers bloom while the stems are short, which may be desirable for small bouquets and potted plants (picture one of those small potted hydrangeas with three enormous blooms—that's a plant that has been forced to bloom on short stems). Even leaves are affected: Easter lilies grown in a DIF-positive environment will produce leaves that point up, but a "zero-DIF" environment will cause leaves to stick straight out. Once the leaves are mature, they'll remain at that angle and a grower can change the DIF to induce flowering without affecting the orientation of the leaves. Understanding this made it possible to offer up perfectly identical flowers year-round. As one lily grower said, "The customer doesn't care if Easter is early or late—they want the plant to look exactly the same again and again and again."

The problem with all this new information is that it was not always cost-effective for growers to tinker with light and temperature to get the kind of flower their customers demanded. Artificial light, heating, and cooling systems add an enormous and unpredictable expense to a growing operation. After all, once the customer comes to expect a particular flower every Easter, they're not likely to accept the explanation that the flowers are shorter because hikes in gas prices prevented growers from being able to set the temperature where it needed to be. But now that growers have more transportation options, they have started looking for locations that more closely meet the light and temperature requirements of their crops. That's how carnations ended up in Denver in the early twentieth century. That's how roses made it to the equator. And that's how lilies came to Humboldt County.

LANE'S ANALYSIS OF climate data proved that a place like Arcata, with cool, foggy summers and mild winters, could produce lilies year-round. As bulb-growing regions go, it could rival Holland. And the bulbs themselves do come from around the world to enjoy this perfect climate. The lily bulbs come from Lane's business partner in Holland. Tulips come from Europe, South America, the Pacific Northwest, or New Zealand. Even gerbera daisies, delphiniums, and asters start not as seeds, but seedlings, delivered by the thousands in time to meet the farm's precise planting schedule. A plant like a gerbera will be pushed to produce for as many years as it can; at Sun Valley's Oxnard facility I saw gerberas that had been blooming for over five years. But a bulb gets just one shot, one season to make its mark. It is not cost-effective for Sun Valley to coddle a bulb along year after year as its productivity declines, so after it blooms once, it gets tossed on the compost pile and a fresh bulb arrives to take its place.

A tulip or a lily shows up in Arcata packed in a plastic crate with air vents on all sides. It has been grown especially for the cut flower trade, which means that it has been fed, chilled, watered, dried, stored, and picked over by a grower who knew that it was destined not for the garden but for the greenhouse. The raising of bulbs for the cut flower industry is a specialty all to itself; most cut flower growers don't bother with bulb production because it is such a highly specialized endeavor best left to the experts.

What makes a cut flower bulb different from any other bulb? When I plant one in my garden, I expect it to come back year after year, but I'm not particularly concerned about precisely when it blooms, just how many flowers it produces or the exact size and color of the blossom. A cut flower grower, on the other hand, requires a bulb that is primed for one spectacular show. It must be packed with stored energy and ready to burst. As one lily breeder put it, the bulb is "a dynamo of energy, in a hurry to grow, bloom, and increase." It must bloom exactly on schedule, produce the precise number of buds that the customer demands (one chain of grocery stores might want four flowers per stem; another may require six), and be just the right size to fit into the space allocated to it in the greenhouse. In other words, not any bulb will do.

Each crate is packed full of bulbs—a few dozen in the case of the larger lily bulbs and a few hundred in the case of the smaller tulips—and it is in this kind of environment that they will spend the rest of their lives. One morning, Lane and I walked through the Arcata processing facility, where pallets of these crates arrive at the loading dock and are stacked above what is, essentially, a mechanized assembly line. Empty crates—the same crates the bulbs arrive in, just cleaned up and recycled as a container for planting—move on to one end of a conveyor belt, and a machine fills them with steam-sterilized soil, which is Sun Valley's own mixture of sand, compost, bark, and other ingredients. Once filled, the crates emerge on the other end of the line, where a row of workers waits to plant the bulbs that are sitting on a shelf above the conveyor belt. Each crate is planted with a specific number of bulbs—one hundred tulips, for example—which makes it very easy to count the number of flowers growing in a greenhouse. A hundred tulips per crate. A hundred crates in a row. Fifty rows on each side of the greenhouse. That's a million tulips under glass.

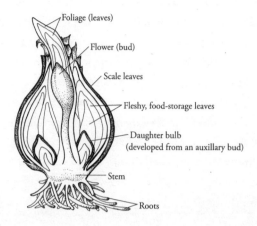

But before they go to the greenhouse to bloom, the bulbs require a cold winter. Growers' understanding of chill requirements has continued to evolve: it is now known that tulips, for instance, cannot go into their cold period too early. The flower's embryo forms inside the bulb like an infant growing in the womb. Before winter begins—whether that is a true winter or simply a false winter in the cooler—the embryo must already contain the beginnings of the flower's petals, the first leaves, and even the female reproductive anatomy, called the gynoecium. A bulb that goes into its cold period before that gestational process is complete will not bloom properly. To make sure that the embryo has developed, bulb growers dissect a random sample of bulbs during this warm phase and look for the beginnings of a fully formed flower inside.

"It used to be that you'd just plant them in the fall outside, and then at a certain point in the winter you'd dig them up and bring them in the greenhouse," Lane told me. "I used to do that as a kid.

But then in the sixties and seventies these Dutch growers started doing what they call stage research. They realized that you can't start cooling the tulip until that entire flower has formed inside the bulb. Now, based on the variety, there are a certain amount of weeks—called an in-between period—where you keep the bulb at sixty-five degrees, and then you start cooling it. If you start cooling earlier than that, you have huge losses. That's what brought the tulip from a very seasonal crop to something we could sell year-round. Now we have lists and lists of the in-between and cooling requirements for every single tulip variety we buy." Some varieties come prechilled; others have already experienced their in-between period; and others are just out of the ground, requiring quite a bit of care and handling before they ever go into the greenhouse. Most bulbs spend some time in Sun Valley's coolers before they bloom.

It is something of a misnomer to call the enormous, tightly sealed, artificially ventilated rooms at Sun Valley "coolers." They can be set to whatever temperature a flower requires, and on a chilly day it can be warmer in there with the tulips than it is outside. Lane and I went through his warehouses and down a long, wide corridor with doors to the coolers on each side. We looked into every one of these rooms, as if skipping a single one would leave me with an incomplete picture of the operation. Each time he tugged one of the heavy metal doors open and let me look inside, I felt like I was peeking into some private, intimate world. Behind each door was a different climate, a different flower, a different growing strategy. Peering into those coolers gave me one quick glimpse into the personal lives of these flowers—their unclothed, inglorious state, before they were presentable to the public, before they were ready to put on their show.

In one cooler, four-foot-square wooden crates of tulip bulbs were stacked as high and as deep as the room would allow. Dry, warm air rushed around the room. This was their in-between period—after the bulbs arrived from Holland but before they were planted in soil and given a chill period. Vents at the base of the crates forced a powerful stream of air through thousands of bulbs at once, keeping them warm and ensuring that mold or rot would not set in. The roar from the fans was so loud that I could barely hear Lane above it. "Feel the bulbs," he said, and I reached across to the top of an open crate. Sure enough, I could feel a warm wind rising from the papery, sand-colored bulbs.

Another cooler held newly planted tulip bulbs that were on hold until it was time to move them into the greenhouse. They sat in the dark, tucked into their dirt-filled, black plastic crates for a winter's nap, during which they would put down roots and push up the beginnings of leaves, but go no further. The temperature was near freezing. I could have skipped these dark, frigid rooms, but hanging out with growers requires moving from one extreme temperature to another, and it also requires standing around while they inspect the crop. I stamped my feet on the concrete floor and struggled into my sweater while Lane, oblivious to the cold, walked up and down each row of crates, checking for premature growth or signs of disease.

Without any sunlight, the pale shoots on these tulips were more yellow than green, and they looked like, well, like something that was not meant to be. In fact, the place had the air of a morgue: chilled, clinical, and impersonal. Stacks of black crates towered above my head, with only a narrow path to allow anyone to walk through them. The tulips in their crates looked like the ghosts of life, but not life itself. In another month or two, these tulips would leave the cooler and come into glorious bloom, washing the greenhouse in waves of purple and pink, yellow and red. But for now they sat by the hundreds, pale and unmoving in the dark.

I raised my camera to take a picture, but Lane waved me away. "Don't photograph that," he said.

"Why?" I asked, surprised. As far as I could tell, Lane had no company secrets. He'd never refused to answer a question and never denied me entrance to any part of his farms.

"It's . . . I don't know," he said, faltering. "They don't look right. I just can't stand to look at them when they're like this. Let's get out of here."

In these coolers, it's not just the temperature that changes. Each cooler is carefully calibrated to control the humidity, movement of air, light level, and even the amount of oxygen in the room. Lower levels of oxygen will slow down transpiration, the movement of water vapor from a plant into the air. Slowing down a process like transpiration can extend a plant's life. The goal is to keep the flowers alive and full of vitality, free of disease and ready to bloom, but also to keep them on hold until you need them. It's all about sticking to the schedule. If, sometime in November, you ask Lane how many weeks are left until Valentine's Day, he'll know without even having to stop to count. Growers measure the year in weeks; Valentine's Day falls during week 6 or 7. Mother's Day lands around week 18. The cluster of holidays in winter and spring put a lot of pressure on growers. Most of them would tell you that from their perspective a summer floral holiday, when days are long, temperatures are warm, flowers are abundant and cheap, would be nice. "We need a holiday around week 33 or so," one grower told me. "Sometime in August. After we've recovered from Mother's Day but before we get going on Thanksgiving."

The last cooler Lane took me to was empty save for two women who were scrubbing the walls with bleach and water. "Once a week we take everything out of the cooler and clean it top to bottom," Lane said cheerily, as if just the sight of something being cleaned pleased him. "You've got to stay on top of disease in this business. It's the only way." He nodded at the two women and called out, in

his Dutch accent, a barely recognizable version of "*Buenas tardes*."
They smiled at him and went back to their mopping.

FLOWERS LIVE A SHORT but pampered life in a Sun Valley greenhouse. For the most part, they don't even have to bother
putting roots down into the earth. Tulips and lilies are tucked into
their plastic crates, and gerberas live quite contentedly in plastic
pots that contain no dirt at all, just shredded coconut fiber that acts
as a clean, disease-free conduit for water and fertilizer. The flowers
are unmolested by bugs, which are kept out by virtue of screens on
the greenhouse vents, destroyed by predator insects released into
the greenhouse for just that purpose, caught on sticky traps, or
sprayed into submission with pesticides. The lighting is perfect, and
if it's not, a battery of equipment and a trained staff are there to take
care of it. It's never too hot or too cold—there are fans and heaters
and hot water pipes to make sure the temperature is perfect.

Water and food move through tiny plastic drip lines that resemble IV tubing, and if something about the meal is not quite
right, it is not incumbent upon the flower to complain. The staff
measure the fertilizer left in the water that runs out the other end
of the drip system; if there is too much of a particular nutrient
left the plants might have been overfed and unable to take up any
more, and if there is too little they might have grabbed all they
could and still felt hungry at the end of their meal. Either way,
it'll be adjusted right away, before the plant shows the first sign of
stress. They're even groomed to perfection. Smaller buds are carefully snipped off to encourage larger blossoms, and any leaf that is
blocking light to the rest of the plant or showing signs of fatigue is
quickly removed. A leaf's duty is to support the flower, not sap its
strength. If it isn't doing an efficient enough job of capturing light
to transform it into energy for the plant, it's got to go.

There are some drawbacks to this sheltered lifestyle. Green-house flowers might miss the company of bees, for instance. They don't get pollinated, because they aren't expected to reproduce and they've been bred to produce huge flowers without it. Even if a bee did sneak in and make a move, it would probably be point-less—breeders often make flowers sterile as a little extra protection for their patent. Greenhouse flowers won't feel the rain showering down on their leaves as overhead watering encourages disease and droplets of water on a leaf can intensify the sun's rays, leading to scorch. Even the wind won't shake their stems unless, of course, a good stiff breeze is needed to cool off the greenhouse, to keep gases like ethylene from stagnating, or simply to toughen up the flowers and make their stems stronger so they'll stand up straighter in the vase. In that case, the fans come on and blow an artificial wind along the rows of flowers.

As comfortable as their time in the greenhouse might be, it also goes by dizzyingly fast. A tulip can shoot up and bloom in three weeks. An Asiatic lily might take only nine weeks. Gerberas are expected to produce one or two perfect blooms every month. And when their time is up, each flower is picked individually by the same person who has cared for the plant, day in and day out, for weeks or months.

WHEN IT COMES time to harvest a flower at Sun Valley, the stem is sliced or yanked off the plant and pressed into a bundle with its mates. After a few minutes, when the worker reaches the end of the row with an armful, they'll go into a plastic bucket that has been disinfected and filled with water and preservative. Any flowers that are damaged or just not up to grade are tossed out at this point, and though it's costly to throw flowers away, it's better to pull them out now than to keep them moving through the pro-duction process. After all, a grower might get only ten or twenty cents for an individual blossom. At that price, it can't be coddled along. Besides, a damaged or diseased flower might spread bacteria to other healthy flowers. In Sun Valley's greenhouses, I was often seized with an irrational urge to dive into their enormous trash bins filled with near-perfect blossoms. A thousand bouquets' worth of gerberas, all headed for the compost bin.

Once a cart has been filled with buckets of flowers, it'll be wheeled into the production room, where the flowers will either be processed right away or put into the cooler for a day or two. (Sometimes the crew simply can't process any more flowers that day, and sometimes the flowers are put on hold because they benefit from a postharvest rest in the cooler—baby's breath, for instance, turns pink if it's allowed to open fully in the field, so it's harvested young and allowed to open in a cool space indoors where the flowers will bloom pure white.)

So they may hit the production room on the day of harvest or perhaps the day after. A different crew of workers grade the flowers, often placing each stem into a metal rack that has been marked with measurements that indicate stem length or blossom size. They'll probably go into different buckets by grade—this is particularly important for roses, whose prices depend greatly on size and length. And they'll toss out any substandard flowers that the harvest crew missed.

Gerberas may be packaged with little plastic sleeves around each blossom to keep the petals together. Some flowers, like tulips, may be harvested with their bulbs still attached, so at this point the stem is sliced and the bulb is tossed out. The stems are cut to a precise length depending on the customer's requirements. The flowers go into bundles, they're wrapped in paper and cellophane sleeves, and they're dropped into a box.

At Sun Valley, the postharvest treatment is fairly automated. There are machines and devices that do some of the cutting and stripping and banding and bagging. There are bar codes and computerized instructions to help the staff figure out what goes where. But it's still a labor-intensive process. I met a Dutch intern at Sun Valley once who told me that he found their operation to be fairly primitive by Dutch standards. "Labor costs are very high in Holland, so we automate as much as possible," he said. "Here you can afford to use more workers and fewer machines." But with workers' compensation and health insurance costs on the rise, not to mention the increased cost of housing in Arcata that puts pressure on wages, it is not so true anymore that labor is cheap in California. I once asked Lane if the Dutch really were so much more innovative with their labor-saving devices. "Not really," he said. "They're always trying something new, but I don't know if it really saves enough labor to make it worthwhile. You know, we Dutch are all such trend followers. One of them starts growing tulips in water, and then everyone does it. Now they're tired of it and they're starting to grow tulips in soil again. They're always trying something new, but I don't know if it really gets them anywhere."

Although Sun Valley's equipment doesn't allow you to stick a bucket of flowers in one end and pull a sleeved bouquet out the other, there's still a fair amount of automation. The production line is both high tech and low tech at the same time. The conveyor belts and the bar codes are all pretty impressive, but it really comes down to a bunch of people in gloves and aprons standing on a wet concrete floor that is piled with torn leaves and wilted petals. No matter how slick and automated the process becomes, there's always something a little messy, a little green and earthy, about a postharvest room.

The flowers are not in water at this point, and they won't be in water again until they reach the flower shop or the wholesale market. Each box is loaded onto a pallet and moved back into the cooler, where the goal is to keep them in the cold and dark so the buds don't open, the leaves don't breathe, and, as much as possible, the flowers don't age. By the next morning, they'll leave the farm for their next destination.

This is the best care these flowers will ever get, and growers are painfully aware of that fact. As the flowers begin their journey to the customer, their fate is out of the growers' hands, and they can only hope that the merchandise will be treated well along each step of the journey so that it will have a long vase life once it reaches its final destination. With any luck, at least some of the trucks will be refrigerated. Maybe they've got an airplane ride ahead of them. It should be cold in the baggage hold once the plane takes off, but how long will they sit on a hot runway in July? How long will they wait in a cargo bay in Los Angeles or Denver? And when they arrive at the grocery store or the wholesaler or the florist, how long will it be before someone pulls them out of the box, recuts the stems (one hopes), and puts them in water? By the time the customer sees the flower for the first time, it may be four or five days old, and the real performance hasn't even begun. Now the flowers have to go home with somebody who expects them to last a week in a vase, even if they drop the stems into water without recutting them and set them in a sunny window or (a grower's worst nightmare) on top of the TV, where the heat from the set will bring about their demise. These are all the things a grower worries about but can't control. And Sun Valley is just one of thousands of growers trying to get it exactly right.

VISITING A FLOWER FARM is kind of like visiting a chocolate factory. In many ways, it's the most ordinary, run-of-the-mill operation, with warehouses and machinery and people doing their jobs and looking forward to their coffee breaks. But the product itself is magical, transcendent, and utterly distracting. How could a person get any serious work done in the presence of a vat of liquid chocolate? The same is true of flowers. I wasn't always prepared for the response those flowers would elicit in me. When I walked through Sun Valley's greenhouses, I'd see several hundred pink and yellow gerberas wheeling past me on a cart, so bright and perfect that it was hard to resist reaching out and grabbing one as they went by. A conveyor belt piled with dusky purple hyacinths made my heart turn over. I wanted to sweep them all into my arms at once and carry them outside, where the warm air and the sunshine would draw out their perfume. Luxurious 'Casa Blanca' lilies and premium French tulips sat by the hundreds—even the thousands—waiting for a buyer, and one time I almost turned to Lane and asked him if I could just take the lot home with me, no matter the cost. But a flower grower can't think like that. To him, this is a farm, an agricultural enterprise like any other. Sun Valley faces all the same issues associated with agriculture—issues like immigrant labor, pesticide regulations, and overseas competition—that any other California farm must grapple with.

Lane has watched many of his fellow flower growers go out of business or switch from growing to importing and wholesaling. Their complaints are familiar to anyone in the trade. Workers' compensation costs are too high. Land is expensive. Energy deregulation in California didn't work; utility bills are astronomical. Worst of all, farmers complain, they are shackled with regulations and restrictions on the chemicals they can use, which leaves them at an unfair disadvantage against Latin American growers who export flowers, tariff free, that have been sprayed with chemicals that are banned in the United States. But Lane just shrugged off those concerns. "We have to find what we do well," he said, "and be the very best at it." He said it with such certainty that it was impossible not to believe him.

Confidence alone isn't enough—getting a hundred million flowers out the door every year requires people. Sun Valley employs over five hundred at its four farms and more during major flower holidays like Christmas, Valentine's Day, Easter, and Mother's Day. Almost all the workers I saw handling the flowers were Latin American immigrants, and the supervisors sitting around the table at meetings spoke a mixture of Spanish, English, and Dutch.

Sun Valley's culture, then, is an odd blend of the nationalities that make it run. In this way, the company seems to straddle the extremes of the global floriculture trade. The Dutch, on one hand, dominate the industry with a kind of cool, calm certainty that comes from having been in the business, almost as a national pastime, for the past four hundred years. Even though cut flower growing has been moving out of Holland for over a century—first to the United States and then to countries along the equator—the Dutch still export new varieties, growing techniques, and green-house technology. They also hold the purse strings, owning patents on varieties grown around the globe and setting worldwide prices through their auctions. And they are still the tastemakers: the most ordinary grocery store bouquet in Amsterdam is more stylish and innovative than anything I might find in the United States.

Increasingly, however, the flowers themselves are grown in Latin America (or, for European consumers, in Africa). Sun Valley's success depends on how well Lane can bring Dutch ingenuity to bear on an operation that also enjoys a few of the benefits of growing south of the border: a temperate climate and a skilled, but lower-paid, workforce.

Immigrant labor is what drives agriculture in California, where only 5 percent of all farmworkers were born in the United States. Sun Valley is no exception. Still, the company seems to encourage families to settle in Humboldt County by employing a fairly stable crew year-round and offering English classes and even health insurance and a retirement plan for employees who have been with them for over a year. (This is no small matter—a Department of Labor survey showed that only about 5 percent of farmworkers reported being covered by an employer's health insurance plan.) That's not to say that picking flowers in a greenhouse is a dream job—it's hard labor, there's a risk of exposure to chemicals, and you have to go in and out of those freezing coolers all day—but as agricultural work goes it's probably not the worst job out there. And perhaps because Lane worked on a farm himself growing up, he seems to genuinely believe that the experts on his crops are the people who handle them every day.

One morning, Lane invited me to attend his weekly meeting with his supervisors. There would be one representative from each crew, a crew being a group of people who have the exclusive responsibility for one particular crop. There's an iris crew and a tulip crew, a lily crew and a larkspur crew. Within the crew, each member takes charge of a few rows of plants, getting to know them intimately, ushering them from their first sprout to their final bloom. Every stem, every blossom, and every bruised and discarded flower is meticulously tracked and charted. These flowers represent profit, and they're counted down to the penny.

The supervisors met in an ordinary conference room that had been equipped with a laptop and a projector. A couple dozen chairs were crammed around the table and more were lined up in the back of the room. I sat in the corner and watched the staff file in and take their seats. With little fanfare, Lane switched on the projector and started working his way through a series of PowerPoint slides. For each flower the farm produced, there was a chart showing the preharvest, harvest, and packing costs (usually a few cents a stem each), natural gas usage, reported injuries, and recovery rate—the percentage of bulbs that produce flowers that are actually sold. One of Lane's managers translated what he was saying for the mostly Spanish-speaking crew leaders. We went through each crop that way—Asiatic lilies, Oriental lilies, gerberas, germinis, asters, delphiniums. Some of the crews would be rewarded for their production. All of them would be reminded that every flower counts.

I tried to gauge the staff's reaction to this slide show. These were mostly middle-aged guys who had probably immigrated to the States when they were young and worked their way up from field hand to crew leader. They said little and took no notes, and because of that the meeting moved along quickly, with Lane doing most of the talking. I wondered how much anyone else cared about these charts and numbers. We were talking about flowers, after all. No matter how much you treat floriculture as a science, it is impossible to pin it down too much. Bar graphs of costs per stem seemed awfully abstract compared with a greenhouse full of living, breathing plants. If I ran the lily crew, I'd probably sit in that meeting wishing I could get back to my lilies.

But after the meeting, I followed Lane on one of his habitual walks through the farm with his crew leaders and realized that they had not only paid attention to his PowerPoint show, they had memorized the numbers for their crops and wanted to talk about them in the field. "Here's our low larkspur numbers," Lane said, looking out over a field of lacy green foliage. "I thought they'd be further along. But it was too cold last week, wasn't it?" The larkspur boss nodded but pointed out that another farm just a couple miles up the road already had larkspur in bloom. Lane took a step back in genuine surprise. "What? Really? They're in bloom before us? See if you can figure out why." In the greenhouse, a few rows of gerberas were hardly producing any flowers at all. "That explains it," Lane said, referring to another production number he wasn't so happy with. His gerbera guy reached down and wrapped his hand around a black pipe that ran alongside the base of the plants. "It's cold," he said. "Went out a few days ago." He explained that he suspected that the lack of heat prevented the plants from taking up enough nutrients, which lowered yields and drove up the cost per stem. "Wow," Lane said. "That much of a difference?" The pipe would be fixed the next day, and I knew that a week from now Lane would be standing in this very spot, checking to be sure the gerberas had caught up, comparing them against the numbers he'd loaded onto his laptop and recited at his morning meeting.

On Lane's weekly walks through the farm, he was usually flanked by five or six staffers, with people arriving and departing from the group as he made his way through their crops. Sometimes, watching Lane, it was hard to remember that I was there to take notes about the flowers. I was too distracted by the way he ran his business, the amount of detail he managed to carry around in his head. He's the kind of guy that management gurus love to tell stories about, but they never will, because I don't think Lane could stand the attention. Whenever I asked him who was responsible for making major decisions about what to plant, how to grow it, or how to sell it, he'd shrug and say, "It's kind of a group effort. We do it as a team." It's clear that he doesn't want anybody to make a big deal about what he does, but this is the largest cut flower farm in the country, and it was impossible to ignore the fact that it was run by someone who spent as little time behind a desk as he possibly could. He runs the place from the field, and it's something to watch.

At Sun Valley's Oxnard farm, Lane stopped before a freshly dug field that was about to be planted with larkspur. "We're doing hoop houses here, right?" he asked his farm manager, who nodded. (A hoop house is a very informal kind of greenhouse made with pipes bent into a half circle and plastic sheeting stretched across them—not much more than a giant umbrella.) "Are we building them ourselves?"

"We don't have a pipe bender," his manager said. "So we'll have to buy them, and it's an odd size we need."

"Hold on," Lane said, and fished his phone out of his pocket. He called the farm in Arcata. "Can we send the pipe bender down?" I heard him asking. "Yeah, on the truck. No, just whenever you can. Okay, tomorrow's good." He turned to his manager. "You've got your pipe bender."

Another hoop house was filled with asters in full bloom. At the end of each row was a rack of white plastic buckets, where the workers would assemble loose bouquets on the spot. "Why are there so many pink asters in the field, but we're only putting one stem of pink in the mixed bouquets?" Lane asked. His aster boss explained that the office—meaning the people who analyze the planting schedule and match it up with orders from customers—had specified just one pink stem per bouquet.

"But the pink ones are coming in faster than we thought," Lane said. "Don't worry so much about what somebody sitting in an office tells you. You're here in the field, you see what's going on. Let's use two pink stems until it evens out again."

Every one of these encounters elicited a shy smile from the staff. There's nothing like having someone breeze in, week after week, who can see the problem in an instant and solve it on the spot. But that wasn't the only thing that surprised me about Lane. He seemed to be able to get his mind around every piece of the business, no matter how small. We stopped in a field that was, by all appearances, empty. He bent down, plunged a bare hand into the dirt, felt around, and pulled out a newly planted iris bulb. His staff gathered around and he explained what he was doing. "I'm looking for soft tissue around the root ring," he said, "and spots. That's a sign of fusarium." He took out a pocket knife and sliced the bulb in half to check the development of the embryo. "Good," he said, tossing the two halves over his shoulder and moving on.

Just outside a greenhouse, he stopped in front of a test plot of yellow spider lilies, an otherworldly flower in the amaryllis family with long, skinny petals that resemble spiders' legs. "I don't know about these," he said. "They take up a lot of space and they don't all come up at once." He bent down to pick one of the flowers and the entire root ball started to lift out of the ground. He groaned, disappointed, and pressed his foot against the base of the plant to keep it in the soil while he snapped the stem off. "And we're going to have to cut them. We can't just pick these." Using a knife slows the work down and spreads disease. There's a trick to snapping a flower off at the heel, and if you can get the hang of it, it makes things easier on the plant and the picker. (Some Dutch growers I met declared that their own countrymen had an innate knack for this technique that was unmatched by any other nation's labor force, but I never heard Lane make that claim.) Lane stood looking over the scraggly patch of lilies. "Hmmm," he said. "We'll see about this." He carried the flower around with him for the rest of the day. That night, on a chartered plane back to Arcata, he reached under his seat and pulled out the flower, which was by now covered in dust and wilted. Sun Valley's bouquet designer was on the plane with us that day. "See what you can do with this," he said, dropping the flower in her lap.

"How much do you need to make on it?" she asked, holding it up and turning it around slowly. "And when is it available?" To get her an answer, Lane opened his laptop and started looking over production data, planting schedules, and per-stem costs. He'd be immersed in spreadsheets and e-mail for the rest of the flight. We'd been up since five, and it was now past dinnertime. He showed no signs of slowing down.

The plane from Oxnard landed after dark. I'd been marching through the fields all day, trying to match Lane's long stride, take notes, and snap pictures all at once. I couldn't wait to get home and crawl in bed. I stood in the parking lot, chatting with another staffer while we watched Lane get into his truck. "Lane is the first one in the office in the morning," she told me, "and we've seen him driving the fields at 2 a.m. He doesn't stop. I've never met anybody so driven." Another employee is fond of saying, "There is the speed of light, the speed of sound, and the speed of Lane." He waved at me as he pulled out of the parking lot, and as I watched him drive away I realized that he was probably not headed home but back to the Arcata farm, where the lilies and the tulips sat under glass, in the dark, waiting to bloom.

CHAPTER 5

How the Dutch
Conquered the World

It is impossible to be around the floriculture industry for any
length of time without running into the Dutch. They're everywhere. At a flower trade show anywhere in the world, you'll see
vendor booths dominated by cardboard windmills, blue and white
Delft vases, and photographs of their legendary tulip fields. Hang
around growers in Latin America, or Miami, or southern California,
and you'll always hear a Dutch accent somewhere in the room. This
is, in many ways, their industry, one they have exported to the rest
of the world and still keep a hand in, watching over it like the wise,
all-knowing company founder who just won't retire.

The Netherlands got into the business over four hundred years
ago. In those days, the Dutch East India Company and the Dutch
West India Company dominated the world trade in spices, furs,
sugar, and coffee. Turkey was an important trading partner for the
Dutch, and flowers native to that area made their way to European
gardeners through Turkish-Dutch trade routes. It is practically a
matter of national folklore that in 1593, a botanist named Carlos Clusius arrived in Holland with his collection of bulbs that
included a relatively unknown wildflower from Turkey and Per-
sia—the tulip. Among Europeans, tulips were so unusual that the
bulbs were sometimes mistaken for onions and boiled and eaten.
Clusius had brought them to Leiden as part of his new post at that

university's botanical garden. This was the first known instance of a tulip arriving in Holland.

It's hard to imagine what gardeners and botanists must have thought of these exotic, but also surprisingly simple, flowers. A tulip is nothing more than six upright petals that form the shape of a bowl. There's rarely any scent to speak of. Each plant supports just two or three strappy leaves, and those wither away in the summer. Some of the wild specimens have such narrow, pointed petals that they hardly resemble the flower we think of as a tulip. But tulips had been cultivated since about AD 1000 in the Ottoman Empire, and the specimens that diplomats, merchants, and explorers brought from Turkey were a revelation. They bloomed in glorious, brilliant colors, curved and drooped on their slender stems, and opened gradually, becoming even more beautiful as the petals dropped, one by one, onto the table. It's no wonder that Dutch masters rushed to paint them in overflowing vases, where they were often portrayed as sensuously drooping blossoms alongside summer peonies and other impossibly out-of-season flowers.

Clusius cataloged the tulips he'd collected, identifying a few dozen by their shape, color, and blooming time. The bulbs continued to arrive in Holland from collectors eager to share their bounty, and soon tulips were all the rage. The brilliant purples and reds were like nothing else horticulturalists had seen at the time, and the flower quickly came to be considered a crowning jewel in the gardens of the wealthy and among flower growers (already called florists in those days), who hoped to make their profits selling not just the cut flower but also the bulblets that the tulip would produce. Individual tulip bulbs fetched higher and higher prices in the seventeenth century, setting off the frenzy known as tulip mania. Wealthy Dutch merchants outbid each other at auctions, knowing that they could buy a bulb one day and flip it for a quick profit the way people flip real estate in a hot market. The analogy is not as far-fetched as it sounds: in those days, a single prized bulb could sell for the price of a Dutch canal house. Among aristocrats, even the cut flowers were sold at outrageous prices. It was the height of French fashion around 1610 for a woman to wear a tulip the way she might wear a jewel.

The speculation was fed by a random, and poorly understood, element to the flower's coloration. Clusius noticed that some tulips had a tendency to "break"—to emerge with wild, flaming white or yellow streaks across the petals. The broken flowers were highly sought after, but no one knew what caused the flamboyant patterns. Any number of worthless potions came on the market with the promise of producing broken tulips. Growers even tried cutting the bulb of a red tulip in half and tying it to half of a white tulip bulb in hopes of producing a single striped flower. (This, of course, was utter folly and had no chance of actually working.) Already, florists were dedicating themselves to pushing flowers to new heights. They would bankrupt themselves in pursuit of the perfect blossom.

At the time, no one could have guessed that the true cause was a virus. In fact, it was not until the early twentieth century that tulip breaking virus, also called tulip mosaic virus, was finally identified. The virus is spread by aphids and works by inhibiting the amount of anthocyanin (the same color pigments that John Mason works with to develop a blue rose or a purple carnation) that is stored in the vacuoles of each cell. When that pigment isn't present, the ordinary white or yellow surface of the petal shows through, creating streaks of white or yellow against a jewel-colored background.

Modern versions of these broken tulips are still popular. Sun Valley grows 'Flaming Parrot', which, with its swirls of raspberry and apricot and its jagged, feathery edges, would have driven the early Dutch flower traders to distraction. But there's no trace of tulip breaking virus in these new hybrids, for good reason: The same virus attacks lilies, with a much less pleasing effect, and even the color patterns it creates in tulips are unpredictable. No commercial grower would want to bother with it. Instead, hybridizers have selectively bred for the mutation and created genetically stable lines of tulips that will reliably produce the streaked petals for generations. These modern hybrids are sometimes called Rembrandt tulips (an ironic choice since Rembrandt was not particularly known for his flower paintings), and they're much more suitable for the floral trade than their diseased predecessors.

But in those days, the inability of botanists to determine the source of the color patterns meant that buyers would pay outrageous prices for the hope of getting a broken tulip. In their search for novelty, a florist might pay a few thousand gilders for one bulb, an amount of money that could have purchased quite a laundry list of ordinary goods: several pigs, oxen, and sheep, a few tons of grain, tons of butter, barrels of beer, and a ship to carry them on.

The crash of the Dutch tulip market arrived quite suddenly at an auction in early 1637, when the bidding for a pound of tulips started at 1,250 gilders. No one bid. The price dropped, and then dropped again, and as the moments passed with none of the assembled group of florists jumping in with a bid, it became clear that the bottom had just fallen out of the market. Before long, the bulbs were worth less than 5 percent of their original price. Bankruptcies were widespread, charges of fraud were levied, and disputes dragged on in the courts for decades.

In spite of the painful lessons of this market craze, the Dutch continued to dominate as tulip growers. Rare and unusual bulbs could sometimes fetch higher prices, but after the tulip mania ended an ordinary tulip bulb would cost a much more reasonable price of one gilder. Dutch farmers also began growing another bulb that Clusius introduced, the hyacinth. A minor frenzy for hyacinth bulbs flared up exactly one century after the tulip mania ended, but prices were nowhere near as extravagant and the craze died out quickly.

Over the next couple of centuries, Dutch growers continued to fill agricultural land with bulbs. Holland is a country that is barely above sea level in its highest spots; as the draining of lakes and the construction of canals and dams made it possible to claim more land, the bulb fields expanded to their present size of more than fifty thousand acres. Production has now reached over ten billion flower bulbs, about 65 percent of the world market. Holland's bulb industry is worth about a billion dollars (at the wholesale level) annually.

Tourists who flock to Holland's famous tulip fields in the spring are actually witnessing more than an overblown horticultural spectacle: those fields are also a part of the cut flower production process. The tulips are usually not being grown for their flowers; they are being raised to maturity for what's belowground—the bulb. About two-thirds of the bulbs from these fields are sold to the cut flower trade to produce more tulips, and the rest go to home gardeners. The brilliant stripes of blossoms every April and May are simply a necessary by-product of bulb production, and a lucrative one considering that the bulb fields bring in 1.5 million tourists each spring.

It's surprising, then, that in spite of all that Dutch growers owe to their tulip-loving ancestors, there is very little effort to preserve the past. Amsterdam is a city of museums: the tourism bureau estimates that there are fifty-one in the city, but I suspect the actual number is quite a bit higher. In Amsterdam I saw museums devoted to tattoos, trade unions, journalism, beer, marijuana, sex, the Ajax football club, torture, and cats, to name a few. But only recently did a small museum devoted to Holland's tulip-growing past open in Amsterdam. Before that, the closest you could come was the Hortus Bulborum in Limmen, where a group of dedicated volunteers, most of them quite elderly, maintain a living museum of the nation's remaining stock of heritage bulbs. Year after year they preserve such rarities as the red and yellow 'Duc van Tol' from 1595, the broken 'Absalon' from 1780, and the parrot tulip 'Admiral de Constantinople' from 1665, among hundreds of others. The Hortus also houses a small collection of equipment from the early days, including baskets, tools, and wooden implements for sorting and grading the bulbs. But even this modest collection takes up more space than the group has available, and some of the artifacts have had to be stored in the shed of a local farmer.

To ensure the survival of these old bulbs, Hortus volunteers encourage the owners of historic homes to plant the old bulbs in their gardens, and they sell limited quantities through bulb exporters in the hopes that gardeners will let them multiply. And old bulbs come in from growers around the country. "They get calls from people who say, 'I have these old bulbs in a shed. I was going to throw them out. Do you want them?' " Leslie Leijenhorst, author of a Dutch book on the Hortus, told me. "And they go get them. They'll go anywhere to get the old bulbs."

The gardens open for a brief period every spring when the flowers are in bloom, but the Hortus volunteers complain that Holland's many tulip breeders and growers don't show up to view the collection or to use its genetic stock in their own breeding programs. One retired board member is quoted in Leijenhorst's book as saying, "Some bulb growers navigate too readily on their automatic pilot. They make crosses using contemporary hybrids, which inevitably leads to inbreeding. Our botanical collection offers unique genetic material with which they could breed new cultivars, thus incorporating the qualities of the old ones." Without adequate support from the bulb trade or some other source, the Hortus Bulborum's future is uncertain. Leijenhorst told me, "I'm quite afraid that the average bulb grower still doesn't know the importance of this collection. They can use the old qualities — not just color, shape, disease resistance, but even scent. The old tulips had a scent, you know, unlike the modern ones. So they should use the Hortus more than they do."

Perhaps the lack of interest in cultivating old varieties is just another sign that the Dutch flower business is in a constant state of change. Tulips were never the only flower that interested growers. By 1880 greenhouses that had been used for vegetables were converted into special glass houses for the forcing of roses and lilacs. Growers figured out how to bring these flowers into bloom well before the spring season, and with that technology came a marketplace. In the early twentieth century, several small flower auctions sprang up in areas where growers were concentrated, and a new floral commerce was born, not just for tulips but also for daffodils, hyacinths, irises, roses, and any other flower that the public demanded. This broad diversification and constant innovation paid off: today the country has about twenty thousand acres devoted to cut flower production, with sales reaching four billion dollars a year. The Dutch auction system serves as a global marketplace for cut flowers, with over half of all international trade in flowers taking place through one of these auctions.

Now that growers are moving to Africa and Latin America in search of better weather and lower costs, the Dutch have adapted once again by exporting their knowledge. Breeding programs, greenhouse technology, and the financial strength of the international flower auction are Holland's major contributions to the industry today. It's not uncommon to meet a Dutch grower who is at once a hybridizer, a grower, a wholesaler, and an exporter, working on the challenge of building a better flower from every angle of the business.

THE VIBRANT ENERGY of the Dutch flower industry is evident the minute you arrive at Amsterdam's Schiphol Airport. You can buy a bag of tulip bulbs or a bouquet of gerbera daisies right in the terminal, before you even claim your luggage. Step off the train in Amsterdam's bustling Central Station and someone is sure to whiz past on a bicycle with a five-foot-long bunch of gladioli perched on the handlebars. Take a tram and you'll find the floating flower market on the Singel Canal, which is open every day until sunset. The market dates back to 1862, when flowers were transported into the city by boat. Today business is done out of sturdy market stalls that just happen to float like houseboats on the canal, and the flowers themselves arrive by truck, not boat. Even with these modern changes, however, this daily flower market in the heart of the city serves as a kind of bellwether for the industry, overflowing with lilies or roses or tulips as they move in and out of season.

Looking through the cash-and-carry mixed bouquets is like getting a preview of what might be popular in the States in a year or two: fat yellow chrysanthemums paired with green opium poppy pods, for instance, or monochrome blends of dark red gerberas, fuzzy burgundy cockscomb, wine-colored foliage, and, tucked around the edges, wild blackberries still ripening on the vine in shades of green, red, and blackest purple. Who puts blackberries in a bouquet, especially in an ordinary cash-and-carry bouquet? The Dutch do, and that means that soon the rest of us will, too. The market serves as a sort of escape valve for the trade, releasing surplus flowers and the latest floral trends into the streets of Amsterdam.

I took a bus from Central Station to the small town of Kudel-staart, where one greenhouse after another dotted a landscape that was otherwise populated by green pastures, sheep, and cows. The bus stopped in front of Terra Nigra's low-slung glass and concrete office. Although the company is known primarily as a breeder, it also uses some of the most up-to-date growing methods in its trial greenhouses to grow roses and gerberas, and the plants are shipped to facilities it owns in California and Kenya so that they can be tried out in different climates. I'd come to see exactly what kind of technology the Dutch were exporting to the rest of the world.

Peter Boerlage, the son of the company's founder, met me in the lobby of the office. It was an ordinary enough place, with a receptionist sitting behind a desk, a magazine rack filled with the company's catalogs and annual reports, and gray-carpeted hallways leading to offices and laboratories. Peter's a young guy, probably in his thirties, with thinning hair and an open, smiling face. He spoke English with a heavy accent, and even in English he was plainspoken and articulate.

Peter, along with his siblings, took over the business from his father and uncles. "They started in 1971, just as rose growers," he told me. "But my dad was interested in how to propagate plants, and he started one of the first tissue culture laboratories in Holland. We still do all our breeding here."

Terra Nigra still produces roses, but it is probably best known for the novel shapes and colors its breeders have managed to coax from gerbera daisies. Peter and I stepped through a sliding glass door and onto a concrete floor, and there we were in a bright, clean greenhouse bursting with flowers. The gerberas seemed to bob and wink atop a sea of foliage, and although they're a fairly small flower, with no scent at all, a greenhouse full of them has a certain uplifting presence.

At first, Peter didn't have to do much in the way of explanation; he simply led me through one room after another, and I pointed and grinned and made insightful comments like "Wow. Purple. Oh look, tangerine." I think Peter must have learned that the sight of his flowers has an intoxicating effect on the uninitiated, and it's best to just give them a little time to adjust. In every greenhouse, a sea of gerberas faced up toward the sky, seeking the light, their petals forming waves of shocking pink and saffron. It's impossible not to be dazzled by the sight of them. Even Peter, who'd grown up around them, would stop me as we walked down an aisle and say, "It is beautiful, right?"

Right. As I stood with him and looked out across several dozen rows of sunny orange gerberas in bloom, I thought that I'd probably never seen so much exuberance in one place. This is not a flower with nuance. It radiates pure, uncomplicated happiness. You have to love it, although I can see how a person could get cynical enough to be irritated by its unwavering good cheer. I know some florists who are sick of gerberas, bored with their endlessly sunny dispositions and their utter lack of mystery or depth, but not me. A single gerbera on my desk makes me smile every time I look at it. I'm grateful to it for that.

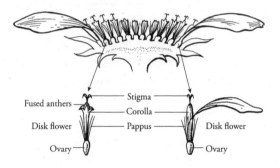

The gerbera is a member of the composite family, which also includes sunflowers, asters, and chrysanthemums. Many of the flowers in this family sport a basic daisy shape, with petals emerging, like rays of the sun, from a yellow center. What most people don't realize is that a gerbera daisy, like other flowers in its family, is actually made up of many tiny flowers clustered together to form the appearance of a single blossom. The flowers in the center are called disk flowers, and they are so tiny that they are almost impossible to distinguish as individual flowers. Instead, they form a green or yellow mound in the middle, and each one may be individually pollinated and produce seed. There can be hundreds of these tiny disk flowers in the center of a single composite. Around the edge are ray flowers, which are often sterile, and it is from these ray flowers that a gerbera's showy, straplike petals emerge.

Look closely at a gerbera and you will see a bunch of smaller, shorter, more tightly clustered petals near the center; these are called trans florets. Some of the most exciting breeding involves making those smaller trans floret petals a different color from the larger ray florets that surround them. A gerbera that shows no trans florets is called an empty gerbera in the trade; there are also half-filled and whole-filled gerberas, depending on how much of the flower's face is taken up by these ruffled trans florets.

The gerbera (also called a Transvaal daisy) is native to parts of Africa, Asia, and South America. The species most commonly grown today was identified by the botanist Robert Jameson in the late nineteenth century and was described for the first time in botanical literature in 1889, bearing the name *Gerbera jamesonii*. The flowers were red or creamy orange, with long, spiky petals that sat atop a leafless stalk called a scape (a stem, according to botanists, is the leaf- and flower-producing part of a plant; a scape is a stem that produces flowers but no leaves). Since its discovery, the gerbera has been bred with other species throughout the twentieth century to produce the perfect specimen for the cut flower industry. By the 1980s, when bright colors and clean, modern shapes were fashionable, gerberas became firmly established in the market. Today it is the fourth-most-popular flower sold at the Dutch auction, ranking just behind roses, tulips, and chrysanthemums in popularity. Americans alone buy over two hundred million stems a year. It's a flower that's hard to resist: the clear, brilliant colors and the iconic daisy shape make it a pop art version of a flower, so cheerful and perfect that it hardly seems real.

About 30 percent of the gerberas sold around the world come from Terra Nigra's stock, and, as Peter told me, "The rest come from our neighbors down the street." The ordinary two-lane road in Kudelstaart is a kind of Madison Avenue for gerberas, with all the big-name designers clustered within a few blocks of each other. I had arrived at the birthplace of almost every gerbera in the world.

"So you keep an eye on your competition?" I asked Peter once I'd stopped gawking at the flowers.

"No, it is not like that," he said. "We talk all the time. If one of us thinks of something—a new innovation—we tell the others so we can all try it."

"Are you kidding?" I said. "That would never happen in the States. None of the flower farmers I've met want their competition to know anything about what they're doing."

"Well. Maybe that is your problem," Peter said cheerfully, as if it was a small triumph that we had seized on this essential truth. Dutch growers are known for working together like this, and after just a few days in Holland I was already seeing the merits of a cooperative approach. This is, after all, a small country with limited space for agriculture and competition coming from around the world. By sharing new techniques and even sales figures, growers believe they can work together to keep their industry afloat.

Terra Nigra's catalog offers 209 different gerberas for sale. The germinis—smaller gerberas with flowers under three inches in diameter—make up over a third of their offerings. Their popularity is due not just to the fact that they're a little more affordable, but also because, like the 'Star Gazer' lily before them, they are easier for the growers to handle. In the packing room, gerberas were sorted and boxed for shipping. A large gerbera with a diameter of four to five inches has to be packed in a shallow cardboard box, not too different from a shirt box, with holes punched in the back of the box. One stem runs through each hole and hangs straight down against the back of the box. The blossoms remain inside the box, flush against the cardboard. The boxes hang from a rack, like so many shirts, until it's time to ship them. Even during shipping, they are always stored upright. Gerberas respond quickly to gravity and the flowers would droop if they were not packed and stored in just this manner. But germinis can simply be picked and stuck in a bucket like any other flower, making it much easier to harvest and ship them. It also helps that germinis have an exceptionally long vase life, surviving up to nineteen days, while some of the larger gerberas might make it only twelve to fourteen days.

Terra Nigra's gerberas are available in a dazzling range of colors — lemon yellow, mandarin orange, cherry red, cotton candy pink — and there are so many variations in the shapes and color patterns that some of them don't even look like a gerbera. The plain white 'Snowdance' could substitute for a Shasta daisy. The ruffled white 'Icedance', with its abundance of tiny trans florets, looks like a chrysanthemum. The rounded 'Terra Saturnus', with over five hundred petals on each flower, looks more like a zinnia or a dahlia. And the deep bronze 'Fireball', with petals that fade to orange at the tips, resembles a miniature autumn sunflower. Some of the colors seem to exist simply because some guy like John Mason, sitting in a laboratory, figured out how to do it. 'Cadillac' is a delicious rich plum, an unlikely color for a flower that is better known for its reds and yellows. 'Crossroad' sports yellow outer petals and a ring of brilliant red trans floret petals around the center, and 'Las Vegas' is sherbet orange with a streak of yellow around the center that looks like it has been tie-dyed into the flower. But Terra Nigra also makes a punk rock gerbera: the flowers in the 'Muppet' and 'Spring' lines each produce unruly, jagged petals that entirely contradict the clean and cheerful look that gerberas are known for. Each petal starts out as narrow as a matchstick and tapers to a fine point, giving the impression that the petals have been through a paper shredder, or perhaps a windstorm. As Peter and I walked past rows of them blooming in the greenhouse, I kept wanting to reach over and tame their tousled petals the way you'd smooth the hair of a child.

These creations come entirely from the laboratory. Gerberas are quite easy to grow from a tissue culture, so there is no birds-and-bees reproduction involved in Terra Nigra's operation. In fact, if you're a cut flower grower and you're interested in purchasing some gerbera plants from Terra Nigra, you have the option of ordering "laboratory plants," which are tiny starts that look like alfalfa sprouts. They come thirty to a jar, all resting in a gelatinous solution derived from algae called agar. These plants have sprouted not from seed but from a few clean tissue cells culled from parent stock. (To accomplish this, Terra Nigra continues to grow every variety it has ever offered for sale. Its genetic library is the most beautiful part of the facility. Rather than a monoculture of red or pink or yellow gerberas, every size, style, and color of flower is allowed to grow together, just a few plants of each, in a happy jumble.)

Terra Nigra is a victim of its own success: the plants are so robust that they keep producing flowers for years in a greenhouse. I've seen it myself. Sun Valley grows gerberas hydroponically, meaning that the plants spend their entire lives in plastic pots, their roots surrounded not by soil but by coarsely chopped coconut husks. Drip lines run in and out of each pot, supplying water and fertilizer. Lane DeVries told me that he'd kept gerberas alive for five years under those conditions. With the plants living so long, Terra Nigra has only one option to increase sales: it must keep rolling out new varieties and hope that growers will dump the old colors on the compost pile and start over with something newer and trendier. During my visit, orange was all the rage. They were also getting ready to roll out 'Evergreen', which was the closest they'd been able to get to another chic color, chartreuse.

Flower growers chase fashions madly: Peter told me that each year at auction, 140 new varieties of gerberas debut. I asked him if he was working on a blue or a black gerbera, and without missing a beat he said, "Yeah, of course. And the bicolors are popular. We each try to come up with something distinctive that nobody else has." The hope among growers, he told me, was that their gerbera would appear on the cover of some major home decorating magazine, and they'd be the only one selling it. "Then you could also sell them your red, your white, your yellow, your pink, everything. That's what everyone is trying to do."

Lane DeVries may have suggested that the Dutch growers are not really so much more advanced than California growers, but Terra Nigra's greenhouses were equipped with all the gee-whiz gadgets a grower could want. It takes time to grow new gerberas in any quantity, get them through their trials, and then introduce them to the market. A new variety of gerbera may spend two years on the journey from laboratory to flower shop; a rose typically takes seven years. So Terra Nigra has no time to waste. The greenhouse has to be more than efficient. It has to be as perfect as the flowers it produces.

The management of sunlight is a constant concern. Greenhouse manufacturers are always at work on a new glass or plastic that can span the largest possible distance without a crosspiece. Just eliminating a few bits of scaffolding inside a greenhouse can increase the light level by 5 percent, and that 5 percent can make all the difference. As we walked through the greenhouses, Peter pointed up at the roof to show me how they manage the light through a combination of old and new techniques. Computer-controlled shade cloths slide along tracks, opening and closing imperceptibly as the light shifts. If the sun moves behind a cloud, the shadecloths part silently to allow more light. On a blustery, partly cloudy day, they might glide back and forth all day long in an attempt to keep the light level on the plants constant. But sometimes the old ways are worth using as well: if the sun is too bright and the plants are at risk of scorch, workers dash outside and toss powdered chalk on the roof. A few hours later, when the sunlight fades, they wash it off with a hose.

High above our heads, vents opened to let in air. We were in a new greenhouse, one that had recently been outfitted with a new kind of fine mesh insect netting. "We cut our pesticide use in half when we started using these," Peter told me. "We keep out about 85 percent of the insects this way. One guy monitors the pests and diseases and designs our spray program. After we built this greenhouse about six months ago, I was going through the bills and I went to this guy and said, 'Something must be wrong.' I thought we weren't getting billed properly. We were using very little chemicals, but the greenhouse was so clean. And he told me it was the netting. Okay, I knew it would help a little bit, but I didn't know how much it would do." This approach is safer and more environmentally sound, but there are also practical considerations: insect netting is quite a bit cheaper than pesticide, and because workers typically have to stay out of a greenhouse for several hours after it has been sprayed, productivity goes up, too.

Fertilizer is also expensive, and its use is heavily regulated. Because of Holland's strict environmental rules protecting groundwater and rivers, Terra Nigra recycles all its water. This eliminates the possibility of contaminated runoff getting into the waterway, and it allows them to reuse the water and the nutrients it may contain. Terra Nigra has a "fertilizer room" where water is collected and reused. For it to be recirculated through the drip irrigation system, water must be sterilized to keep disease from spreading. This is accomplished by running the water through a chamber in which it is exposed to very strong ultraviolet light. If the water contains even a few particles — tiny bits of rock wool, a minute chunk of coco fiber — those particles might shield a few harmful microbes from the light and allow some contamination to sneak through. For that reason, only water that has run, undisturbed, through the drip irrigation lines is reused to deliver fertilizer. Other water — rainwater that runs off the greenhouses into drainage ditches outside, water used to wash down the floors, water that drips off the plants and into the troughs that run beneath them — is instead channeled into a separate system of pipes that is used only for heat. During the day, when electricity use is at its peak, the water in these pipes cools the generators, and at night, after the generators have heated the water up, it runs through pipes near the plants' roots and delivers a subtle and steady source of heat until the sun comes up.

The water that is destined to return to the plants' roots gets an ultraviolet cleaning, then a computer-generated mix of fertilizer is added to it before it is sent back out into the drip system. Every nutritional need a gerbera might have is included in the computer's calculations, and those calculations change, week by week, as the plants grow: nitrogen at first to support leafy green growth, phosphorus and potassium later to put the plant into bloom, and then micronutrients like boron to boost the color. It's an extraordinarily precise system that is designed to supercharge the plants and get every bit of energy out of them. As I leaned against the wall and listened, over the roar of the machines, to Peter narrating the movement of water through the room, I realized that flower production really does happen in a factory. But the factory is not just the greenhouse. The plants themselves are also factories.

Just outside the fertilizer room, Peter pointed to the leafy, mature gerberas spilling out of their one-gallon pots and said, "Look at the size of these plants. The growers are always thinking about labor costs. They only want to have people picking flowers, not tending the plants. If the plant itself is too big, the workers have to do maintenance on the crop itself. They have to pull out leaves to try to find a balance between too many leaves and not enough. If there are too many leaves"—and here he bent down and splayed the leaves of a plant apart—"then this leaf will shade the one below it. So the one below is not producing energy, it is costing energy. That's what it's all about. People want a plant that is smaller, more compact, so every leaf gets enough light." Terra Nigra's gerberas are designed not just for the qualities the customer wants—color, size, vase life—but for the qualities a grower needs, too. As I looked closely at their plants, I saw that they had been bred to produce compact leaves that emerged in a kind of alternating pattern around the base of the plant, allowing each leaf to get some light—light that it will use to produce food and create one flower after another.

Terra Nigra has to deal with some other considerations that the average grower doesn't. Because the plants are raised from tissue culture and are potted up gradually as they mature from the alfalfa sprout stage to the green young plant stage and on to the adult, flower-producing stage, the labor costs can be very high. As any gardener who starts his summer annuals from seed will tell you, all this potting up is a time-consuming and backbreaking chore. Terra Nigra uses machines to do it, sliding a tray of seedlings into a machine that uses optical technology—basically three cameras that photograph the seedlings and a computer that measures the height of the leaves—so that a robotic arm can pluck out the seedlings that are large enough to be transplanted. The arm doesn't even grab the fragile seedlings: it just injects a puff of air into the tray to push out the seedlings it wants to harvest.

"We are the only grower who can do this kind of work outside the laboratory," Peter told me. "So we don't have to grow them in the agar jelly. We can start them in a little soil or rock wool and grow them up to whatever size the customer wants." Larger plants get potted up by hand, and those plants usually move along a conveyor belt or a rail to the worker, so there's very little reaching, bending, or stooping. I thought about California's high worker compensation costs. "So you do all this to keep people from getting injured," I said.

"*Ja,*" Peter said. "That's a problem in Holland. You really need to be careful with your people."

THE EXPERIENCE OF WORKERS in Holland's floriculture industry is different from that of California workers, and like everything else in the Dutch flower business its labor force is also in a period of transition. Some of the workers at Terra Nigra were Dutch, but many were Polish immigrants who had arrived in Holland in search of higher wages. The Dutch growers I met seemed to be of two minds about this transition. On one hand, they were quick to claim that their fellow citizens were the best qualified, through some combination of birthright and lifelong experience, to work in the floriculture industry. They implied that certain techniques, like snapping off a stem at the heel or carefully bending a rose cane to get it to grow in exactly the right direction, required a Dutch touch. On the other hand, they had their share of complaints about Dutch workers: "We have to keep going seven days a week here, at least during our busy season," one grower told me. "But the Dutch? You cannot get them to work on the weekend. These Poles will come and work. Every hour they work is an hour they get paid."

Coming from California, I was surprised—and then unsettled by how surprised I was—to see blond-haired, blue-eyed workers toiling in Dutch greenhouses, after having spent so much time in American greenhouses that are staffed almost entirely with immigrants from Latin America. One day in Holland I saw young Polish workers, in their khakis and blue polo shirts, in a test field of dahlias on their knees picking flowers. The scene looked like something out of a J. Crew catalog. A Dutch grower who was with me nodded at them and said under his breath, "Poles," as if to alert me to the situation. But I never thought, "Oh, the poor exploited Polish people, toiling in the terrible Dutch flower fields." I saw no parallels to *The Grapes of Wrath*. I didn't worry that they'd been burdened with a dead-end and dangerous job that would keep them from their home and their family and call their entire future into question. The Poles looked mildly bored, the way you might look if you were working at a coffee shop at the mall, but that wasn't enough to incite stirrings of moral outrage over their situation. My own reaction worried me. Isn't farm labor the same world over? Could it be that on some level I was assuming that if white people would do this work, it must be safer, better, more rewarding than American farm labor? Or was I just less adept at recognizing Europe's version of the impoverished working class?

Over time, I came to realize that the plight of the flower worker in Holland probably is a great deal different from that of the flower worker in California (or, to an even greater extent, Africa or Latin America). Environmental and worker safety laws are stricter. Greenhouses are outfitted with more ergonomic equipment. Wages are higher. And even the worst health care option in Holland is better than what most U.S. farmworkers get. That's not all: Poland may be a poor country relative to the rest of Europe, but according to rankings of poverty worldwide it's nowhere near as poor as, say, Mexico. These kids could earn some money and take it back to Poland and have a pretty decent urban life, maybe going to college or moving into some kind of office job. Not so for many of the immigrant farmworkers in the United States.

The Dutch flower farmers are in need of ever-cheaper labor, but with tight immigration restrictions they can't always get it.

What I'd heard about Dutch greenhouses was true—they can practically run themselves. As I walked through Terra Nigra with Peter, I saw only one or two workers in every greenhouse. Their vast facility employs only seventy-five people year-round, including scientists, greenhouse workers, and office and sales staff, with more hired on for peak growing seasons. They're trying to get by with even fewer workers. Now, in their rose greenhouses, they're working on designing roses that could be grown and harvested almost entirely by machines.

ROSES ARE SERIOUS business in Holland, as they are in every other flower-producing country in the world. They dominate the Dutch auctions, accounting for over seven hundred million dollars' worth of trade at auction. That's more than double the amount spent on the next-most-popular flower, chrysanthemums, and more than triple that of tulips, the flower in the third-place spot. Germany, France, and the United States make up about half of the worldwide demand for roses, with U.S. consumers alone buying almost 1.5 billion stems a year. Whatever the reason—tradition, habit, poetic Shakespearean notions—people simply prefer roses to any other flower.

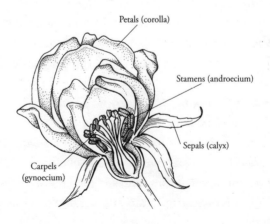

Petals (corolla)

Stamens (androecium)

Sepals (calyx)

Carpels
(gynoecium)

Although the rose is an ancient flower—there are imprints of roses in the fossil record dating back thirty-five million years—a florist's rose bears little resemblance to its wild ancestor. Wild roses produce flowers bearing just five simple petals, usually in red or pink. And in fact, any rose, even a florist's rose, has only five true petals. Those additional petals that fill the centers of modern roses are actually modified stamens (the male part of the flower) that have changed their shape and size so that they look less like an orange or yellow filament in the middle of the flower and more like a petal. Even a rose's thorns are not what they seem: in botanical terms, a thorn is actually a short branch that comes to a point, like the thorns on a hawthorn tree. Cacti produce spines, structures that are actually part of the leaf, and roses put out what are called prickles, which are an outgrowth of the plant's outer covering—its epidermis. (As long as we're getting technical, a rose's stems are more properly referred to as canes, a cane being a strong, flexible stem that dies back after only one or two years, as is the case with roses and another plant in the same family, the blackberry. I hope botanists will forgive me for lapsing into the more familiar "stems," "thorns," and "petals," although in my heart the anatomy of a rose will always include canes, prickles, and stamens.) These prickles often curve downward to keep small creatures from climbing up the stems in search of food, but protection is not their only function. Wild roses climb, bramble-style, like their blackberry cousins, and the thorns allow the plants to gain a foothold and keep moving.

Roses are native to China, northern Europe, and the United States. References to them showed up in Greek and Roman writings, and one rose in particular, *Rosa gallica,* was well known in Roman times for its scent, which persisted even after the petals dried up. Another well-known rose that dates back to ancient times is 'Autumn Damask,' a repeat bloomer that was also used for perfume. Gardeners still grow this rose today, but in spite of its fragrance and its popularity, it's still not sturdy enough to stand up to the modern roses sold on the cut flower market.

The hybridizing work that created the typical flower shop rose began in Europe in the eighteenth century. A new class of roses started arriving from China, and because they were often sent on ships carrying tea leaves, they came to be called tea roses. These roses had a mild fragrance and slender stems, but the wide range of colors, including the previously rare yellow, made them very popular. Tea roses were crossed with another class of roses, hybrid perpetuals, which bloomed repeatedly throughout the season and tolerated cold weather better than tea roses. These crosses were quite successful, and in 1867 the first hybrid tea rose, 'La France', was introduced. The long, straight stems and large blossoms of hybrid teas were perfect for cut flowers, and today they dominate the industry. The blooms on these roses also have what is sometimes called a pinpoint center or a high center, meaning that if you look at it in profile, it forms a pyramid shape. For cut flowers, this is more desirable than a flatter, round shape. The reliable red 'Mister Lincoln' is a hybrid tea, as is the gorgeous orange and red 'Cherry Brandy'.

Gardeners know that hybrid teas can be difficult to work into a garden. They tend to grow in a rigid, upright fashion that makes them seem uncomfortable and out of place in a billowy perennial border. By contrast, their stiff, vertical posture makes them ideal candidates for life in a greenhouse, where stems as straight and long as a yardstick are not uncommon, and blossoms the size of my fist, with petal counts above forty, are becoming the norm.

Terra Nigra's rose offerings include 'Grand Prix', one of the few roses that people will actually order by name. Calling a florist and asking for a dozen 'Grand Prix' is kind of like going into a restaurant and ordering a bottle of Dom — it's the obvious choice, but a good one nonetheless. The upscale British retailer Marks & Spencer offers an individual 'Grand Prix' on Valentine's Day for a whopping five pounds, or just over nine dollars for a single flower. There's no misinterpreting the message this rose sends. It's the quintessential romantic red rose, with blooms over four inches across, a long, straight stem, and deep velvety red petals. There are new varieties of roses coming on the market every day — for instance, a creamy rose with a blush of pink and a hint of green called 'Talea' was all the rage at auction in 2004 — but retail customers will keep coming back for a classic like 'Grand Prix'. And that rose gets its start at Terra Nigra.

The company offers thirty-seven varieties of roses, including a straightforward assortment of whites, pinks, yellows, and reds; a delicious raspberry mauve named 'Beauty by Oger' after the Dutch fashion retailer; and a few of the popular bicolors like 'Sambina,' a two-toned rose with pale pink petals that rise to a wild cherry blush at the tips. Most of Terra Nigra's roses bloom on stems over a yard long, with advertised vase lives of as much as twenty-one days. The trick for a Dutch breeder and grower like Terra Nigra is to create a rose that will grow well not in the Netherlands, where it is bred, but in Kenya, Colombia, or California, where it will be grown.

PETER AND I LEFT the gerbera greenhouses, stepped outside, and followed a muddy path to see where the rose trials take place. We walked into a low glass building that was thick with rosebushes and utterly silent and abandoned. The roses seemed particularly self-sufficient: they grew hydroponically, with black tubes snaking between each plant to deliver water and nutrients, and they'd each been forced to grow in an awkward, undignified posture that a rose would never choose in a garden setting. To make sure that the stems grew perfectly straight and that the non-flower-producing leaves didn't shade the rest of the plant, only three or four stems were allowed to grow straight up and bloom, while the rest were gently bent down to a horizontal position on either side of the plant. In that position, the leaves could take up light to help feed the plant, and the long side shoots trailed into the paths between the rows, leaving just enough room for one person to walk, and only by stepping carefully.

A room full of roses is not nearly as joyful a sight as a room full of gerberas. There is something serious and solemn about the dark green shrubs with their burgundy thorns and their tightly closed buds. The few flowers that were trying to open were, on that particular day, under restraint. It's a common technique among rose growers to place a rubber band or a mesh cap (in Ecuador, they call them *condones*) around the bud to hold the flower closed a while longer while the stem gets taller. You can imagine how handy this trick is before Valentine's Day. In this case, Peter was getting ready to lead a group of buyers through the greenhouse and was trying to keep the roses closed until his guests arrived. A few rosebuds refused to wait; here and there I saw half-opened flowers with a white rubber band suspended around the stem, evidence that some quick and silent worker had moved through the greenhouse, releasing the most robust blossoms from their restraints with a flick of the hand.

Unlike gerberas, which can be genetically modified and cultured in a laboratory, Terra Nigra still breeds roses the old-fashioned way, by introducing the pollen from one plant to the stigma of another. Once they're pollinated, the roses will finish blooming and produce a rose hip, a reddish capsule that contains seed. Those seeds have to be grown out to young plants and forced to bloom (sometimes by grafting the young plant onto another, more mature, rose rootstock), so the breeders can see what they've got. If a rose looks promising, they will make cuttings and grow out six more. After a year, if the plant still looks good, the breeders take more cuttings and grow thirty-six plants. In another year, they might fill a row with them. Eventually the plants are shipped to Terra Nigra's facilities in Kenya and California for more trials. Sometimes they'll send a few boxes to a Dutch auction to see what kind of price they'll fetch in the market. And once a grower places an order for one of Terra Nigra's roses, the company's breeders still have to grow the roses out in sufficient quantity to fill the order. Out of three thousand crosses, just one or two new roses complete this process and make it to market. The journey usually takes seven years, and as Peter explained, that's a long time to wait when you're trying to chase trends in the ever-fickle flower market.

"We'll always have our classics like 'Grand Prix,'" he told me, "but now there is a demand for more open roses, with bigger flowers. Have you ever seen a rose shaped like a dahlia? We have one." And I followed him up and down the rows until he found it: a red rose so open and round that it looked like it would just fit inside half a tennis ball. It perfectly resembled a medium-sized dahlia and looked almost nothing like a rose. The advantage to a rose like this was that it met the market's demand for roses that would open fully and hold their shape, fitting into the dense, tightly clustered arrangements that have come into fashion lately.

Terra Nigra pushes so many roses through its breeding program not just to select the color and shape that might be popular some seven years from now — almost an impossible task anyway — but also to look for other characteristics that will make the plant a success. Is it resistant to botrytis, the dreaded fungal blight that causes gray and brown lesions on the buds? Is it compact, so that more plants will fit in a hectare of greenhouse space? How many flowers can the plant produce each month? How well can the cut flowers handle the postharvest process? When a worker is handling the flower to strip the lower leaves, cut the stem, and grade the size, do the leaves bruise? Do any petals fall off?

Now and then I'd see a thornless rose in the greenhouse. I asked Peter if customers were demanding them. Brides, perhaps, who didn't want to risk snagging their veils? "No," he said, "It is for the growers. Now in the flower factories they are growing these roses on conveyor belts so the worker doesn't go to the plant — the plant comes to the worker. You have machines moving plants around. If one rose has too many thorns, it might tear the leaves of the rose next to it. That lets disease spread and it damages the crop. It's the growers who like the thornless roses. Also, it saves on labor costs. If you are making a bunch of roses, you can put the bunch together twice as fast if there are no thorns. But I think the customers still like the thorns. It's part of what makes a rose a rose. Without the thorns, is it still a rose?"

It was uncomfortably warm and wet in the rose greenhouse. My glasses fogged up; my camera was useless. Peter seemed entirely at home in this steamy environment, but he noticed that I was wilting in the heat, and after we wandered through a couple of rows he'd lead me past an open window or a door so I could stick my head out and get a breath of air. Above the roses hung sulfur vaporizers, which burn at night as a less toxic way of controlling mildew. Yellow sticky traps captured any aphids or whiteflies that dared fly into the greenhouse. The roses grew in surprisingly small containers — their roots were confined to plastic-wrapped rock wool cubes that were only about three inches high. Every plant, each as large as anything I'd grow in my garden, grew from those tiny cubes, putting up abundant foliage thanks to the constant supply of nutrients moving past their roots. The environment was close and steamy, and I thought I could feel the urgency in the plants' thick, rapid growth. The ordinary life processes of a rose — transpiration, photosynthesis, leafing and branching, unfurling and ripening — all seemed powerfully magnified and accelerated in the hothouse.

I FOLLOWED PETER out of the greenhouse and back to the office, and as I walked I thought about this sudden turn of events for the rose. For centuries, it was something beautiful and romantic and wild. Eventually, in our own crude way, we started to cultivate it, selecting for the brightest color and the most elegant shape, figuring out how to grow it indoors and make it bloom in winter. But now, just in this last century, roses have become science experiments, lab rats. Now the perfect rose is one that can live in a factory and be fed by machine. It is built to suit the needs of the grower, not the lover. Does that change anything—for me or for the rose? Does it kill the romance?

I started to ask Peter what he thought about the significance of mass-produced roses on the art of seduction, but he was done with roses. He shifted the subject away from them and onto his latest project.

"Come and see one more greenhouse," he said. "We are putting in ranunculus. I think this will be a good crop in the future for us. It does very well flowering when it is colder." Growers love to find off-season crops they can grow when the greenhouses are empty. In fact, I had noticed that Terra Nigra was growing poinsettias in one greenhouse to keep the crew busy and the space in use. A crop that can handle cooler weather also saves on greenhouse heating bills, making it even more profitable to grow. And it helps if the flower has a common enough shape that it can stand in for other, more expensive flowers. Ranunculus and lisianthus both owe their popularity to peonies and roses—in a tight, monochromatic bouquet, slipping some lower-cost ranunculus in between the more expensive peonies, or pairing lisianthus with roses, will make a larger, fuller bouquet for less money.

But Peter wasn't thinking of ranunculus in comparison to peonies or roses, even though the flower has a similar round, ruffled shape. "With some imagination, you can compare it a little with the gerbera," he said. "It has the same range of colors, and also you can multiply it in the tissue culture laboratory, just like we do with the gerbera." In other words, the ranunculus fit with their technology. It was a good flower for them for that reason alone.

"What about the harvest?" I said. "Can you pick them by hand the way you do with gerberas, or do you have to cut them?"

He shook his head. "Cut. You really have to cut them. But okay, that's not a big deal. So we are breeding now and working on our varieties, and maybe in a couple of years we will have a catalog of ranunculus."

Growers work entirely in the future. In November they are thinking about Valentine's Day. At a trade show in 2005 they are thinking about what they might grow in 2007. And for a grower and breeder like Terra Nigra, the crop that shows promise today will roll out in two, five, or seven years. The only question is, will the public want it when it arrives?

I left Peter's office in the early afternoon and took the bus back to Amsterdam, arriving just in time to walk through the floating Singel flower market before it closed. This is a market geared for tourists. Every shop sells cheap Dutch souvenirs like ceramic windmills and refrigerator magnets in the shape of canal houses. Bags of tulip bulbs are sold for one price to locals, and another price, which includes shipping and a U.S. agricultural certificate, to tourists. The cut flowers themselves are mostly cash-and-carry bouquets that have been out on the street, away from refrigeration, all day. There are no great finds here by Dutch standards, just the most inexpensive flowers that were readily available at auction that week. Still, this is where the public chooses. Is everyone tired of sunflowers? Are carnations really making a comeback? Will green flowers stay in vogue? What about opium poppy pods, the ropy strands of 'Love Lies Bleeding' amaranth, or the purple, red, and apricot hypericum berries? In or out? Asclepias—butterfly weed—was showing up more and more in Holland, but would it catch on in the States? Ultimately, the customers decide, and growers just have to hope that they guess right more often than they guess wrong.

The Singel flower market is a kind of microcosm of the industry, where you can buy just one, or one dozen, of something that is auctioned by the millions just a few miles away. When I was there, hyacinth and daffodil bulbs sold for just under a euro apiece. I bought a bag of a hundred assorted tulip bulbs and had them shipped to me for only forty euros. I found a bunch of Terra Nigra's gerberas for sale and took them to the counter, where I got this reminder from the saleswoman: "Put them in just a couple inches of water. They don't like any more than that." (Later, at the hotel, the desk clerk would see me walking in with my gerberas and would call after me, "Just one or two inches of water!" As anyone—perhaps everyone—in Holland will tell you, gerberas will absorb too much water through their stems if you plunge them into a full glass of water, so keeping them in a small amount of water extends their life. It is apparently a national priority in Holland that gerberas be kept alive as long as possible.)

In spite of the high-tech operations and global marketplace just outside the city, here in Amsterdam, flowers still possessed abundant romance. I saw the tulips at the market, the geraniums in the window boxes, and the roses poking out between the handlebars on a bicycle, and I could not convince myself that flowers had lost their magic. Even now, when the growers themselves call their farms "factories," and even in a day when gerberas are sprouted in laboratories and shipped by the hundreds to Kenya or Bogotá— even now, when you walk through a floating flower market in Amsterdam, there is something thrilling and irresistible about a bunch of bright yellow sunflowers or a bouquet of sweetly scented narcissus.

HOLLAND MAY BE the birthplace of the flower industry, but even Dutch ingenuity couldn't compete with the perfect climate, cheap labor, and minimal government restrictions that Africa and Latin America had to offer. In the last several years, Dole Food Company has been buying cut flower farms in Colombia with the intention of applying its fully integrated strategy — it owns the farms, the trucks, the processing plants, the wholesalers, and distributors — to flowers. Their idea was that customers would walk into Safeway and ask for a Dole Bouquet. That hasn't happened yet because, as Peter Moran, executive vice president of the Society of American Florists, speculated, people don't want a generic, undifferentiated bouquet of flowers. "Flowers aren't Big Macs," he told me. "People want to believe they're buying something unique, something grown and assembled just for them. They don't want to be able to buy the same bouquet of flowers at every grocery store in the country."

I returned home to California, but before my Dutch tulips arrived, it was time for Agriflor, Latin America's floral trade show. I got on a plane for Houston, and from there I headed to Quito for a look at one of the flower trade's final frontiers.

CHAPTER 6

Flowers on the Equator

Quito is a grand, gorgeous, crumbling old colonial city. It drapes itself alongside the slopes of the Pichincha volcano like a shawl, slipping down the mountains and gracefully covering the valley. I wasn't prepared to love Quito—it just happened to be the city nearest to Ecuador's major flower farms—but I fell for it anyway. It is a city of sweet decay and unexpected vitality, of kind and generous people and mysterious old ways, of glorious contradictions. Just outside the grand Spanish plazas are tiny, dark shops selling the cheapest shoes imaginable and plates of hot homemade food that I longed to eat but knew that I should not. An enormous statue of the Virgen de Quito looks down from a hill called El Panecillo (which means "the bread loaf"). She wears an expression of ethereal kindness that radiates comfort down on the city.

But just try finding a bouquet of flowers in Quito. It's not easy. Ecuador may produce some of the highest-quality roses in the world, and the flower trade may be taking up an increasingly large share of its economy, but this is not a country of flower buyers. I didn't see a flower shop, or even a woman selling flowers on the street, for the first two days I walked around and tried to acclimate myself to the air at ninety-two hundred feet above sea level. The open-air markets in Quito's old downtown sold battered and polished tin pots, ancient television sets, outdated automobile repair manuals, and burlap bags of dried beans, but no flowers. Even the lovely El Ejido park, which sits at one end of the newer Juan León Mera tourist district, offered no flowers for sale, although you could buy everything else — street scenes painted on feathers, hand-knitted shawls, and homemade ice cream. Eventually I found a flower stand near a church and bought a tuberose that I carried around with me all day, pushing my nose into it and inhaling every time I walked past a man relieving himself on the street. (If you're a guy and you go to Quito, the city is your urinal. You'll know where to make your mark by the stench.)

I was staying at the freakishly clean and modern Marriott on the edge of the tourist district. The hotel had a marble lobby, a curvy, heated swimming pool with waterfalls where my husband, Scott, and I floated every night after the sun went down (and when you're on the equator, the sun comes up at six and goes down at six, no matter the time of year), and a bland little bistro where we ate pizza and the Marriott's version of *locro de papa,* the national soup of Ecuador, which is made of potato and cheese and sometimes has a hunk of avocado submerged in the center.

But I mostly avoided the hotel in favor of the rundown but comfortable tourist district nearby, which offered cheap Internet cafés, surprisingly good Indian and Chinese food, plenty of bars, and a few small drugstores and bookshops. It was in that neighborhood that I finally found a proper *florería,* a tiny shop just large enough for three or four people to stand in, that sold bunches of Ecuadorian roses straight from the grower and, in a small glass cooler, an assortment of stiff, formal arrangements of roses and carnations.

It wasn't clear who this flower shop catered to. I rarely saw my fellow Marriott guests this far from the hotel, and most of the people staying in the neighborhood seemed to be students traveling on a shoestring. But I went in anyway and picked out a bunch of peach roses whose petals opened gently to green. They were the oldest roses in the bucket, the most shopworn, but I didn't care. I was just going to keep them in the ice bucket in the hotel for a few days, and I was looking for an excuse to chat up the owner.

I paid five bucks for the flowers, and sure enough, in exchange for my purchase, the shop's owner, who was plenty willing to chat but didn't want his name used, leaned across the counter and talked to me for the better part of an hour. During that time, no one else even set foot in the store. My Spanish is passable, and like many Ecuadorians I met he spoke very little English, but we managed to understand each other. He was a jowly guy with thinning hair, probably in his fifties, with deep-set, heavy-lidded eyes that watched me over the top of his glasses.

He told me the story I'd heard most often before I came to Ecuador. The flower farms had become a dominant trade in this small country, gradually rising to be the third-largest industry after oil and bananas. Flower farms, he said, churn out a luxury commodity that does not serve the locals as well as they would be served by growing their own beans or by raising dairy cattle, which would at least put food on the table. They use up important resources like water and fertile farmland. Not only do workers in the flower industry become less self-sufficient because they're working on the rose plantations and not at home tending their own farms, the country as a whole becomes less self-sufficient as well. When the United States wants to renegotiate trade deals with Ecuador, flowers are the bargaining chip. "The United States says to us, 'You take our milk and our corn without an import tariff. If you don't do this, we will impose a tariff on your flowers,'" the florist told me, switching to English to make sure I understood him. "Ecuadorian flowers are—what is the word—when I take someone in your family and won't give them back until you pay me?"

"Kidnapped?" I said. "Held hostage?"

"Yes, he said. "Hostage. Our flowers are held hostage. So we take your milk and your corn. But what about our own farmers? Now they don't produce milk or corn. Now we depend on the United States for our food."

Ecuadorians already have a nervous relationship with the United States. They switched from their own currency, the rapidly devaluating sucre, in 2001, and now their commerce is based on the dollar. (You can still buy thousand-sucre notes in the markets, as a novelty item, for a few cents each.) This makes their financial situation uncomfortably dependent on U.S. fiscal policy. When the dollar fell against the euro, Ecuadorians found themselves paying more for products like cars or greenhouse supplies that they were in the habit of purchasing from European countries. By adopting the dollar as their currency, they've hitched themselves to our financial future, for better or for worse.

Just the night before, from my hotel room, I'd watched the 2004 U.S. presidential debate that centered on foreign policy. It was astonishing to this florist that throughout the entire debate, no one mentioned Latin America. When I told him that most Americans probably had no idea that Ecuadorians used dollars as their currency, much less that the roses they bought at the grocery store may have come from this country, he just shook his head in amazement. I didn't have to spend very much time in Ecuador before I came to see the United States as a large, blundering elephant of a nation, oblivious to a tiny bright bird like Ecuador that watches us constantly.

Floriculture didn't seem, to him, to be a way out for his country or for his fellow citizens. The work is hard, he told me, and it exposes workers to toxic agricultural chemicals in exchange for a low wage. "If the flower industry does better," he said, "do you think the workers will get paid more? I don't think so. The owners will keep that money." I listened and nodded and thought, Okay, that's about what I thought. These flower plantations are dumping chemicals in the river and exploiting the workers. Such a beautiful flower, the Ecuadorian rose, and such a terrible story behind it. That was the refrain I'd heard about Latin American flowers before I left, and it was what I expected to hear when I got there.

It was also one of the only times I'd hear that particular version of the story while I was in Ecuador. I'd come to a trade show, after all. This was the industry's chance to put its best foot forward. But even setting aside the opinions of the industry representatives, I was surprised at how many people—taxicab drivers, rug weavers, waiters in restaurants, and even floriculture workers themselves—saw the flower industry as something other than an unmitigated evil. Perhaps it was one of a limited number of dubious choices for the country's difficult economy, but most people did not possess the level of outright vitriol I expected to find.

Let's back up for a minute and look at how the industry came to Latin America in the first place. Between World War II and the 1960s, growers in the United States made big advances. They figured out how to ship flowers across the country quickly, making it possible to set up a farm wherever the climate was most favorable. Greenhouses converted from coal heat to oil or natural gas after the war. Growers in the United States supplied almost all the flowers for a country that was enjoying an economic boom—and we were a nation of people who wore corsages, decked out parade floats in carnations, and ordered themed floral arrangements for banquets and dinner parties.

Then a group of businessmen turned their attention to Colombia and figured out that the country had the ideal climate for growing flowers, with much lower labor costs and fewer regulations. Thomas Keller, a Harvard MBA who'd gained experience in exports when he was a fisherman in Kenya, came to Colombia with an interest in exporting, but he had no idea what crop would do best. He met a California flower grower who thought (correctly) that the rising prices of land and utilities would make it difficult to continue growing flowers profitably in California, and they formed a company called Floramerica along with two other partners. One of those partners was David Cheever, who, as a university student, had done a study on the best places around the world to grow flowers. Colombia proved to be the ideal spot, with its high altitudes, proximity to the equator, and predictable weather patterns. The men founded Floramerica in 1969, and six months later, they were loading flowers onto airplanes and shipping them to the States. Over the next two decades, they grew the company to the point where it was generating $50 million in sales. Gradually more companies, many of them Colombian-owned, began growing flowers for sale in the U.S. market. In 1998, the Dole Food Company bought Floramerica. (Its operations have expanded since then — the company now owns fourteen hundred acres of flower farms in Colombia and Ecuador, grows eight hundred varieties of flowers, and reports sales of about $168 million.) Cheever, along with other industry leaders, was recently honored as a kind of founding father at the thirtieth anniversary celebration of Asocolflores, the Colombian flower growers' association. Floramerica was a pioneer, a company that practically invented the floriculture industry in that troubled country.

And Colombia's troubles are, ironically, part of what has contributed to the flower industry's success over the years. The Andean Trade Preference Act, signed into law in 1991, allowed Colombia, Ecuador, Bolivia, and Peru to export products to the United States duty free, with the expectation that this favored trading status would encourage farmers to grow some other crop besides coca, the plant used to make cocaine. While the drug war is widely considered to be a failure — the White House's own statistics show an increase in the acreage devoted to coca production at the end of

2004 in spite of its eradication campaign — these preferences for Colombian and Ecuadorian flowers and other products continue.

Colombia is the dominant Latin American player in the cut flower business, with over sixteen thousand acres under production, while in Ecuador, production is roughly half that. Colombia is also more focused on the United States: 85 percent of its cut flowers are exported to the United States, while Ecuador exports 71 percent to the United States. The rest, particularly the very high-end flowers, go mostly to Europe and Russia. Colombia's production is also more diverse, with about half its floral crops devoted to roses and the rest to carnations, mums, and other flowers. In Ecuador a solid three-fourths of the production is in roses, and most of the remaining production is in flowers like gypsophila that are intended to complement the roses in a bouquet. Still, Ecuador has the advantage of being a more stable country, both in terms of its economy and its overall safety. The prevalence of drugs and violence in Colombia can make it a difficult place to do business. Security is a top concern for any international grower who wants to set up an operation there, and the risk of drugs being smuggled out of the country in boxes of flowers attracts an unwelcome level of scrutiny to the industry.

While I was in Ecuador, Colombian growers often asked me if I would come see their farms after I left Quito. I tried to find a polite way to explain why I had chosen Ecuador over their country, but eventually they'd say, "You are afraid to come, right?" I'd raise an eyebrow as if to say, Should I be? and they'd shrug their shoulders in a defeated way. "It's not as bad as you think," they'd say. "There aren't as many kidnappings anymore. Well, in some areas there are. You do have to be careful." These kinds of lukewarm endorsements were never enough to convince me to book a trip. Besides, the reputation of Ecuadorian roses had surpassed that of Colombian roses. One U.S. importer told me, "When it comes to buying roses, my first choice is Ecuadorian roses. My second choice is Ecuadorian roses. Third choice, Colombian or Californian. Those are third-tier flowers as far as I'm concerned." Ecuadorian roses are known for their gigantic heads, long stems, and brilliant colors. They have come to be seen, thanks in no small part to the industry's marketing efforts, as a sought-after luxury flower. That's what I'd come to Ecuador to see.

The Agriflor trade show is held every other year by Expoflores, the Ecuadorian growers' trade group. (In off years, the Colombian growers put on a show.) In a crowded convention hall about an hour outside Quito, growers showcase their most fantastic flowers and make deals with wholesalers and retailers from around the world. Breeders display their latest hybrids and hope to convince growers to try them. Shipping companies and airlines hand out charts showing their delivery schedules and transport times. Manufacturers of tools, pesticides, and Spanish-language agricultural instructional videos demonstrate their products and take orders.

There were plenty of European buyers around, including the ever-present Dutch, growers from other countries who are considering the feasibility of growing cut flowers, and Americans from just about every segment of the market. I met an Israeli woman who manufactured cellophane sleeves for bouquets, a Chilean agricultural consultant who was looking to expand growing operations in Chile, a German importer who sold African roses to European supermarkets but was considering adding Ecuadorian roses to his line, and a high-end Nashville florist who traveled around the world to personally select flowers for his big-name clients.

The florists I have met over the last few years are, ironically, the least familiar with the inner workings of the industry. Most of them have never visited a large farm or talked directly with a grower. The flowers appear in their shop as if by magic from a wholesaler. I realized that one reason why customers have so little idea where flowers come from is that their only point of contact in the industry—the florist—may have little idea, either. But for the florists who made the trip to Ecuador, the possibilities were endless, the choices dazzling and overwhelming. Terra Nigra carpeted its booth with perfect, geometric stripes of gerberas in even more colors than I'd seen a few months earlier at their greenhouse in Holland—brown, burgundy, more multicolors. There were booths filled with carnations, alstroemerias, and even native Ecuadorian tropicals. But everyone was there to see the roses.

As I write this, there is a half-wilted bunch of bicolor grocery store roses on my desk. They're pretty enough—creamy yellow at the base, with a pink blush that rises along the petals and turns dark pink around the tips—but they might as well not even be the same species as the roses I saw at Agriflor. Walking among Ecuadorian roses is like walking through a forest of roses. The preferred way to exhibit these gigantic roses was to set them inside sturdy, waist-high floor vases, and then arrange the blooms so they formed a dense, perfect sphere that could reach four or five feet in diameter. They were so tall that I had to look up to see them.

And what roses they were. I walked a dozen times past 'Esperance,' which seemed to epitomize what was happening in the high-end market. It's a tricolor rose, with colors that fade from pink to creamy white to pale green. The flowers are picked when they are about halfway open, and they hold that shape in the vase. (This is a concession to customers who are tired of buying rosebuds that never open. It's almost impossible to find a rose that ships well, has a long vase life, and opens in the vase. Take your pick. Lately the choice is to have the rose open halfway just before harvest and then stay that way in the vase.) What was most amazing about these flowers was their size. In their almost-open state, they were nearly the size of baseballs. I'd seen enormous, blowsy roses like that in a garden—a 'Just Joey' in full bloom makes any florist rose look meager and stingy—but I'd never seen it in a commercial cut flower. These roses were larger than peonies, even larger than some dahlias.

Everything else about the flowers was perfect, too. The stems were absolutely straight and as big around as my finger; the leaves were unblemished, never torn or wilted, and polished to a faint shine; and the thorns, if there were any, were large and sculptural and perfectly spaced along the stem. This, I realized, really is a luxury flower, an elite flower. You won't find it in a grocery store. You might not even find it at your neighborhood florist, unless you live in a very different kind of neighborhood than I do.

It was distressingly easy, in this environment, to forget the terrible stories about worker abuses and environmental problems on Latin America flower farms. The flowers themselves were a powerful distraction. 'Cherry Brandy' was a swirl of tawny orange and candy pink that looked good enough to eat. 'Limbo' was a delicious sherbet green like no color I'd ever seen in a rose before. 'Forever Young' was just that—scarlet and luscious and perpetually on the verge of breaking into full bloom. I used to be somewhat indifferent to roses as cut flowers, but that day I found myself turning into a rose snob. This was haute couture for flowers, and I got completely sucked into it. If I could find a florist in my small hometown who carried the icy pink and red 'Latin Lady' or the burgundy and mahogany 'Black Baccarat', I'd be in there every week buying more. These weren't just roses. They were high style. It didn't bother me, all of a sudden, that they didn't seem natural or that they were entirely divorced from their garden cousins. They were something else entirely—the floral equivalent of a Tiffany diamond, all polished and carved and styled to perfection.

But here's where the problem lies. As the quality of Ecuadorian roses continues to go up, the pressure mounts. Norma Mena, an Ecuadorian economist and an advocate for the rights of the country's flower workers, told me, "Each flower has to be the best flower so it can compete in the marketplace. It can't just be any old flower. There are growers here with more technology, some with less, and there are good companies and bad companies, but you know what? They all have to produce the same flower." That is, they all have to grow a perfect flower. And that creates pressure—pressure on workers, pressure on natural resources, pressure on trade negotiations, pressure on infrastructure.

The result is a host of problems, not just in Ecuador, but also in other Latin American countries and in Africa, that attract criticism from human rights and environmental groups around the world. Workers rarely earn more than the minimum wage; in Ecuador, a typical wage on a flower farm is about $150 per month. In an industry that revolves around a few major holidays, labor rights advocates charge that workers are not paid overtime in the busy season, are forced to work unreasonably long hours, and are hired through third-party contracting companies that rotate employees from one farm to another to avoid having to provide the benefits or higher pay that more senior workers might earn. Child labor is also a serious problem: a Human Rights Watch report on child labor in Ecuador's banana industry brought heightened scrutiny to the country's entire agricultural sector. As a result, UNICEF has been inspecting both banana and flower plantations and has discovered hundreds of children working on farms. UNICEF estimates that 6 percent of children in Ecuador ages five through fourteen are engaged in child labor.

Interviews with children reveal that the actual prevalence of child labor may be much higher. Even children who claim not to work in greenhouses can give a surprisingly detailed account of how the work is done, leading one to believe that at the very least, they have spent a great deal of time there. A study by the International Labour Organization showed that of the children interviewed in flower-growing regions, 78 percent began working by the time they were fifteen years of age. Of those who reported that they worked, roughly half had jobs in the cut flower industry. Some worked for subcontractors; others were employed directly by the farms and worked alongside adult relatives to help them meet their quotas. Some of the children also received a medical examination as part of the study. Thirty percent had headaches, 32 percent had tremors, 27 percent had migraines, and 15 percent had experienced some kind of fainting or blackout. The results of these diagnoses and bloodwork "suggest that contact with neuro-toxic substances" could be the cause of health problems among the children.

Workers, both children and adults, are exposed to pesticides and other chemicals that are illegal in the United States, and a small study by the International Labour Organization showed that only 22 percent of Ecuadorian flower companies trained their employees in the proper use of these chemicals. The level of protective gear, the limits on re-entry time for greenhouses that have been sprayed, and the quality of medical services at the workplace vary widely. The same report showed that up to two-thirds of Ecuadorian flower workers suffer some sort of work-related health problem, from headaches and nausea to miscarriages and neurological problems. (By contrast, less than a third of California agricultural workers complain of similar problems.) I can attest personally to the hazards that some of these chemicals present; in one processing room, the fumes from a barrel of fungicide were so strong that I could hardly breathe. I kept my sleeve over my mouth, fighting the urge to run outside, wondering how the two dozen workers cutting and grading roses were able to tolerate it. They had no more respiratory protection than I did, not even a paper mask that might provide some symbolic comfort.

The Pesticide Action Network of North America (PANNA) serves as a kind of watchdog for the floriculture industry, monitoring the public health effects of agricultural chemicals and also reporting on specific incidents of worker poisoning. It tracks increased incidence of miscarriages and birth defects, as well as reduced fertility rates, among flower workers exposed to harsh chemicals over a long period of time. In late 2003, just when the industry was gearing up for the peak Valentine's Day demand, PANNA reported on a chemical spill at a Colombian farm that resulted in 384 workers going to the hospital for treatment. Among the pesticides in use were two organophosphates, which are known as endocrine disruptors and likely culprits in long-term neurological damage. Their effects are cumulative and long term. According to PANNA, the Colombian Minister of Public Health investigated the incident and found that the chemicals were stored, mixed, and used improperly. "The tools for measuring chemicals were inaccurate," PANNA reported, "procedures for mixing chemicals were not clearly identified, some pesticides were stored in containers previously used to store other chemicals, and workspaces and floors were narrow and/or uneven."

Sexual harassment complaints are also widespread. It's ironic that an industry that manufactures expressions of love would be riddled with such complaints; labor rights groups are quick to publicize this fact on Valentine's Day and Mother's Day. "This Mother's Day," a 2005 press release from the International Labor Rights Fund read, "we hope you will consider the situation of the women who have worked to produce the beautiful roses that you buy." A documentary on the flower industry called *Amor, Mujeres, y Flores* (*Love, Women, and Flowers*) compares the flowers themselves to the women who grow them. One flower worker says, "It's sad, really, to see one flower growing beautifully at the expense of the other."

Norma Mena coauthored a study about sexual harassment in the Ecuadorian cut flower industry. She interviewed 101 women from forty-seven companies in the countryside north of Quito. More than half of the women she interviewed reported some form of sexual harassment, and among young women aged twenty to twenty-four, the percentage was higher—over 66 percent. Reports of whistles, gestures, jokes, and catcalls were widespread; about a third of women reported some kind of unwanted physical contact; roughly 18 percent had been asked out or propositioned by a supervisor; and a tenth of the women had been sexually assaulted. The study showed that women who work in cultivation and production areas were particularly vulnerable. "In the flower industry," Mena reports, "cultivation activities are done alone. There are generally only one or two people working in each section of the greenhouse. This makes workers an easy target for sexual harassment and abuse by coworkers and superiors."

Another major concern among environmental groups is the impact of the floriculture industry on a country's natural resources. More attention has been focused on this problem in Africa, where flower farms around Kenya's pristine Lake Naivasha have faced a heightened level of scrutiny. Agricultural runoff into the lake and declining water levels owing to irrigation have placed this important natural resource in serious jeopardy. In Latin America, the primary concerns include fertilizer and pesticide runoff, the disposal of chemicals into streams or hazardous dumps, and the impact on livestock eating contaminated grass. Without a serious natural resource management program, the floriculture industry could pose a real threat to the countries' natural resources. And Ecuador is no stranger to such threats: the Rainforest Action Network has reported extensively on foreign oil companies' destruction of Ecuador's rainforests as they build pipelines and drill for

new sources of oil. The promise of riches, although tempting in
this poor country, comes at a high cost.

The complaints about labor and environmental problems have
been part of the flower industry's legacy for as long as it has been
in Latin America. Although the situation has been thoroughly
reported by investigative journalists, it doesn't appear to have
changed American's buying habits. Every year, a greater share of
flowers sold in the United States come from Latin America. Over
the last decade, sales of domestically grown roses have dropped
from almost 500 million stems to just under 100 million. Mean-
while, imports of cut roses have increased to over 1.3 billion stems
a year. All the while, none of the American retailers or wholesalers
I met reported having any customers who wanted to know where
their flowers came from or how they were grown. And the needs
of those customers are foremost in the minds of Latin American growers, since most of their flowers go to the United States.
Right now, Americans seem primarily concerned with price, and
that's where Latin America has the advantage. (There is also a
competing need to increase vase life in the face of long shipping
distances. California growers would argue that the reason customers are demanding lower prices is that Latin American flowers don't last as long, so people feel they aren't getting much for
their money and want to pay less and less, which may contrib-
ute to a downward cycle of ever-cheaper flowers and even lower
quality.)

The industry has been under pressure to change, but that pressure has not come from the people who buy most of the flowers
and take them home. Instead, the demand for better labor and environmental standards comes from retailers and wholesalers who
make large purchases—for instance, a grocery store chain with a
code of conduct for its suppliers—and from the more demanding

European market. Although Europeans purchase only about 15 percent of Ecuador's flower exports, many of the growers I met believe that it was only a matter of time before American consumers adopted the Europeans' interest in purchasing flowers through more socially responsible channels.

IN FACT, THE situation in Latin America is similar in many ways to that of Kenya, which supplies flowers to the UK and European markets. The debate over imported foods and flowers has left growers scrambling to answer to charges of unfair labor practices, depletion of water supplies, environmental damage, and greenhouse gas emissions caused by transporting the flowers thousands of miles. Kenyan flowers now make up the largest share of imports to the European Union, providing twenty-five percent of the EU's floral imports, ahead of Colombia and Israel, which each hold sixteen percent of the market. While most of the flowers coming from Kenya go to one of the giant flower auctions in Holland, twenty-five percent of them go directly to the UK, often to supermarkets.

The UK anti-poverty group War on Want published a report on the global cut flower trade called "Growing Pains" in March 2007. The report called attention to ongoing problems on flower farms and advocated government regulation rather than what it called "ineffectual voluntary standards." Among the problems it addressed: low wages, estimated at about £23 per month, an amount that it said was not adequate to cover basic needs; pesticide and fungicide exposure accompanied by a lack of proper safety equipment and training; repetitive strain injuries; a lack of clean drinking water at work; and the use of short-term or temporary contracts to avoid having to provide better wages or benefits, among others. In Kenya, the situation is made particularly acute because of the impact the flower farms are having on Lake Navaisha.

This enormous freshwater lake northwest of Nairobi stretches across 53 square miles and is fed only by underground springs. An important source of drinking water for local villagers and a habitat for hundreds of species of birds and other wildlife, the lake has also attracted flower farmers who need a reliable source of water for irrigation. Polluted runoff into the lake as well as steady depletion of water levels is causing Lake Navaisha to turn into what Maude Barlow, national chairperson of the Council of Canadians and board president of Food & Flower Watch called "a putrid puddle." In 2007, she traveled to Kenya to see the impact of the flower farms on the lake for herself.

"Think of the movie *Out of Africa*," she said. "The homes on the lake are simply beautiful. Most of the people living on the lake are quite wealthy. Behind those homes are the flower farms, and they pipe water up from the lake to the farm. Beyond the farms you'll see a road, and on the other side of the road are the homes of the workers. It's really a tiered world. The difference between the way the land owners and the farm owners live and the way the workers live is just beyond comparison. Pit latrines for bathrooms, no running water, just incredible poverty."

Barlow acknowledges that some farms, particularly those that have been certified by the Kenya Flower Council, are working to provide better conditions for their employees and to take steps to minimize the impact of flower farming on the lake, but it's not enough.

"The water levels are down about 25 percent," she said, "and the hippopotamuses — the largest wild tribe left in east Africa — are dying. They're baking in the sun. The lake can't sustain this any longer." The farms, she said, are simply taking more water out than they put back in. Even the most responsible farms are participating in a form of agriculture that is simply unsustainable. And although workers may depend upon those jobs to feed their families, she called it "cruel" to offer up a livelihood that is dependent upon a resource that will soon be gone.

"Every single big lake in Africa is in crisis," she said. "Europe does wonderful work preserving its own water, but the way it's doing that is to use other people's water. If you're destroying water systems and other people's countries [through the use of imported goods], that has to be factored into your own report card. It's great that there are salmon back in the Thames—that's wonderful—but look at the water footprint of the goods you are importing."

Although Food & Water Watch and the Council of Canadians stopped short of calling for a boycott of Kenyan flowers, Barlow herself has stopped buying imported flowers. She wants people to start considering not just their carbon footprint, but their water footprint as well. "This practice of using somebody else's water for the things that you want, but don't want to use your own water for, is going to have to get factored into the analysis. Nature put water where it belongs, and we are removing it from watersheds and shipping it around the world in the form of imported goods. This is another argument in favor of local, sustainable agriculture."

But what about those jobs, and the idea that many countries—the United States included—originally built their own economies around exporting goods to wealthier nations? James MacGregor and Bill Vorley, researchers for the International Institute for Environment and Development, wrote a paper in 2006 exploring the idea of "fair miles" in the food miles debate. They pointed out that the worldwide distribution of carbon dioxide emissions is as unequal as the distribution of wealth, and that people in developing nations should be allowed to occupy more "ecological space" to grow their economies. "Economic development for the poorest in a low-carbon future necessarily means expanding emissions for some," the researchers wrote. "Export horticulture is one of the few genuine opportunities for developing countries that have direct and indirect benefits to reach into poor rural areas . . . all environmental and social aspects need to be analyzed, and trade-offs assessed."

Ian Finlayson is technical director of World Flowers, a cut flower importer that sells over 1.5 billion stems around the world. The company supplies Kenyan flowers to most major retailers in the UK, making up about a third of the flowers sold at supermarkets and other large retailers. Finlayson defends the practices of the Kenyan farms that supply flowers to World Flowers, pointing to riparian areas around the farms that purify water before it runs back to the lake, and a new water act that charges companies for extraction from the lake to encourage conservation. But he admits that there's more work to be done. "There's certainly no room for complacency," he said. "The efforts need to continue to be made, and certainly the lake shouldn't be taken for granted."

And the economic impact of the flower industry in Kenya cannot be overlooked. Finlayson pointed out that with unemployment rates hovering around forty percent, the loss of jobs on flower farms would be a serious blow. Tourism was the country's top source of foreign revenue, bringing in close to $1 billion annually, before violence broke out following disputed election results in December 2007. But with tourism down, flowers may become the leading export: in 2006, floriculture exports were valued at $300 million, with fresh produce at $230 million. An estimated 1.2 million people derive their income from Kenya's floral export business.

In 2007, World Flowers commissioned a study on flower miles in partnership with Sainsbury's. The study, which was conducted by Dr. Adrian Williams at Cranfield University, compared the environmental impact of growing roses in Kenya's favorable climate and flying them to market in the UK, versus growing them in an artificially heated greenhouse in Holland and trucking them to England. The study showed that carbon dioxide emissions from the Dutch flowers were about 5.8 times higher than those from Kenya.

In the debate over the environmental impact of imported flowers, and the carbon footprint associated with them, some advocates for international trade point out that socially-responsible consumers should start by making significant changes in their own lifestyles that would not take a job away from a poor person in a developing country.

Hilary Benn, Secretary of State at Britain's Department for International Development, cited the Cranfield study in a speech just before Valentine's Day in 2007. He advocated greater transparency when it comes to the carbon emissions of the products people consume. He suggested that attempts by grocery stores to label airfreighted food with an airplane symbol might not give consumers complete information about the environmental impact of growing, packing, and shipping the products they buy, and might cause them to focus their attention disproportionately on the produce they eat as compared to other, more significant lifestyle changes they could make.

"Air-freight fruit and vegetables from Africa account for less than one-tenth of one percent of the UK's greenhouse gas emissions," he said, adding, "but more than this, we should remember that people living in the vast majority of African countries are responsible for only a tiny amount of carbon emissions. In Kenya, carbon emissions are 200 kg a head; here it is 50 times that." He pointed out that people in wealthy nations could do a great deal to reduce carbon emissions without impacting jobs for people in developing nations. Taking public transportation to work, switching to energy-efficient appliances and light bulbs, and insulating attics are all "simple and easy things". Those are lifestyle changes that poor people could not make, he pointed out, because they don't have that lifestyle in the first place.

One British florist, the Real Flower Company, is grappling with those issues in an unexpected way—by selling fresh, field-grown English roses in season, and supplementing them with roses from a sustainable flower farm in Kenya that is located in the Nanyuki region, far away from Lake Navaisha. The farm, run by an Englishman named Tim Hobbs, employs 470 people, most of whom live within two miles of the farm. The flowers are shipped on passenger jets, meaning that no new flights have to be added to transport the flowers. The farm has also planted over 20,000 trees to help reforest the area, in addition to participating in a carbon credit program.

Water depletion is less of a problem in Nanyuki. The area receives ample rainfall, so the only challenge is to do a better job of capturing and storing water. Hobbs has set up new water storage systems that provide irrigation for the farm and improve water quality for people who live in the area. The farm supports local schools with donations of food and water tanks. Its agricultural and labor practices meet the Kenya Flower Council's "gold standard", which requires 120 days paid maternity leave, a complete ban on the most hazardous pesticides as determined by the World Health Organization, and advanced wastewater recycling measures, among others.

The Real Flower Company got its start in England in 1995, when a woman named Rosebie Morton planted fragrant roses and herbs on her farm in Hampshire, which she intended to sell as old-fashioned bouquets. That may not sound like an unusual move, but anyone who has brought a supermarket bouquet to their nose searching for a hint of fragrance knows that something has been missing from commercial cut flowers for a long time.

Morton brought her flowers to the Covent Garden market in London, and sold them directly to florists who were looking for something different than the standard offerings available from importers and brokers who sell flowers from the Dutch auction houses to florists in the UK. The response was overwhelming —people got tears in their eyes when they got a whiff of that old-fashioned garden scent—and what started as a sideline on a busy farm turned into a floral empire all its own. When Morton met Hobbs, who was already farming in Kenya, they decided to join forces and grow her fragrant rose varieties in both countries. By 2003, the company had re-launched under its new name and started selling flowers online and in flower shops in London. Today the Real Flower Company ships just under a million stems a year of luxurious, scented roses and herbs. Managing director Karen Watson has spent time on both farms, and she believes that the flowers are more than a luxury brand; they also represent a better way of farming. "It's not just about making money, ultimately," she said. "It's about social responsibility."

I THOUGHT ABOUT these questions of social responsibility and farming practices as I wandered the exhibition halls at Agriflor, Ecuador's floral trade show. I was surprised at how eager growers were to demonstrate that times had changed, that the tarnished reputation of the floral industry was undeserved, and that the industry was good for Ecuador and for Ecuadorians. I had noticed, as I traveled around the world talking to growers, wholesalers, and retailers, that many people preferred to keep a low profile and weren't interested in talking about their industry's inner workings. It usually took some effort to convince people to let me pull out my tape recorder and start asking questions. But at Agriflor, growers and industry representatives chased me down in the aisles. "Are you the American writing the book?" they'd ask. "I want to talk to you." I found myself sitting in one exhibitor's booth after another, hearing essentially the same story: Yes, there have been problems, but we are turning it around. We cannot afford a bad reputation. We're a small country next to Colombia, which has twice as much land devoted to flowers and can sometimes take advantage of devaluations in its peso to dump roses on the U.S. market at a very low price. Besides, without the flower industry, they argued, people in the countryside would simply leave and move to Quito, which is already overcrowded and short on job opportunities. The flower industry provides a way for people to remain in their homes and near their families. (Ecuador has a serious problem with worker emigration. Many go to Spain in search of work, where Ecuadorians make up one of the largest immigrant communities.)

In addition to providing jobs, the argument in favor of the flower industry continues, flower farms bring infrastructure like sanitation and electricity. Some help build schools, roads, or medical clinics. New research on the well-being of Colombian women working in floriculture suggests that providing women paid work outside the home gives them more power within their own family, which may make them safer from domestic abuse and allow for greater gender equality at home.

And the alternative—no flower farms at all—is worse. "If you go home and buy California roses," one grower told me, "you are not supporting an American worker. You are supporting a Mexican worker who is away from his family. If you buy Ecuadorian roses, you are allowing an Ecuadorian family to stay together." If Americans stopped buying Ecuadorian roses and the jobs vanished, he said, what options would these workers have but to travel in search of work—work which, by the way, is made even scarcer by the fact that Peruvians and Colombians come across the border in hopes of earning wages in U.S. dollars rather than their own currencies.

There was the debate, neatly framed and set before me. On one hand, work on the flower farms was low paying, exhausting, and hazardous. All this to produce a short-lived luxury product for Americans who demand ever lower prices for a better and better flower. On the other hand, people need jobs. There may not be a lot of economic opportunity in Ecuador, but what the country has is the perfect climate and altitude to grow flowers and a labor force to tend to them. As one grower told me (and I'm roughly translating here), it would be easy for somebody like me to say that rural Ecuadorians were better off before the flower farms came, when they lived a more pastoral life. But I've never had to scrape by with a bare patch of land, a few chickens, and only marginal access to electricity or drinking water, have I? Would I like to try it sometime? No, I had to admit, I wouldn't.

I visited a half-dozen flower farms that week, along with a group of buyers and growers who had also attended the trade show. Most of the farms were clustered around Cayambe, a village about forty-five miles northeast of Quito. To get there, you take the Pan-American Highway out of town, holding on to your seat as the road gets narrower, winds around ever-higher mountains, and accommodates more trucks, buses, and motorcycles, moving at faster speeds, than you might ordinarily be comfortable with. As we ascended, I was struck by how much the landscape looked like the high desert of New Mexico or Colorado. The hills were increasingly rocky, and the plants were mostly low-growing, scrubby trees and shrubs that clung to the gray earth. Occasionally our little tour bus would round a hairpin turn and I'd get a glimpse down a steep ravine, and at the bottom there would be a fast-moving stream pushing its way through boulders, rusted cars, old clothes, and trash. I tried not to look down. I kept my eyes on the ever-present volcano looming above us, which is also called Cayambe. It's covered in a permanent snowcap and reaches almost nineteen thousand feet into the sky.

Once or twice the road swerved across the equator; each time
the driver would point it out to me, and I'd imagine a bright orange dotted line draped over the landscape, like the one on my
globe at home. We were at the very midpoint of the earth. If you
spun the globe along that orange line, you'd see Kenya, another
major flower-growing region. Spin it again. Singapore. They're
growing them there, too—mostly orchids but also chrysanthemums and carnations, and some roses, for the Asian and European
markets. I felt, as we wove back and forth across the equator, that I
was traveling on a tight thin line that held all the emerging flower
growers together. If you wanted to open a flower farm, you'd follow this line around the globe with your finger, looking for a place
that had enough rainwater, a cheap labor force, a decent airport,
and roads that could handle big refrigerated trucks. That's where
you'd build.

The standard of living in the Cayambe region is not too different from that of other flower-growing equatorial countries around
the globe. Homes in the countryside around Quito tend to be
small—just a couple of rooms—and constructed of cinder block
with a corrugated tin roof or, if it's an older, more dilapidated
house, mud brick and plaster with a Spanish tile roof. In town,
people sometimes live above little shops in a building of brick or
cinder block, and many of those buildings were in what looked
like a perpetual state of construction, with a second or third story
mostly built save a roof or a couple of windows. Although only
about 55 percent of households in rural Ecuador have electricity,
we never strayed that far off the grid. Almost every house I saw
had a snarl of electrical lines near the front door. In fact, as remote
as Cayambe may seem, I realized later that we were never more
than an hour's drive from an Internet café.

But a modest amount of infrastructure is one thing; a thriving
economy is another. The nearby village of Otavalo depends on

tourism — its colorful open-air market supplies Ecuador's visitors with rugs, shawls, carvings, and thousands of Panama hats, which are not, as the name may imply, made in Panama. (Let me take a moment to dispel a rumor about Ecuador and hats. The Panama hat has always come from Ecuador, and Ecuadorian vendors are fond of telling tourists that the hat got its name from a photograph of Teddy Roosevelt wearing one when he visited the construction of the Panama Canal. In fact, the *New York Times* has references to a "Panama hat" going back to 1851, and a *Times* report dated September 2, 1900, clarifies that the hats got their name because Panama was a central distribution center for them.) The village of Cayambe itself has less to offer tourists in the way of straw hats and trinkets, not to mention hotels or restaurants. I was also struck by the fact that, unlike Holland, in Ecuador there are no tourist attractions that revolve around the flower industry — no visitor's center, no guided tours, no roses for sale.

So without tourism, what's left of the local economy? Most villages in the area had a couple little grocery stores, an auto repair and machine shop, and tiny restaurants the size of living rooms that served home-cooked soup and other *platos típicos.* There were no malls, no offices, no factories. I had to admit that the growers' description of country life outside Quito was not far off: to get by, a family might have a small vegetable garden, a goat and a couple chickens wandering around the yard, and sometimes a beat-up car parked nearby. This was a lean existence. A job on a flower farm, despite its drawbacks, would be hard to turn down.

THE GREENHOUSES WERE a startling sight in this countryside dotted with tiny houses, crisscrossed with dirt roads, and sheltered by only a few trees. They dominated the landscape, filling an entire hillside with long, shiny blocks that fit together like a puzzle and reflected back Ecuador's dazzling bright sunlight.

They were perfect and new, and seemed entirely foreign, as if they had been dropped into the countryside from somewhere else—as, indeed, they had.

By now I knew better than to expect fields of yellow and blue blossoms around the farms. Very few flowers are grown outdoors in Ecuador, even though temperatures reach sixty-five degrees year-round and the sun rises and sets at almost the same time every day. Gypsophila, larkspur, and some filler greens do better in fields, but roses need protection from wind and rain. The greenhouses (which are, for the most part, just hoop houses with walls of plastic sheeting, not glass) also keep pests and weeds out and help contain pesticides and other fumigants.

We approached the flower farms along narrow dirt roads lined with fast-growing eucalyptus trees that were planted as windbreaks and privacy screens. Sometimes, depending on the time of day, we'd have to sit alongside the road and wait while a bus carrying workers made its way to or from the farm. Occasionally we stopped to let goats cross the road; the farms used them to keep down weeds around the greenhouses.

Every farm visit began the same way. We were greeted at the gate by the owner or manager and a group of supervisors with expertise in each aspect of the operation—growing, harvesting, postproduction, pest control, and so forth. The men (and they were always men) were dressed in crisp button-down shirts bearing the company logo, and they were all Ecuadorian with the exception of a few Colombians and a couple of German or Dutch owners. They'd lead us on a tour of the facility, followed by a short stop in the office for soft drinks and cookies that young women from the administrative office served us. We'd leave with a rose or a ball cap or a notepad printed with the company logo. I was keenly aware that these tours were designed to impress us. The growers had no idea who had signed up to visit their farm, and I could see them trying to sort out the buyers with large accounts from the more casual onlookers. In our group there was an editor of a magazine for American florists, a Dutch wholesaler, a retail florist, a broker who bought and sold flowers out of an office in Bogotá, and several Latin American wholesalers.

I'd come expecting to see low-tech operations that relied more on labor than expensive equipment. Sure enough, Ecuadorian roses are usually planted directly in the earth, not grown in pots or plastic crates as they might be in the United States or Europe. The greenhouse structures are built of metal or polyvinyl chloride poles with plastic sheeting stretched across, and they are usually entirely open at each end, allowing air (and insects) to move in and out freely. Birds flew into the greenhouses and chattered at us from the rafters. Weeds sprung up between the rows. These people were actually growing plants in the ground, I kept thinking. This is almost like gardening.

Well, not entirely. These farms ran on the same strict schedule you'd see on any flower farm, anywhere in the world. Each individual plant had its own monthly production quota to meet, its own tight deadline. The farms that grow large-headed flowers for high-end markets expect to get only one rose per plant per month and might put about twenty-eight thousand bushes in an acre. Farms that grow roses for a more middle-of-the-road American market will push those numbers to nearly two flowers per plant per month and upward of fifty thousand plants per acre. Holidays throw everything off; to get ready for Valentine's Day, workers start pinching back the plants before Christmas, and in January they place little mesh *condones* on the buds to hold them back until harvest and force the stems to get taller before the flower opens. Even so, meeting the demands of the major flower holidays is such an overwhelming task that growers will leap at the chance to sign on customers whose demand for flowers is less seasonal, allowing them to keep to the same schedule all year.

In most greenhouses, roses grow two to a row, side by side, and the rows seem to march on to a distant vanishing point, with so little space in between that one can barely squeeze between them to get a better look at a flower. The bushes, planted in beds of carefully mounded soil, towered overhead. Many of the blossoms are so high that a six-foot-tall man couldn't reach them. These were premium roses, the same varieties I'd seen at Agriflor. I always asked the growers what their favorite variety was, and it was never a fancy, showy rose like the sunset-hued 'Cherry Brandy' or the red rose with fine, tie-dyed streaks of yellow called 'Hocus Pocus'. Most growers preferred the workhorses, the plain varieties that sold week in and week out, shrugged off pests and diseases, and stood up well in transport. Try as I might, I couldn't get them to consider the roses from a purely aesthetic standpoint. In fact, most growers had a hard time understanding why anyone would want a novelty rose if it didn't hold up well in the greenhouse, as if customers somehow knew, when they were choosing a rose, what the grower had to go through to produce it.

Carlos Krell, the president of Plantador, a company that propagates rose plants to sell to growers, put it this way: "Look at the variety 'Circus'," he said, referring to a gorgeous bicolor rose with rich yellow petals and orange-red tips. "We looked at this variety four years ago and said that it is a typical three-hectare variety. That means that we thought we could sell about two hundred thousand plants and that's it. It's very nice in the vase, keeps the color, long vase life, open bud, but the production is not the best. To manage the plant is not easy. The stem length is fifty centimeters, so it's nothing special. But, in the last two years, it's our best variety. The Russian market buys it, the Dutch market buys it, the USA market buys it. Why? I don't know. But they like it. You can't try to understand. Only the market knows the market."

Then he pointed to 'Red France', which looked to me like the most ordinary red rose, the sort of thing I'd pass over in a flower shop in favor of something more interesting, and said, "This is very nice—excellent production, excellent in the vase, nice petals, nice color—nobody wants it. That is the market."

I can understand why growers favor the plants that are easiest to handle in the greenhouse. It takes an extraordinary effort to get several million perfect roses out the door every year. I saw every kind of greenhouse management practice in use at one farm or another: workers in rubber gloves picking diseased or damaged leaves off and dropping them into bags tied around their waists; yellow sticky traps to attract aphids; tiny laboratories where biological pesticides resembling moldy blue cheese grew in glass jars; enormous steaming piles of compost that would eventually be added to the greenhouse floor; tanks of methyl bromide leaning against a shed; NO ENTRY signs outside of greenhouses that had recently been sprayed, usually with a little plastic clock to indicate the hour when workers could return; and foot baths at each entrance, where we would rinse the soles of our shoes in muddy disinfectant water before entering.

Ecuadorian greenhouses are a mixture of the old and new. Every greenhouse manager I met knew about hydroponic growing techniques, organic pest controls, sophisticated water recycling systems, and mechanized racks that bring the plants to the workers rather than the other way around. After all, this is a global marketplace. They knew what the Dutch were doing, and the Kenyans and Ethiopians and Israelis and Californians. But the deciding what equipment to buy, what technology to employ, and when to rely on human labor instead of automation is entirely a function of economics. It all comes down to what the market will pay and what it will demand in terms of quality, freshness, and size. It's a complex calculation, and it's apparent in the greenhouse, where every square foot of growing space, every plant, every gallon of water, and every drop of fertilizer counts. This is even more obvious in the postharvest process. As soon as a rose is picked, it begins to die. As the clock ticks, profits evaporate. From the moment a stem is cut, time is money.

LET's CHOOSE A ROSE — the lime green 'Limbo', for example — and follow it through its journey from greenhouse to retailer. We'll begin on a Monday morning, when 'Limbo' is cut from a rosebush in a greenhouse in Ecuador. This is a fairly good-sized rose: stem length is just over two feet, petal count around forty, and it's expected to live ten days in the vase. The person cutting 'Limbo' is looking not just for a clean, unblemished flower with a straight stem; he or she is also choosing the flower that has opened to exactly the right point. At some farms a customer can choose from among seven "opening stages," starting with a small, tight bud just over an inch tall that will probably never open, to a half-opened flower almost three inches in height that will, with any luck, hold this half-opened shape throughout its vase life. Most roses are harvested "at the crack," the stage when the first petals begin to unfurl. This might be considered stage 3 for most roses. 'Limbo' doesn't look like much in its bud form, so it's

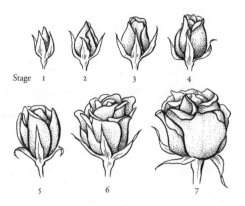

Stage   1   2   3   4

5   6   7

getting picked today at a stage 6, almost half-opened, when its petals have matured from pale yellow to brilliant chartreuse.

'Limbo' doesn't go into water right away. It gets bundled up with a few dozen others and carried to the end of a row, where it will wait on a metal cart, wrapped loosely in sturdy plastic, until the cart is full and ready to leave the greenhouse. After a half hour, it takes a short, dusty journey down a dirt path between the greenhouses, where it is one of perhaps ten thousand roses that will get wheeled into the production room that day.

Flower farms start early; work may begin at seven in the morning, and fresh batches of roses will continue to make their way into the production area until after noon. I was never prepared, as I followed 'Limbo' and other roses from the warm, steamy greenhouses into the warehouse, for how cold the production areas are. Growers in Latin America talk about the importance of preserving the "cold chain" from harvest to delivery, and that cold chain begins here, in the chilly processing rooms. The workers wore long pants and long sleeves, rubber aprons, gloves, a hat, maybe a mask, and some had on scarves and a sweater as well. But you wouldn't just be cold working in here; you'd be wet, too. Staying dry in this job would be almost impossible: the concrete floors were wet, the roses were wet, and water was always sloshing around.

'Limbo' goes first to a worker who strips off the lower leaves. There's a technique to this: some growers prefer little metal tools called rose strippers with a circular blade that you fit around the middle of the stem and pull the rose through to remove the foliage. Other growers issue their workers gloves made out of chain metal. You wear a rubber glove underneath, a metal glove on top, and to strip the rose, you just grab it and yank. If any of the flower's upper leaves or outer petals are damaged, you pull those off, too.

Once the leaves are stripped, the flower is graded by blossom size and stem length. Most farms use metal racks for this purpose:

you hang a rose in the rack and match it up against a metric ruler, then drop the roses into a bucket or onto a shelf according to size. This is also the second opportunity to check the rose for damage and discard anything that can't be sold. (The first is in the greenhouse — any roses that don't look salable right off the bat go into a bin and become compost.) I watched damaged roses, or roses whose petals fell off during handling, or roses that were just too small, go into buckets, and I could see, from an owner's perspective, that even though the flowers had been harvested only an hour or two earlier, the profits were already falling away. That's why growers are always looking for a gentler postharvest process, some new way for the employees to get more flowers out the door and fewer into the compost pile, or just a rose that can withstand rough handling.

Once 'Limbo' has been sorted and graded, it's packed into a bunch of twenty, thirty, or twenty-four, depending on the market it's headed for. (The European market is accustomed to buying in increments of ten, but Americans still want to buy a dozen roses. Increasingly, big box retailers like grocery stores and discount clubs are selling growers bunches, which means that they might be sold in multiples of five or ten instead of by the dozen or half dozen. It's also easier, on the wholesale level, to buy and sell in increments of ten, because the per-stem price is easier to calculate.) The longer stems are usually headed to Europe, Russia, or high-end American florists, and shorter stems go to grocery stores and other mass-market retailers in the United States.

'Limbo' is headed to a wholesale market, where it will be sold to a retail florist for its shop. It's packed into a bunch of twenty stems for its journey. The workers arrange the blossoms in a neat square, usually with two rows of five roses each, and then lay another two rows of five each just below the first, so that when you look down into a growers bunch, there will be ten flowers looking up at you, and another ten packed in tightly right below them. Usually there's a strip of tissue paper between the rows to protect the petals; in some cases, each bud might be individually wrapped in tissue paper. A layer of corrugated cardboard with the company logo goes around the blossoms, and often workers will use two wooden blocks to pack the roses closer together and make sure that the size of each package is uniform. They staple the cardboard closed, trim the stems one more time, and lay them on a conveyor belt. Still another worker checks them again, maybe adds a bar code sticker to indicate the bouquet's final destination, plucks off a few more stray leaves, and puts them into a bucket.

Depending on the grower, the time of year, and the flowers themselves, there is sometimes another step before the flowers reach this point. Before 'Limbo' leaves the production room, it and the other flowers in its bunch might be dipped, blossom first, into a barrel of fungicide to prevent botrytis, the fungus that causes unsightly gray or brown splotches on roses. This practice is especially prevalent during rainy weather, when botrytis spreads easily. (Ecuador's highest rainfall happens in March and April, but in general winters are rainy and summers are dry.) The growers know that these flowers will be inspected when they arrive at their destination country, and they also know that customers don't want roses with spots. Because botrytis can appear on a rose after it's left the farm, growers can't rely on a visual inspection to tell them whether the disease is present. And even if the flower makes it past inspection, any damaged or blemished petals or leaves will get picked off by the florist, which just means that the flower will be handled and defoliated even more before it goes home with a customer.

So I watched as bundles of roses went into the barrel of fungicide, head first, then got turned over and dipped again stem first. This had to be the nastiest job in the production room. The men handling the roses wore respirator-style masks and carried the flowers to the opposite end of the production room to do the dip, but there were no masks for the rest of us and the smell was horrible. Every grower assured us that they were taking all necessary precautions to protect their workers and keep chemicals out of waterways, but keeping runoff contained seemed like an impossible task. The guys in charge of the dip were drenched in the stuff. It spilled on the floor. It dripped off the flowers. For the first time in all the months I'd spent looking behind the scenes at the cut flower industry, my heart hardened against the flowers themselves. If those rich velvety petals had to be dipped in a chemical to make them ready for market, I didn't want them.

Let's pause for a moment and think about this dip. Although there are many more chemicals used in the growing process that may pose more of a threat to workers, this final fungicidal dip is the thing that turns consumers off the most. It's one thing to know that your flowers have been sprayed at some point in their lives. It's another to imagine them dipped — completely coated — in fungicide right before they are shipped to you. One Ecuadorian grower told me that he used a few different fungicides for the job, including two products from Bayer CropScience: Teldor and Scala. These products are designed to be sprayed on strawberry and grape crops, and it is worth noting that although they are rated as less toxic than many other agricultural chemicals (neither has been identified as a "bad actor" by the Pesticide Action Network [PAN], a designation that indicates that a chemical is a known groundwater pollutant or harmful to humans in a variety of ways), they are also not identified by the manufacturer or by PAN as suitable for use as a fungicide dip. Of the thirty-seven products that PAN has identified as a rose dip treatment, seventeen are classified as "bad actors" for their possible toxicity to humans or the environment.

I should also mention that the masks the workers were

wearing appeared to be what are called negative pressure air puri-
fying respirators. Those respirators have to be fit-tested to the individual person using them. If they're not fitted properly, they offer
no protection and they're actually worse than useless, because they
give people a false sense of security and they'll take more risks than
they would with no mask at all. Large government agencies in the
United States have difficulty meeting the Occupational Safety and
Health Administration's fit-testing requirements; it seemed nearly
impossible to get it done in this environment. Many fungicide
dip products include on their Material Safety Data Sheets a rec-
ommendation to use the masks. Given the International Labour
Organization's study showing that only 22 percent of workers had
proper training in the use of chemicals, it seemed unlikely that
these masks were properly fitted all the time.

"So . . . ," I said to one of the production managers, trying to
sound casual as I watched the flowers being dunked in fungicide,
"about this dip. Does it remain on the flowers long?"

"No," he said, "the more time that passes, the more it loses
its effectiveness. As a contaminant for humans, it's very low.
But"—and he flashed me a warm smile—"I would never recommend that you take a bath of rose petals. Never."

It's now Monday afternoon, and 'Limbo' has been
harvested, graded, trimmed, dipped, and packaged. It's in a
bucket on its way to the cooler. What happens next is critical to
its survival.

The moment 'Limbo' was cut, a series of physiological changes
began, all of which lead to senescence—the eventually drooping, withering, and aging of the flower. First, the flower starts to
breathe faster, and in the process it takes stored energy—sugar or
carbohydrates—and breaks it down, releasing energy, water, and
carbon dioxide. Normally, the plant uses this energy to build more

cells, move food around, and generally stay healthy. But once the flower is cut, it breathes faster to help heal the wound. It's burning up resources in an attempt to survive. The fact that flowers are cut in a warm greenhouse doesn't help—at higher temperatures, a plant breathes faster anyway. That's why growers are in such a hurry to get flowers into a cold room—they are in a rush to slow down the respiration of the flower and allow it to conserve resources.

'Limbo' is using up its stored sugars at an alarming rate. Running out of carbohydrates creates a real crisis for the flower, forcing it to make some tough choices. Its job is to produce seeds, so what can it let go of in pursuit of that goal? The lower leaves are the first to get their food supply cut off, which forces them to wither, turn yellow (as much-needed chlorophyll is transferred back to the plant), and fall off. The manufacture of scent is too costly, so scent production, if there was any, usually declines as well. The outer petals are shed, and any younger petals that are still developing may be smaller and less colorful as energy that would have gone into the production of pigments is redirected to seed formation instead.

That's not all. 'Limbo' also starts to lose water the moment it is cut. A woody plant like a rose is less vulnerable to water loss than a flimsy flower like a sweet pea, which is one of the reasons why sturdy flowers with thick stems are more popular as cut flowers. Plants lose water through a process called transpirational pull in which water, and the minerals it carries with it from the soil, is quite literally pulled from the roots to the leaves, where it evaporates into the air through pores called stomata. (Roots also exert pressure upward to push water into the plant, but it is this transpirational pull that finishes the job and gets water to the tips of leaves and even to the tops of trees.) When a stem is cut, that pull continues long enough for the cut flower to actually draw air into the vessels that normally carry water. These air bubbles block the flow of water, which is why stems must be recut every time they've been out of water for even a few minutes.

To counteract this chain of events, a grower has to push water into the flower as quickly as possible. As soon as 'Limbo' makes it through the production room, it, along with the other nineteen flowers in the bunch, will be plunged into a special hydrating solution. This is called "pulsing" the flowers because it gives the flowers a quick pulse of food before they leave the warehouse. A pulsing solution will contain citric acid, which lowers the pH of the water, creating an acidic solution that will move into the flower's tissue faster, along with a disinfectant, because when you cut a stem, you create the perfect environment for bacteria. It may also contain sugar—that's the food—although some growers use a hydrating solution without sugar for the first pulse. The exact levels of sugar, disinfectant, and citric acid vary by plant, but sometimes flowers will get a pulsing solution with a sugar content of up to 20 percent. These supercharged solutions aren't intended to sustain the flower through its entire vase life. This is a short-term treatment. Most growers I met in Ecuador preferred to pulse their flowers for twelve to twenty-four hours, keeping them in the solution and storing them in a cooler at near-freezing temperatures, where guys in heavy gloves and ski masks could keep an eye on them and eventually sort and pack them. This can add a day to the process, but it's the only way to prepare the flowers for the next, and most difficult, leg of their journey.

By Tuesday morning, 'Limbo' has been pulsed, taken out of water, wrapped in a plastic sleeve, and packed into a long, rectangular cardboard box that can hold four to six bunches, with the flowers laying at either end and the stems meeting in the middle. A worker straps six boxes together and stacks them on a pallet with the rest of the day's production. Once a pallet is full, it's ready to leave the farm by truck. A single pallet, packed full of boxes, might hold seven thousand roses. Even a small farm will fill a couple of pallets a day.

What happens next depends on the grower. Some haul their flowers directly to the airport in a refrigerated truck. Others use a freight forwarder, a company that takes the freight, bundles it with other freight going to the same place, and forwards it on to its destination country. Some might sell their flowers to an exporter or a bouquet maker who could repackage the flowers, or arrange them into bouquets, before they leave the country. Regardless, once the flowers leave the farm, they usually become someone else's responsibility.

There are several passenger flights leaving Quito for Miami every morning, and each flight is likely to have flowers in its cargo hold. Air transport can be one of the major bottlenecks in the flower supply chain: Quito's small, outdated airport in the city center, which was built in 1960, cannot meet the demands of passengers or cargo companies. Just outside Quito a new airport is under construction, but until then Colombian growers have one major advantage. The airport in Bogotá has many more direct flights to Miami and Houston, and Colombian growers have the option of either loading their flowers onto passenger planes, where they must be unloaded with other baggage, sometimes on a hot runway, then travel to a separate cargo area, or loading them onto a cargo plane that flies directly to the airport's freight and inspection facility.

Either way, by Tuesday night 'Limbo' is on a passenger jet out of the country. This is only the second day of its life as a cut flower, and already it's been on a long journey. And after a couple more days of making the rounds of flower farms, it was time for my long journey, too. I would meet up with 'Limbo' again in Miami.

When I left Ecuador, I wondered about the roses that were traveling with me. The passengers all around me probably had no idea that several thousand roses were packed into the cargo hold alongside their baggage. The plane lifted off, and for a few minutes all of Quito was spread out below, its tile roofs, Gothic cathedrals, and uneven roads blurring together to form a kind of patchwork that stretched luxuriously across the valley. It was easy, as I looked down from a passenger airplane in the early morning, to wonder if I'd dreamed the whole thing. From above, it looked like an ancient lost city, wonderfully uneven and handmade. Just beyond the city, the land was impossibly green, a brilliant gem of a color that I somehow missed at ground level. Then, before the plane pushed up and on to Miami, a cluster of greenhouses shimmered and winked in the distance.

PART **3** *Selling*

CHAPTER 7

Forbidden Flowers

'Limbo' landed in Miami, and so did I. I checked into my hotel late at night and when I walked outside the next morning, Bunny Schreiber was smoking a cigarette and waving at me from across the parking lot. She's a marketing specialist for Miami International Airport's cargo division, and she had agreed to help me figure out what happens to 'Limbo' when it gets on the ground.

"We've got 88 percent of all the cut flowers coming into the country," she told me as I settled into her comfortably disheveled airport-issued car and we drove around the back of the airport to the cargo facility. "I tried to do a pie chart one time that showed which airports handle most of the flower imports, but the other slivers were so small that you couldn't see them. So I took the airports that have some flowers—LAX, Boston, New York, Chicago—and gave them each their own slice, then grouped all the others together. But basically, we're it."

I'd arrived ten days before Valentine's Day, when flower shipments are at their peak. Twelve million to fifteen million stems arrive every day during the two weeks leading up to the holiday. I could tell that Bunny was running on full steam, fueled by coffee and the sheer energy of the season. She seemed to be eager to have someone to talk to, someone with whom she could reflect upon her work. A slightly hoarse smoker's voice and a no-nonsense attitude made her come across as tough, someone who could go toe to toe with the guys who ran the warehouses, but she was also friendly in an almost maternal way, looking after me and showing genuine concern about how I might spend the rest of my time in Miami. A large chunk of her job involved going to meetings among airport staff, government officials, airlines, importers, and exporters, and I could just see her sitting happily in the middle of it, trying to hold the whole thing together. She was clearly at home here, and she seemed to thrive on the muscle and grime of international transport.

"This is the craziest time," Bunny told me. "We'll see another spike at Easter and Passover, and again at Mother's Day, but it won't be so crazy. You know why? Here's why. Believe it or not, we get a higher volume at Mother's Day than we do at Valentine's Day. There's a reason for that. Valentine's Day is all about roses. But when people send flowers to their mothers, they tend to send arrangements, not just roses. They'll put in carnations, larkspur, gypsophila. So you might send more stems to your mother at Mother's Day than you do to your wife at Valentine's Day. Also, most people just send flowers to one person on Valentine's Day. Let's hope so, right? But on Mother's Day, you might send flowers to your mother, your mother-in-law, your grandmother, your wife—that's a lot of flowers." And a lot of sentiment, I thought, imagining the planeloads of filial love clearing customs every May.

We pulled into a service entrance behind the airport and Bunny showed the guard her badge. "But even with higher volume coming in at Mother's Day, there's more pressure around here for Valentine's Day," she said as we drove alongside an unused runway. "If you're sending your sweetheart roses, they damn well better arrive on February 14. If it's February 15, go buy her a diamond bracelet. It's too late for flowers. Whereas mothers are very happy just to get them at all. Whether the flowers come Friday, Saturday, Sunday, or Monday, your mother doesn't care so much. There's less pressure."

We drove past a new United terminal that was under construction. The need to expand at this airport is unrelenting, she told me. "We get so many airlines through here. Ninety-seven as of last month. A lot of Latin American carriers. Some of them come in here one day and they're out of business the next."

Bunny is seriously into cargo. She used to work at the seaport, where she calculated rates and routing for freight operators. "I'd get shipping lines calling me and saying, 'Okay, how do I get something up to Seattle?' and I'd have to figure out the local drayage fee to get it to the rail and then speak to truckers and railroads all over the country. So I'd figure out the routing and start them out on FEC Railroad, then it'd go to Norfolk Southern or CSX, and then Burlington Northern." Somehow she made this sound exciting. "It was fun," she said, "but the airport is much more exciting. It's a faster-paced industry." Today she works with the airlines to make sure the logistics of getting their planes and cargo in and out of the airport work smoothly.

We drove through a tunnel under an active runway. Jets rumbled overhead. "Sixty-five percent of our cargo comes in on freighter aircraft, which is just a passenger plane that's been stripped down," she said. "That's true of flowers as well, especially in high season. Although American Airlines has no freighters, they bring in plenty of flowers. It's all belly cargo on passenger jets. That's why, as a passenger, you're restricted to two pieces of luggage. They want space for cargo, because cargo pays."

We came out of the tunnel and drove across an expanse of concrete crisscrossed with yellow and white lines. Bunny followed one set of lines and then another, making her way past trucks and taxiing airplanes according to a set of rules I couldn't figure out. Then we came to an abrupt stop. "This is an active taxiway," she said, and we waited while a jet took off in front of us. Across the way was a series of low concrete buildings. This was where the flowers, along with all the other perishable cargo, arrived. "You're looking at what we call the land side," she said. "Anyone from the public can go to it. You can see all the doors for trucks to back up to. For every three doors on the land side, you'll see one door on the air side. Air side is not open to the public. We call these warehouses, but that's really a misnomer. This is a transit shed. If it's something that can be warehoused, why fly it anywhere? You'd be putting it on a ship, not a plane."

It was a chilly, overcast morning in Miami. When I'd imagined what it would be like to come to Florida in February to see the flowers arrive from Latin America, I'd pictured explosions of color: thousands of red roses, hundreds of purple carnations, blue sky, white beaches, pink Deco hotels. Instead I was sitting on a gray runway next to a gray building under a gray sky. The cargo planes parked on the air side of the building were just as Bunny had described: stripped down and devoid of company logos, with their windows covered up, which made the planes look as if they had been blindfolded. I knew I should take a picture, just for the record, but would I even remember, months from now, what I had been photographing?

I wondered if flower growers of a century ago could have ever imagined flowers moving around the world like this. In 1900 flowers were wrapped in old newspaper or in cardboard boxes that the growers cut and pasted together themselves, then loaded onto a buggy and taken, by horse, to the train station. There was no refrigeration; they had to think carefully about what the weather would be like along the route and only ship the flowers that could handle the heat or the freezing cold. By 1910 a few innovative growers used automobiles to ferry flowers from the greenhouse to the market, and in the 1920s express bus lines started transporting flowers. Refrigerated cars gradually came into use. But then the possibility of airline transportation after World War II changed everything. A 1944 issue of *Florists' Review* reported on the new opportunities air freight opened up for California growers: "The idea of picking flowers this afternoon and laying them down in the New York and other eastern markets tomorrow morning presents a fascinating and challenging merchandising opportunity."

I can imagine a grower in 1950, packing his flowers in damp, frozen newspaper or dry ice, and standing at the airport to watch them get loaded into an airplane's cargo belly. It must have felt like the beginning of a new age, and indeed it was. But that grower probably could not have predicted all the changes that it would bring. He probably could not have imagined a jet full of Ecuadorian roses sitting on a runway in Miami.

Bunny stubbed her cigarette out and exhaled one last breath of smoke. "All right," she said. "Let's go see some flowers."

MANY OF THE PERISHABLES coming in from Latin America leave on the last flight in the evening, when the cool air makes it easier for freighter planes to take off at high altitudes and there's less danger of the cargo sitting on a hot runway. They arrive as early as four o'clock in the morning; by ten the inspections are over and the freight is on its way. By the time we got there, it was nearly nine and the majority of the flowers that had arrived that morning were already leaving the airport.

We parked on the air side and Bunny flashed her badge at one of the security guards posted at the entrance. Four or five planes were parked around the U-shaped building. Cargo handlers zipped around us in forklifts, picking up pallets as they came off the planes and wheeling them inside. One plane was nearly empty; Bunny cocked her head toward it, and pretty soon I was following her up a metal staircase and climbing on board.

If you've ever seen a soldier parachute out of a military plane in a movie, you have a general idea of what the inside of a freight plane looks like. There's no galley kitchen near the front, just an open section of cabin with jump seats for the crew to strap themselves in. There are no passenger seats, no overhead compartments, no reading lights or call buttons to summon the flight attendant. The floor is made of metal and rubber and embedded with rollers that make it easy to slide pallets around. The sides of the plane's body, where the windows would be, have been covered by sheets of what appear to be metal or fiberglass. Overhead is nothing but shiny foil insulation and fluorescent tube lights. One by one, the pallets of flower boxes, which were wrapped in plastic and covered in netting, rolled out of the aircraft onto a lift that would lower the cargo to the ground so the forklift operator could take it away. As the flowers rolled away from me, I saw some names I recognized: Esmeralda Farms. Miramonte. Florimex. Eden Floral Farms. FLOWERS, the side of a box read. ALIVE WITH POSSIBILITIES.

We followed a forklift into the transit shed, where the flowers would get wheeled into a cooler to await inspection. The cooler was not the same tightly sealed compartment I'd seen at Sun Valley. It was simply a room with air conditioners, and it was not nearly as cool as I would have expected. If the temperature outside was about seventy degrees, it probably wasn't much below sixty in the cooler. And flowers weren't the only kind of cargo being stored there: as we walked around and looked at the boxes, Bunny read the company names and called out their contents: "Sea bass. Asparagus. Tilapia. Lots of fish coming through here. Charlotte? Oh, okay, that's a type of rose."

As we left the cooler, Bunny turned to face me. "One thing. Whatever you do. Don't photograph the inspectors."

"Don't photograph the inspectors," I repeated.

"They're Department of Homeland Security," she said. "You

can't photograph them. You can take a picture of the flowers with their hands on them, but that's all."

I'd been hearing about Miami's flower inspection facility for years. It's a narrow point, a kind of bottleneck, in the supply chain, and almost all the flowers coming into the country must pass through it. This one point in the process is also where much of the pressure on Latin American growers comes to a head: if the inspectors find one bug or one spot of fungus on a flower, the whole shipment either gets tossed or it has to be fumigated at the airport, which creates more costs and delays. (In some cases, an infected leaf might be sent for further testing, and the shipment held, to be sure that a new disease is not coming into the country where it could hurt U.S. crops.) But unlike imported fruits and vegetables, flowers are not tested for illegal pesticide residue. After all, they're not going to be eaten. That creates a situation in which growers have an incentive to use the maximum amount of pesticides to eliminate the possibility of a single gnat turning up in a box. The goal of over a thousand Latin American cut flower growers who ship through Miami is to get their product past the inspections that take place in the very room where I was standing.

I expected to see something extraordinarily sophisticated. People in white lab coats. Gleaming stainless steel tables. Scanning equipment, microscopes, conveyor belts. But Bunny and I walked out of the cooler into an ordinary section of warehouse where a row of uniformed Homeland Security officers stood at a long, wooden table covered in peeling white paint. Shop lights, each holding two fluorescent tubes, hung from brackets above the tables. The whole setup looked like it had been built long ago by a couple of maintenance guys who had been given some spare lumber and instructions to build a waist-high table with lights above them. No taxpayer dollars had been spent on fancy equipment here.

"This is it?" I whispered to Bunny.

She shrugged. "Yeah. It works."

The inspectors wore latex gloves. As flower shipments came into the inspection area, they'd select one or two boxes to sample and those would come off the pallet and onto their table. They opened each box—this is where our pale green 'Limbo' might take its first breath of Miami air—and shook a bunch of flowers over the table. If any bugs fell out, that was bad news. They checked the leaves for spots. They made sure there was no contraband hiding in the box. (Bunny said that since September 11 security measures have made it harder for drugs to get through, and as a result the inspectors have seen fewer attempts over the last few years. In the old days, inspectors knew all the tricks. Even the stem of a rose could be hollowed out and filled with cocaine.)

Bunny told me that the inspectors look at about 2 percent of the flowers on a pallet. "Roses are easy," she told me. "Roses don't have a lot of bugs. But we see more bouquets coming in. Those might have baby's breath, and baby's breath has a lot of bugs. So we have to make sure they label the flowers properly so the inspectors know what they're getting into."

The USDA's handbook on inspecting cut flowers identifies varieties of flowers by their country of origin and indicates the level of risk of pest infestation based on the pests that are found in that country and the methods growers use to treat them. Alstroemerias from Europe, for example, are considered at high risk of a pest infestation, while the same flower from Ecuador is not. Asters from Colombia are high risk; asters from Costa Rica are not. Roses from any country are low risk; Thai orchids are high risk. Depending on the risk level, the inspectors might look at only one or two boxes of each flower and might inspect anywhere from 25 percent to 100 percent of the contents. It's interesting to note that although little is ever said about the risk to consumers of pesticide residue on cut flowers, the USDA's manual does include safety precautions for the inspectors, "to guide your inspection and protect your health." When inspectors smell a chemical odor or suspect that a box of flowers has been treated, they are instructed to aerate the containers, avoid breathing near the open box, have the importer's representative vacuum residue out of the box, wear gloves, and throw the gloves away after handling the flowers.

Many exporters already have an agreement in place to cover what will happen when a box of flowers fails inspection. The flowers can be sent back, which is usually too expensive to be practical, they can be burned, or they can be fumigated in a special methyl bromide fumigation chamber at the airport. "Fumigation takes an hour and a half," Bunny said. "You just back the truck into the facility and hook it up. Problem is, it has to air out for another four hours after the fumigation. Some of the trucks are built with special fans now so that can go a lot faster and the truck can get on its way. But yeah, that slows them down."

And in case you were wondering, flowers aren't the only perishable product subject to fumigation. Bunny told me that all of the asparagus coming in from Peru was fumigated as a matter of course. "I see these signs at natural food stores for organic, non-fumigated asparagus from Lima," she said. "One time I tried to tell the manager that if the asparagus came from Lima it was fumigated, and he didn't believe me. I told him, trust me, I would know."

Bunny and I got back in the car and drove along the edge of the airport near the cargo entrance. Just outside, a long line of semi-trucks waited for their floral freight. Many of them were plastered with gigantic, up-close images of lilies and roses in full bloom. It would be a distracting sight, while driving down the highway, to pull up alongside a twenty-foot-long image of a parrot tulip. These trucks were mobile billboards for flowers, the manifestation of how enormous this industry really is. It's easy to think of flowers in terms of one stem or one bouquet; it's something else again to see trucks parked by the dozen, waiting to load up hundreds of thousands of flowers and carry them to market.

There was something else you could learn about the flower industry just by looking at the trucks parked outside the airport before Valentine's Day. Once a flower leaves the grower, it does not necessarily follow a neat vertical path from grower to exporter, exporter to distributor, distributor to wholesaler, wholesaler to retailer. Those channels of distribution do still exist, but they're far from the only option for getting flowers to market. Several of the trucks going in and out of the airport that day belonged to Esmeralda Farms, for instance. It is a breeder and a grower—I'd seen its representatives in Ecuador showing off new varieties of limonium, a feathery filler flower—and it exports its flowers, ushers them through the airport, and brings them to its own distribution facility in Miami, where they will be sold to wholesalers all over the country. Some importers are also bouquet makers, creating bouquets in Miami that are sleeved and packaged to be sold as cash-and-carry flowers at flower shops and grocery stores. Large chain stores often buy directly from growers, bypassing all the intermediate steps, and some growers are even shipping directly to consumers by FedEx.

Because Miami has a major port, a major airport, and its own free-trade zone, it is easy to move flowers by air, rail, truck, and even, in rare cases, by ship, using the infrastructure that's already in place. Around the airport, there are seventy-five companies that do nothing but import flowers. Importers and related companies occupy 1.4 million square feet of office, warehouse, and cooler space in the city, and over six thousand people are employed by Miami's flower-importing industry alone.

How does 'Limbo' make its way through this maze? Once it leaves the airport, it disappears into a vast network of importers,

exporters, shippers, distributors, auctioneers, wholesalers, and retailers. Where it goes next is anyone's guess. But let's say it's headed
for a wholesale market in Manhattan. It was cut on Monday, boxed
and trucked away on Tuesday, and arrived in Miami on Wednesday morning. It's been out of water and stored at temperatures just
above freezing for twenty-four hours. The inspection at the airport
goes quickly, and by 10 a.m. it's headed to a distribution center in
Miami. Green roses are all the rage, so 'Limbo' is lucky enough to
get out of Miami and on its way to New York that afternoon. It's a
twenty-four-hour drive up the coast; 'Limbo' makes its Manhattan
debut by Friday morning, when it shows up at a wholesaler in New
York's flower district on Twenty-eighth Street.

The shop is closed to the public; you've got to have a resale
license to buy anything. A boutique florist on the Upper West
Side sends a buyer to the market to look for anything new and
interesting; the green roses catch her eye. 'Limbo' is in the shop
by Friday afternoon, and on Saturday it leaves the store in a tight,
monochromatic arrangement of green roses, green pompom chrysanthemums, and pale green opium poppy pods. It's a trendy arrangement of long-lasting flowers; the customer will get at least a
week out of these flowers, and maybe two if he takes good care of
them, which means that 'Limbo' may survive up to twenty-one
days from the day it was cut until the day it goes in the garbage.

This is an upscale neighborhood; the shop charges $150 for the
flowers and the square green pottery vase it comes in. If you were
to price it out, you might find that the customer paid close to $5
for each 'Limbo' rose in the bouquet. The florist bought the roses
for a $1.50 or $2 dollars per stem, and that's a premium price that
befits an upscale rose. When that same flower left the farm on
Monday and made its way down a dusty, eucalyptus-lined road
toward the Pan-American Highway and on to Quito, it earned
thirty cents for the grower who nurtured it along and prepared it

for its long journey. And what about the workers who cut the stem, stripped its leaves, graded it, packed it, and loaded it on the truck? Their wages represent less than four cents for every 'Limbo' sold.

THE MIAMI AIRPORT seemed impossibly far away from that Ecuadorian worker earning six or seven bucks a day harvesting 'Limbo' on a flower farm. The plane ride from Quito or Bogotá might take only a few hours, but when the flowers landed here they were in another world. Before I left, Bunny drove me around the back of the airport, the part that nobody ever sees. There was a customs and immigration office for nonpassenger aircraft. A repair facility, including a junkyard of defunct planes that are used for parts. An airplane wash. ("Like a car wash," Bunny said cheerfully. "If your plane is dirty, it costs you more money to operate. You've got to wash it.") There was a separate terminal for private aircraft, all steel and glass, like a tiny airport inside an airport. A new air traffic control tower was under construction. A holding facility sheltered animals—cows, horses, ostriches—that arrive or depart by plane. A blast fence offered a place for planes to back up and rev their engines, which is something that planes have to do from time to time. There was even a decompression chamber to test belly freight for explosives before takeoff. The inner workings of an airport are extraordinarily complex. It's a wonder that something as fragile as a flower can navigate this world of concrete, steel, and jet fuel.

She pulled back into the cargo terminal where we'd begun. By this time all the planes were unloaded and the facility was almost empty. We watched as the last couple of planes rolled away from the air side of the building. "Usually we see ten to twelve flights a day from Colombia," she told me. "Around Valentine's Day, it might be forty flights. You wonder why roses cost so much this time of year? I'll give you one reason. With this many planes coming in every day, they've got to fly them back empty. And fuel's not cheap these days. It costs a fortune."

When Bunny dropped me off at the hotel, I asked her if being around millions of flowers like this had changed how she looks at them. She sighed and shook her head. "I never even dreamt that flowers were like this," she said. "I buy many more flowers now than I ever did before. But I buy them around the airport. On a street corner around here, you will pay four dollars for a dozen roses. You would never believe the flowers I get. Magnificent."

AS A CONSUMER of flowers, Bunny Schreiber happens to be very well informed about what flowers go through to get to her. Still, she wants what most of us want from a flower. It should be gorgeous and long-lasting. It should be perfect — no spots, no bruised leaves, no bugs — and although nobody ever says it like this, that means that our flowers must be sprayed and dipped and fumigated. As consumers, we're not particularly concerned about season — we'd like a rose in winter and a tulip in the fall — and although it wasn't your idea or mine that flower-growing operations should move to Colombia and Ecuador, it was our determination to buy flowers out of season that meant that they had to come from the equator and travel by plane and truck to get to us.

Most of all, we care about price. While all the other costs associated with growing, shipping, and selling flowers have gone up, the price a retail customer is willing to pay only declines. A supermarket near my house sells beautiful 'Leonides' roses for ten dollars a bunch, and nobody can claim the quality is poor: they last over a week in a vase on my hall table. So when Bunny said she could get a bunch for four bucks — just a few pennies per stem more than what the grower was paid for them — of course I was tempted. I'll spend more than that on a latte, and it would be gone in half an hour. Who wouldn't want flowers at that price?

But I've been to the farms where those flowers are grown, and I know what kind of pressure-cooker situation this relentless drive for lower prices can create. Do I really want that cheap bouquet of roses if I know it's been sprayed with pesticides that are illegal in the United States and that were applied by a minimum-wage-earning Ecuadorian worker in an ill-fitting gas mask? At least I can buy a latte that is brewed with fair-trade coffee, and that alleviates my guilt somewhat. At the grocery store, I can buy organic wine, fair-trade chocolate, and hormone-free milk from a local creamery. But the flowers in buckets by the cash register are unlabeled, unmarked, entirely undifferentiated. There's no basis on which to compare and choose, except for price.

Now that I'd been to Miami, I understood why. A mixed bouquet for sale at a supermarket could contain roses from Ecuador, carnations from Colombia, and larkspur from California. Where they came from, how they were grown, what was sprayed on them, and how the workers were treated—all these issues get harder and harder to sort out as individual flowers are packed into boxes, bundled into crates, loaded onto cargo planes, and unloaded at international airports. Once flowers begin the final leg of their journey to the consumer, they lose their identity. They blur together in a sea of petals and leaves, of sweet carnation pinks and fiery dahlia reds. It is at this stage, all massed together, that flowers seemed to me for the first time to be utterly faceless, anonymous.

If it seems like flowers have lost their soul in this process, well, they have. There's nothing romantic or sentimental about toxic pesticides and underpaid workers. "Green label" flower certification programs, which establish standards for the reduction of pesticides and other chemicals, conservation of natural resources, worker safety, and labor rights, represent the best hope flowers have of winning back their souls, their purity. But as Norma Mena, the Ecuadorian economist, told me, once a flower gets to Miami, it makes no difference whether a grower is a good grower or a bad grower. They all have to produce the same flower. And that flower has to pass the same inspection at the airport, whether it was grown organically or sprayed with every chemical on the market. Once it gets through inspection and enters the fast-moving river of floral commerce, it has to compete on the same basis all the other flowers do: price, beauty, and vase life.

THE ANONYMITY OF cut flowers has made it difficult for customers to demand anything different. In response to that problem, there has been a drive to introduce certified flowers to the European market since the mid-1990s. These eco-label programs tend to fall into one of three categories: first, those created by advocacy groups for consumers, such as the Fairtrade Foundation label and the Rainforest Alliance seal. Consumers look for those labels and vote with their wallets by choosing certified products over non-certified products. The second category comes from growers' associations that have created their own programs with varying standards. The Kenya Flower Council has its own set of standards called the KFC Code of Practice; Colombia's Asocolflores created FlorVerde; and Ecuador's Expoflores certifies its members' flowers under the Flor de Ecuador label. And the third category is a kind of hybrid: programs created by industry insiders, not marketed to consumers, but aimed at making substantial and measurable changes on flower farms.

One such program in this third category is the Dutch floriculture program, Milieu Programma Sierteelt (MPS). This program certifies flower growers in Europe, Africa, Asia, Latin America, and the United States. About 4500 growers participate, and a full 85 percent of flowers sold at Dutch auctions are rated under the MPS program and given a rating of 'A', 'B', or 'C' for their level of compliance with environmental and worker standards.

The MPS program operates largely behind the scenes, rating the practices of growers and passing that information on to wholesalers and bidders at flower auctions. Although 70 percent of flower farms in Kenya are MPS-certified (along with 70 percent of Ethiopian farms and nearly 100 percent of Ugandan farms), news reports of troubled conditions on African flower farms rarely mention the role of this Dutch program in monitoring and certifying their environmental and labor practices. But according to MPS general manager Theo de Groot, the certification model developed for farms in the Netherlands is working in African countries as well. "After ten years in the Netherlands, we've done very sophisticated research and we've calculated that the program has reduced fertilizer, chemicals, and energy use by 60 percent on a per-stem basis," he said. Although the program does not require growers to use entirely organic methods, the substantial reduction in chemical use contributes to worker safety and keeps those chemicals out of groundwater, a major concern in areas like Kenya's Lake Naivasha.

According to de Groot, MPS's emphasis on third-party inspections and concrete measurements that can be tracked from year to year help illustrate the impact that certification programs can have. "You see the progress on the farms," he said of conditions in Kenya. "We see improvements in hospitals, medical care, education, good equipment, and wages that are fair. We do the audits every year, and we can see the progress."

But because MPS is a business-to-business label, the logo does not appear on bouquets in the flower shop. Instead, a variety of consumer labels fill that need. The Fair Flowers Fair Plants program (FFP) is a European consumer label with standards comparable to those of MPS. In the UK, ninety-three retailers and traders are authorized to sell FFP flowers and plants. All participating growers have received an 'A' rating from MPS, and comply with the International Code of Conduct for floriculture workers, a code that was developed by trade unions and advocacy groups to ensure freedom of association, fair wages, and other basic worker rights.

In the UK and in European countries, flowers have been added to larger, better-known certification programs that customers are already familiar with. Switzerland's Max Haveelar Foundation, for instance, is named after the idealistic, reform-minded protagonist of an 1860 Dutch novel called *Max Haveelar: Or the Coffee Auctions of the Dutch Trading Company*. Roberto Nevado, founder of the much-certified Nevado Roses in Ecuador, explained the connection by saying, "In schools in Holland and Switzerland, children learn about Max Haveelar. When they introduced the trade name Max Haveelar, everyone knew already what it meant. Now when a gentleman goes into a shop in Switzerland and sees a rose without the Max Haveelar sign, and a rose with the Max Haveelar sign, he goes immediately to the Max Haveelar rose, and he pays more for it. Because he knows what it means." The foundation licenses its label to producers of coffee, tea, honey, sugar, fresh fruit, and cut flowers, among others. Customers pay a small premium for a Max Haveelar product, and as Roberto Nevado said, "That goes directly to my workers—not to me, but to my workers—and they can do whatever they want with it." In 2004, eighty-nine million stems were sold under the Max Havelaar label, which represents almost a third of all flowers Swiss customers bought.

And in the UK, the best-known flower label program comes from the Fairtrade Foundation. Like the Max Havelaar program, the Fairtrade flower label is familiar to customers who buy Fairtrade coffee, wine, chocolates, and other products. In 2004 the British superstore Tesco started selling Fairtrade roses from Kenya in its shops. Like the Swiss program, workers at farms certified through Fairtrade get a premium—in this case, 8 to 10 percent of the export price—that can be used for a community project like better housing or a school.

Jane Snell, business development officer for the Fairtrade Foundation, visited Fairtrade-certified farms in Kenya in 2007. "I usually work with the retailers here," she said, "so for me to go and see the flower farms was quite impactful. The idea that all these beautiful flowers are coming from small-scale farmers—it's just not the case. These are very large plantations with between eight hundred and a thousand people working on them. It's a very big business."

While she was in Kenya, she met with the Joint Bodies, committees of workers who decide how to spend the revenue that comes from the sale of Fairtrade flowers. Although the funds are used for projects that make a tremendous difference in the lives of the workers and their families—micro-finance programs, health care, and other community improvements—Snell was quick to point out that the amount of money that they have to work with is relatively small because certified farms are not able to sell all of their flowers through the Fairtrade program. On Fairtrade farms in Kenya, for example, only 1 to 20 percent of flowers sold on a certified farm actually receive the Fairtrade premium.

"Wait a minute," I said. "If the farm has been certified through the Fairtrade program, why wouldn't all of its flowers be sold under the Fairtrade label?"

She took a deep breath. "Because they are not able to secure buyers for all of those flowers."

I still didn't get it. "So let's say I'm a farmer and my farm produces a million stems a year," I said. "My whole farm is certified, and we're doing all the right things across the board—"

"Right," she said, picking up my train of thought in the voice of this hypothetical farmer. "We're meeting the standards, it took us six months to be certified, we're being audited probably every twelve to eighteen months, we have to meet the environmental credentials in terms of spray regimes and protective equipment, we've got places for people to separate out clothing so they don't have to work in the same clothes they were spraying in, we've got fresh drinking water—quite basic things, but all things that are specified as standard. They do all this, but then they're only selling such a small proportion under the terms of Fairtrade."

"So they would love to sell the entire farm's production under the Fairtrade label, but they need to find a buyer who's willing to pay the extra premium for that," I said.

"Right," she said. "In the UK, about 60 percent of the flowers we buy are sold at the big retailers—the Tescos, the Marks & Spencers. And almost 100 percent of the flowers sold through Fairtrade are going to these big retailers, not the small florists."

"So it is the retailer who decides how many flowers they want to buy under the Fairtrade label?" I asked. "And then they just say that they'll buy the rest without the Fairtrade label?"

"I think they're buying as many as they feel they can," she said, "across all products, not just flowers." She pointed out that the premium—roughly eight percent of the price the farm gets—is quite small. "If you work it out, it's a few pence extra, as opposed to pounds," she said.

This points to one of the more perplexing problems in the pricing of these certified flowers. As flowers travel from farm to distributor to retailer, the price may be doubled or tripled or quadrupled at each step of the way to cover the cost of sorting, packing, refrigerating, and transporting the bouquets. But the Fairtrade premium, the "few pence extra" Snell describes, does not necessarily have to be doubled or tripled along the way. "There's no reason for additional costs along the supply chain," she said, "when really, the only difference was that initial premium paid straight to the grower."

I told her that I thought most people in the United States would certainly pay five or ten cents more for a bouquet in support of

Fairtrade, but they might not pay an extra dollar or two, especially if most of the increased cost didn't go back to the farm. But few consumers understand—or even want to understand—how the price they pay relates to what the farm gets. Snell said that the buyers who work for the retailers, sourcing and pricing flowers, are the ones who can make a difference.

"I think we're actually starting to see people who want to really understand the supply chain," she said. "The retailer buyers can be really influential here. Instead of just saying, oh, this is the price, and I'll either pay it or I won't, we need buyers who want to understand the supply chain and break down the costs. With more engaged buyers, you can really make that work."

In 2007, 83 million stems of Fairtrade-certified flowers were sold. This may be less than one percent of the flower market in the UK, but Snell is quick to point out that supply is not the problem because so many certified farms are not able to sell their entire production under the Fairtrade label. "There are plenty of products where the problem is supply," she said, "but that is not the case with flowers. We've got more flowers than we know what to do with."

In the end, the number of flowers sold under the Fairtrade label may not be the most important piece to this program. When Snell met with workers in Kenya, she was surprised to hear them say that the money was less important than the standards themselves. "It was less to do with what the premium would let them do, and it was much more to do with the standards, so that both the workers and the management knew what was expected of them. Time and time again, what came up was the protective equipment and the separate storage areas for that equipment and their normal clothes so that nothing became contaminated. It seems like such a basic point, but it kept coming up."

THE UNITED STATES, as one of the largest importers and consumers of cut flowers in the world, is a latecomer to the certification game. (Germany leads the world in flower imports. Germany imports just over one billion dollars' worth of cut flowers and foliage per year, and the United States came in second with about three-quarters of a billion dollars in wholesale value. However, imports don't tell the whole story: when domestically grown flowers are factored in and differences in markup from import to retail value are factored in, overall retail spending on cut flowers in the United States is about double that of Germany.) It's worth noting that those countries that consume the most flowers on a per capita basis are also the ones with the most well-known certification programs. The Swiss outrank all other countries by a long shot, spending over one hundred dollars on flowers per capita annually, with Holland, Germany, and Great Britain all spending forty to sixty dollars per capita. The United States, by comparison, spends about twenty-six dollars per capita on cut flowers, and most of that spending is concentrated in a relatively small number of households. Just 28 percent of U.S. households regularly buy flowers, compared with 76 percent of German households. It's no surprise, then, that even though the United States is a behemoth among flower-consuming countries in terms of overall numbers, it has been slow to come around to the idea of certification. With Americans spending relatively little on flowers, the demand for such a program just hasn't been there.

But that changed when Gerald Prolman, founder of an online flower retailer called Organic Bouquet, entered the marketplace in 2001. The bouquets he sold on his Web site were designated "green label," "organic," or both, and in his search for a consistent certification standard that he could use to sell eco-friendly flowers to U.S. customers he and some other flower growers and wholesalers approached SCS (Scientific Certification Systems) about developing a national certification standard. SCS already certifies forest products for the Forest Stewardship Council and seafood for the Marine Stewardship Council, and it provides organic and pesticide residue–free certification services for produce. It began working to develop VeriFlora, a green label for flowers sold in the United States.

Jeff Stephens, communications director for SCS, told me that when the company set out to create a certification for U.S. flowers, it wanted to do something different than other certification programs around the world. "Let's face it," he said, "the flower industry is not as far along in terms of its research and technology for organic methods as other types of agriculture. So we didn't come right out of the chute and say that they had to be organic, but we listed the chemicals they could not use—we used World Health Organization standards for that—and told them that they had to start incorporating certain organic elements that we know are feasible." Growers have to pledge to move nonorganic crops to organic as soon as the tools to do so become available.

SCS also saw a need to put some quality standards in place. Right now, cut flowers sold in the United States are not graded or evaluated according to any kind of quality rating. "We didn't set out to incorporate quality," Stephens said, "but people in the industry said that it was really lacking." Growers and handlers have to submit a plan to demonstrate how they will keep the flowers fresh, including postharvest treatment, preservation of the cold chain, and vase life testing. The other components of VeriFlora's certification program include conservation of water and ecological resources, waste management, and social responsibility, including labor standards.

Labor issues are among the trickiest that a certification program has to deal with. It's one thing for an employer to show an auditor payroll records or personnel policies, but it's another entirely to

ensure that workers actually have a right to organize, get appropriate overtime pay, and aren't exposed to hazards in the workplace.
Nora Ferm of the International Labor Rights Fund (ILRF) points
to the need to strengthen labor standards within the VeriFlora
program, which mostly just requires growers to comply with their
own national labor laws. "Ecuador needs the flower industry," she
said. "It's brought in a lot of jobs. And workers at a given plantation are better off than they were before the certification arrived.
But some of these certifications come in and basically give a prize
for complying with local laws. Well, they should all be complying
with local laws, and the certification should go to those who go
above and beyond." The ILRF is in the process of reviewing the
VeriFlora standard and suggesting ways to strengthen the labor
standards before it begins the next stage, which is to go through
a national standards accreditation process that may help it to become a national, and even worldwide, standard for the industry
through the American National Standards Institute (ANSI).

This kind of credibility is critical to VeriFlora's success. "This
is not just some rose grower in Ecuador who has three acres,"
Stephens told me. "We're not just a fringe movement of eco-hippie
liberals. Big players in the industry are involved now." Delaware
Valley Wholesale Florist, a major U.S. wholesaler, and Sierra Flowers, one of the largest Canadian distributors, are both involved
with the program. Sierra has been marketing flowers under its own
eco-label for years. "We realized that the more socially responsible
growers were producing better flowers anyway," said Tom Leckman,
president of Sierra. "We made a decision in the year 2000 to start
moving to a hundred percent certified flowers. At that point we
had no certified growers, but today over half of our growers are
certified." This is no small matter. One of the ways in which Sierra
has encouraged its growers to become certified is by agreeing to
buy flowers at a fixed price all year, guaranteeing them a steady

income while they make the transition. Within a few more years, Tom expects all the flowers they sell to be certified, and VeriFlora will be a big part of that. "Once the VeriFlora standard becomes the ANSI standard, that's really going to shake things up. This may become the dominant standard in the industry."

Nobody's more ready for that than Gerald Prolman and his company Organic Bouquet. Prolman, a stocky guy in his forties with brown hair and rimless glasses, looks like any other Bay Area entrepreneur. He could be selling software or real estate, but I've never seen anybody light up about software the way Prolman does when he talks about flowers. At a sustainable floriculture symposium he sponsored in San Francisco, he said, "Walk into any Starbucks. You'll see a little flyer that talks about their social and environmental responsibility. They've now embraced fair-trade coffee and organic coffee. From a business standpoint, there are sixty-three million educated and affluent consumers who are spending $230 billion annually on socially and environmentally responsible products. What we call this is the LOHAS market. LOHAS stands for 'lifestyles of health and sustainability,' and it represents 30 percent of all U.S. households. Eighty-five percent of these consumers believe themselves to be environmentalists. They like to do their part."

Prolman knows this market. In 1989, he founded a food company called Made in Nature and sold organic food under that brand in supermarkets. Dole Food Company bought the business in 1994, and by 2001 he'd founded Organic Bouquet. Prolman and his colleagues hope that these LOHAS consumers, the kind of people who drive the demand for organic food in grocery store chains, will snap up flowers with the VeriFlora label — if they can find them.

Apart from Organic Bouquet, there aren't many retail outlets where people can buy certified flowers. "Retail florists are just one leg in the distribution channel," Jeff Stephens said. "It's just part of the changing nature of the floral industry, with more flowers sold in supermarkets or online." A wire service like FTD would have a hard time marketing a VeriFlora bouquet unless it could ensure that every florist in its network had certified flowers in stock. Supermarkets might, as part of their own corporate standards, decide to purchase only certified flowers, but they might not label the flowers so that customers know they are buying VeriFlora bouquets. Even industry groups are slow to come aboard. "Some associations are afraid of the issue," Stephens told me. "And it's challenging for a trade association. They need to represent all their constituents, so they're more careful about what they do."

So far, the fledgling program has certified just six farms. I'd spent time at two of those farms: Nevado Ecuador and Sun Valley Floral Farms.

I WAS AT THE Organic Bouquet symposium in San Francisco on a sunny summer afternoon when I found out about Sun Valley's VeriFlora certification. Michael Keyes, an auditor who certifies farms for the VeriFlora label, did not come right out and announce to the audience that Sun Valley had been certified. Instead he said, "We've certified close to three hundred acres of flower farms, including growers of roses, a lot of different field varieties, and a certificate was just issued yesterday for a large California grower who produces lilies, irises, tulips and freesia." That could only be Sun Valley.

I knew that Lane had some interest in organic flowers—he'd supported the VeriFlora concept from the beginning, and Prolman had convinced him to supply tulips to Organic Bouquet. Lane agreed with a little trepidation. "Organic tulips are not for the faint of heart," he once told me, but the experiment had continued and Sun Valley tulips became a regular offering through Organic

Bouquet's Web site. Still, in all the time I'd spent at Sun Valley, Lane had never mentioned that he was in the middle of certifying the entire farm to become if not organic, then more environmentally friendly. I had every reason to believe that Sun Valley already used the least toxic chemicals to do the job, and I'd seen firsthand Lane's commitment to his workers, but the VeriFlora certification would make it official. He'd go on the record, so to speak, as an eco-friendly and worker-friendly grower. And like all VeriFlora farms, he would develop a transition plan to continue to reduce the use of chemicals and to eventually convert to fully organic methods. Because Sun Valley is the largest cut flower grower in the country, this is no small matter.

I tracked Michael down in the lobby after the symposium and asked him about the certification. "I live near Arcata," I told him. "This lily grower you just certified . . ."

"Yep," he said, "that's Sun Valley."

He was reluctant to say too much about the certification process because the ink on the certificate was barely dry. "Seriously, this just happened yesterday," he said. "But I'll tell you, this was a great fit. We're picky about who we take, because the certification process is expensive and time-consuming. The grower had to be willing. We don't want some guy who says, 'Okay, just tell me what I have to do to get that certificate thing.' They have to be committed before we'll even talk to them. So Sun Valley was like this big, low-hanging fruit because Lane was already on board."

Michael spent a great deal of time at Sun Valley interviewing workers and watching what they did. He installed monitors in their irrigation system to make sure they weren't overwatering or overfertilizing—a mistake that would cause them to deplete natural resources and create a situation in which fertilizers could run off into aquifers or streams. He walked through every warehouse and looked for chemicals that they wouldn't be able to use under the VeriFlora label.

"And we found a few things," Michael told me. "I'd sit there in Lane's office, with all his staff around him, and tell him that we found chemicals in his warehouse he didn't even know he had. 'We haven't used that for years!' Lane would say, and I'd say, 'So now you've got to get rid of it.' And I found a few places—not many but a few—where they were overwatering or overfertilizing. I'd tell Lane about it and he'd say, 'You mean we're spending more money that we have to?' I told him, 'Yeah, you sure are.' That put an end to it."

He opened a file folder he had tucked under his arm. "Look at this," he said, pulling out a handful of receipts from Humboldt County's hazardous waste disposal center. "These guys are serious. Here's a receipt for every leftover chemical they had in their warehouse that they shouldn't have had. They took it all down and got rid of it. They even sent me this"—and he showed me a photograph of a section of warehouse with empty shelves. We both laughed. It's not easy to prove that you don't have something, but clearly Lane was trying everything he could think of.

Michael's story about Lane's finding cost savings in the reduction of water and fertilizer points out a surprising truth about certified flowers: they can be more profitable for the grower. The more hazardous the chemical, the more of a nuisance it can be, especially for highly regulated California growers. It's expensive to buy; it must be replaced with a newer, often more costly product every time the bugs and fungi develop resistance to it; there are reporting and tracking requirements; and growers have to pay for extensive worker protection, from protective gear to special training to longer re-entry times during which workers can't get back into the greenhouse after a spray. And even the worker-friendly practices that certification requires might at first seem to cost more, but paid maternity leave, incentives and bonuses, and on-site facilities for schools and day care may also pay off in terms of higher productivity and lower turnover. Growers hope that consumers will be willing to pay more for certified flowers, but even if they don't, there may be a way to do this profitably. One of the major hurdles to overcome is the idea that many growers have that there simply are no viable organic alternatives.

Pamela Marrone owns a company called AgraQuest that creates biological pesticides for organic growers. "Some growers just look at the cost of the product," she told me, "and as far as that goes, we're in the middle-high range compared to chemical pesticides. But when growers factor in the labor savings, it's significant."

Her company collects and catalogs microorganisms that might have some pesticidal or fungicidal quality. "When I started this company," she said, "I never imagined the resistance of farmers and distributors and even university researchers to wanting to adopt biopesticides. I thought it would be a no-brainer. But there's a perception out there that these products don't work—that they're snake oil. What's remarkable about that is that most human pharmaceuticals are derived from natural products. After all, aspirin comes from tree bark. Digitalis. Antimalarial drugs. Antibiotics. They all come from natural ingredients."

Of course, natural ingredients can be a mixed bag. Chinese, Greek, and Roman farmers all used highly toxic pesticides based on arsenic they had mined. Arsenic oxide was first used as an ant killer three hundred years ago; it's still in use today. And some organic techniques also have ancient roots: the Chinese introduced a chrysanthemum extract called pyrethrum that is widely used as an organic pesticide today. Greek and Roman farmers used sulfur on their crops, which is another less toxic product that is still deployed for controlling powdery mildew on asters, chrysanthemums, and other flowers.

In the nineteenth century, when flower growers began constructing large greenhouses and looking for easy pest control methods, they turned back to arsenic-based chemicals. One common pesticide in those days was Paris green, an emerald green concoction that was also used as a pigment in paint, wallpaper, and fabric. At the time, there was little understanding of how deadly it could be in the greenhouse or in the home. If the pigment got moldy in damp weather, the molds could react with Paris green and create a noxious gas. It was so poisonous that historians speculate that Napoleon's lengthy exposure to the chemical through the wallpaper in his home might have been the actual cause of death, not stomach cancer, as his doctors reported. Growers used it generously, spraying it not just on flowers but also on food crops, and they applied it to ponds and lakes to control mosquitoes.

Finally, around World War II, the earlier arsenic-based chemicals were phased out in favor of newer synthetic chemicals that may have solved some pest control problems for growers, but introduced new health and environmental hazards. The insecticide DDT was introduced in 1939 and banned in the United States in 1972 when it was implicated in the widespread deaths of birds. Organophosphates, originally created for use as nerve gas in World War II, are still used as pesticides (malathion is one of the best-known organophosphates) but are subject to increasing criticism because of their known toxicity to humans. Some growers have started to realize that the costs of agricultural chemicals—worker safety gear, training, regulation, paperwork, and the need to replace older products with newer ones when the insects become resistant, not to mention the public objections and the damage to people and the environment—might outweigh the benefits.

So Marrone's research team continues its search, turning over compost piles and scratching mold off tree bark to find organisms to use in the new generation of organic products. AgraQuest has cataloged and tested over twenty-three thousand different microorganisms to find the ones that work. "Our first product, Serenade, comes from a bacterium— *Bacillus subtilis*—that we found in a peach orchard in Fresno," she said. "One of our farmer investors called us and said, 'You know, there's never any brown rot in this one field.' So we went out and took a sample of soil under a tree and I went back to the lab and put it in a petri dish, and it was warding off all the other microbes that were on the plate. There were these big zones of inhibition. We found out that these bacteria were producing what we call lipopeptides that are antibacterial and antifungal. We're selling it in fifteen countries, and we should have it for sale in Colombia and Ecuador soon for flower production."

Marrone was surprised to learn how extensive pesticide use was in the cut flower industry, even after the flowers have been cut. "I wasn't aware that growers were dipping cut flowers in fungicide until one of our customers asked us how to use our products for that," she said. "I was like, 'You mean, they actually dip the flowers?' So we added instructions for dipping onto our labels."

AgraQuest also developed a fumigant that can control botrytis on cut flowers once they leave the farm. A rose can appear to be blemish free when it goes into the box, but botrytis will continue to grow and by the time the customer gets the flowers, there may be unsightly grayish brown patches on the petals. To combat this, AgraQuest has developed a fumigant called Arabesque that is derived from a fungus—a newly discovered genus and species—that was growing on the bark of a cinnamon tree in Honduras. When the fungus is in water, it releases a gas that works as a powerful fumigant. Marrone's staff packaged it into tea bags and found that if you get the tea bag wet and put it in a box of flowers, the gas will kill pests and fungi on flowers during shipment.

These products aren't just for strictly organic growers. Using biopesticides between applications of chemical sprays can slow down the resistance of microbes and pests and allow the chemicals to be used less often, but over a longer period of time, before resistance develops and the farmer is forced to switch products again. But no matter how they're used, Marrone is quick to point out that organic farming is about much more than simply spraying a different product on the crops. Workers have to be trained to detect problems early and prevent infestations before they get out of control. "Growers tell us that they'll put workers on the organic crops first and if they work out, they'll use them on the conventional crops, too. There's so much more management involved, and you use these biological products as a last resort. That's a lot different than doing a once-a-week calendar spray of a chemical pesticide."

There is one more benefit of biopesticides—you can spray them right up until the day of harvest, and they won't leave a harmful residue. "Of course, that's a much bigger issue for fruit and vegetables," she said. "You don't eat flowers. But once you make consumers aware that there are all these chemicals on flowers that are in your home—and you're sniffing them—I think people will start realizing that maybe organic flowers are a better choice."

I THOUGHT BACK to Miami and the millions of flowers flooding into the country. It's one thing for a large, domestic grower like Sun Valley to win a green label certification and start marketing its flowers to eco-conscious retailers like Whole Foods or Trader Joe's. But what about the crush of flowers from Latin America? In a flower shop, a red rose is a red rose. You'd never know that you were buying 'Forever Young,' which was grown by

Nevado Ecuador and picked three days ago. If, as a customer, you don't even know that much, how are you ever going to know—or care—that you're buying certified flowers? And if that's the case, why would a Latin American grower even bother growing certified flowers for the U.S. market?

It would be easy to say that certified growers in Ecuador or Colombia are simply responding to the market, growing Max Havelaar–certified flowers for the Swiss or MPS-certified flowers for the Dutch markets because that's what the market demands. But there's something more than blind economic forces at work here. The certified growers I met were committed to more environmentally friendly and worker-friendly practices from the beginning, and the certification programs simply provided a kind of common language to allow them to describe and market what they were already interested in doing. Hernan Chiriboga, owner of an organic rose farm in Ecuador called Biogarden La Pampa, said, "We were already on that track. We were biological. We were ecological. We wanted to become organic. Gerald Prolman contacted us and asked us if we would like him to put us in touch with someone who could certify that what we were doing was organic. We said yes. We had to change very little of what we were doing, and we became the first organic rose producers."

He explained his motivation for growing organic roses during a speech he gave at Organic Bouquet's symposium. After we'd seen representatives from labor rights and environmental groups show slides of terrible conditions on flower farms, Hernan put up a slide of a little girl standing next to a row of rosebushes. "That is not child labor," he said to nervous laughter from the audience. "That is my granddaughter. We live on the farm, and we wanted the best conditions, of course. Those are the conditions where we were going to live with the workers.

"We have received three certifications," he continued. "The first came from USDA, certifying us as organic. The second came from Germany, allowing us to sell our roses in Europe as organic. The third certification came from nature directly," he said, and put up a slide of a bird's nest built inside the canes of a greenhouse-grown rosebush. It held two tiny, bright blue eggs. "A little bird nested in one of our rose plants. That little animal is telling us that we are doing things correctly. With just instinct, it knows that it is not in any danger. The chicks were born right there on the plantation. Nobody helped them, but nobody hurt them, either.

"It's not an easy task," he concluded. "When a problem happens on the farm, the organic solution takes longer. And if we have any problems, we have to get rid of the roses that do not meet the standards for exportation." An organic grower like Biogarden might have to prune and discard up to 30 or 40 percent of the rose crop if it shows early signs of infestation or disease. I thought about Lane's comments about organic tulips. This really wasn't for the faint of heart.

I WAS AT ROBERTO Nevado's farm in Ecuador just as it was working toward its VeriFlora certification. Nevado Ecuador is situated in the Cotopaxi province, south of Quito, where the snowcapped volcano of the same name reaches over nineteen thousand feet and dominates the horizon. This region, with its sweeping plains, good soil, and a ready workforce from the countryside and from the province's capital, Latacunga, has become a kind of secondary flower-growing region to Cayambe.

Nevado bills itself as "Roses with a Conscience," and it's got the plaques on the wall to back that claim up: it's won certifications from the Swiss, German, Dutch, Ecuadorian, and the new American VeriFlora programs, among others. Its goal is to remain the most certified grower in the world. Every time a new certification was developed, it would go after it. It isn't always easy to conform to the various standards that each country imposes, and simply keeping track of paperwork and inspections must be a bureaucratic headache. But Nevado Ecuador has managed to do it, and on a long, whitewashed, cinder-block wall outside the production room is posted the seal from each program.

At first I was surprised by how much the world's most certified flower farm looked like any other farm I'd seen. There were the same rows of hoophouses, the same towering plants pushing rosebuds high above my head, the same radios blasting popular music (some growers believe that a particular type of music makes the plants grow faster, but most agree that the best strategy for the plants is to play whatever music the workers like best). A few greenhouses held hydroponic roses, the only ones I'd seen in Ecuador, but for the most part it was hard to distinguish this farm from its neighbors. In the production room I had to ask why the workers wore so little protective gear—just a rubber apron and gloves—and one of the managers smiled at me and said, "When you use less chemicals, you don't need all that protection." That's when I realized that what I couldn't see made all the difference. What they weren't doing was every bit as important as what they were doing.

Less toxic pesticides mean shorter re-entry restrictions in green-houses. Careful management of the plants means that fewer roses require a postharvest dip, and those that do require treatment are dipped in the least toxic fungicide available. Like other high-end growers, Nevado plants under twenty-eight thousand plants per acre, which allows for more air circulation and lets them pay more attention to each plant. They also limit their production to about thirty-five varieties, but within their selection I found many of my newfound favorites. The lime green 'Limbo' grows there, as does the tricolor pink, cream, and green 'Esperance' and 'Red Intuition,' a red rose with a kind of variegated pattern on its petals, as if darker red paint had been splashed over them.

'Red Intuition' is a good example of the kind of premium rose that is almost impossible to find in the United States. Each flower has an enormous head that grows on perfectly straight, five-foot-tall stems. At the farm these roses were exhibited in sturdy glass floor vases, which was the only way to show them off. It would be hard to imagine a room, except perhaps a ballroom, that would be large enough to accommodate a bouquet of these sitting on a table.

These flowers would be headed to the Russian market, where there are buyers for these kind of high-end roses. (About 30 percent of Nevado's roses go to Russia, and almost all the rest go to Europe.) Nobody in the United States would know what to do with them, as I found out later for myself. Nevado had supplied some of the flowers for Organic Bouquet's symposium in San Francisco, and there, on either side of the podium, were those glass floor vases filled with impossibly tall 'Red Intuition'. After the event was over, I took a rose with me and walked through the Ferry Building, a marketplace on the bay that houses the farmers' market and a number of high-end shops, including a caviar bar and a mushroom shop. I held the rose next to me, just high enough to keep it from dragging on the ground, which meant that it looked to be about as tall as I was. I have never attracted so much attention in public. Nobody bothered to hide their amazement. People sitting in cafés turned and pointed, and I could take only a few steps before someone would stop me and ask where the flower came from. "Ecuador," I'd say. I might as well have said that it came from the moon. Everything about this flower—its size, the patterns of color on its petals, its country of origin, its many certifications—was entirely exotic.

By commercial rose-growing standards, Nevado is small—the

farm occupies only about seventy-five acres and produces twenty million roses a year, two million of which go to the U.S. market—and it employs only four hundred employees, all of whom enjoy the protections and benefits mandated by their many certifications. That means that they have the right to organize and the right to present grievances, and they get additional protections against pesticide exposure, harassment, and forced overtime, among other hazards of the job. The use of subcontractors is strictly prohibited; this ensures that workers can gain some seniority and are enrolled immediately in Ecuador's social insurance system, which offers pensions, survivor benefits, and a form of workers' compensation. About two-thirds of the people who work on the farm live close enough to walk or ride their bicycles to work. The company provides an on-site lunch, a community room, and medical and child-care programs. The premium from the Max Havelaar program was enough to allow the employees to start an Internet café in their village.

These modest amenities probably wouldn't mean much to an American worker, but Nevado was making an effort to be a good employer in this community and to give its workers some kind of stake, an identity of their own, in this often anonymous industry. Each bunch of Nevado roses is sold with a sticker inside the sleeve that reads NEVADO ECUADOR, ROSES WITH A CONSCIENCE. Below that, it reads HANDMADE BY and a blank where the worker writes her name. Those stickers are there so that each woman can leave her mark on the roses before they go out into the world. A person harvested these roses, the sticker implies, a person who matters. I don't know who made the blue jeans I'm wearing, or who assembled the keyboard I'm typing on, but knowing the name of the woman who bundled my roses and sent them to me makes the vast flower market seem a little smaller, a little more connected. That's the story Nevado Ecuador is trying to tell with its roses.

GREEN LABEL PROGRAMS are not without their critics. Felicity Lawrence, consumer affairs correspondent for the *Guardian*, ruffled a few feathers with her March 5, 2005, story "Why I Won't Be Giving My Mother Fairtrade Flowers," in which she asserted that even a certified farm would have trouble maintaining high labor standards—such as avoiding compulsory overtime—when demand for flowers rises and falls dramatically at holidays and "everyone must have the exact same floral tribute on exactly the same day." She criticized the Fairtrade Foundation for certifying a large farm that employs "large clusters of migrants in shanty housing, sucked into the area by work in the horticultural companies." She said that such an environment was "not the villages many shoppers paying a Fairtrade premium might expect." She wondered why the customer should pay more for workers to have "decent housing, reasonable hours and sufficient pay" when such costs could reasonably be borne by a large, profitable grower. "If we are not careful," she asserted, "we will find the burden of behaving decently has been thrown back to the shopper. We will be offered a choice of one shelf full of more expensive goods for those rich enough to take their morals shopping and a shelf next door of bargain goods produced without worker's rights for those who don't care or can't afford to care."

The Fairtrade Foundation responded that farms must adhere to restrictions on working hours even during times of peak demand and pointed out that workers at large farms deserve the same protections as those at smaller farms. Also, the higher price shoppers pay for Fairtrade products goes back directly to the workers, not to the farms' owners to offset the costs of decent working conditions and compensation.

Not all growers are quick to jump on the green label bandwagon, either. Lee Murphy, formerly president of the California Cut Flower Commission, which represents California growers, told me that it was almost impossible to grow a cosmetically perfect flower using organic methods and that those growers who did devote some of their production to organic flowers were doing so as a "marketing ploy." When I asked him how many of his members were growing any organic flowers at all, he said that "most organic flowers are grown by Mama and Papa . . . They go out and shoo the bugs off the flowers."

He continued, "Our chemicals are so benign, so safe that you have trouble killing the bugs with them. How are you going to kill the people? We have these conversations about methyl bromide, but if somebody handed me a methyl bromide burger, I'd eat it . . . People talk about how dangerous pesticides are, but the world never had a safe food supply until you had pesticides." If anything, Murphy seemed to see environmental restrictions as an obstacle that put California growers at an unfair disadvantage against Latin American growers who face fewer restrictions. "If you cut a rose two hours too late, you take a forty-cent rose and make it a ten-cent rose because it's too cracked to ship," he said. "So you've got a forty-eight-hour re-entry time on a chemical, but our workers have to get in there twice a day or else they have to throw away the crop . . . so in the last four years, we've been functioning as an industry that's not really in compliance with the laws. My rose growers have to harvest illegally whenever they need to."

Murphy told me that he was more in favor of developing standards for heavier worker protection gear that will allow quicker re-entry times. At the same time, he said that he advocates residue testing so that consumers will know that California flowers have fewer chemical residues than Latin American flowers, a stance that puts him at odds with the Society of American Florists, which represents retailers who sell Latin American as well as domestic flowers.

"Peter Moran at Society of American Florists—I consider him a friend of mine," Murphy said. "But when we were pushing for residue testing, Society of American Florists said, 'No, you can't do that, because that's admitting we have a problem.' And we backed off."

Moran was recently quoted in *E/The Environmental Magazine* as saying that the Society of American Florists has not taken a position on VeriFlora or other green label programs. "I don't see the problems on flower farms you read about in the newspapers," he was quoted as saying. "You don't eat flowers; it's not the same as food." The retailers he represents also don't seem motivated to market certified flowers to their customers. I asked dozens of florists if their customers ever asked for organic flowers or even wanted to know where their flowers came from, and not a single florist could recall getting such a question from a customer. If someone did ask, most florists would have to confess that they didn't have a single organic blossom in stock.

Ironically, it may turn out that most certified flowers purchased in the United States will be sold to customers who don't know exactly what they're buying. A retailer like Whole Foods will make the decision for them, purchasing flowers from growers that meet the company's procurement standards. Shoppers may assume that flowers sold at an eco-friendly grocer are somehow more socially and environmentally friendly, but for the most part they'll choose a bright bouquet of tulips or roses because they're beautiful, or because they'll match the place settings at the dinner party, or cheer up a friend, or make the apology or confession of love that they can't find the words for otherwise.

It's a lot to ask of a flower—all that and a promise of worker safety and environmental stewardship, too—but if I've learned one thing about flowers, it's this: they're tougher than they look. Somewhere out there is a flower that will do whatever you want it to do. That's what the flower industry has given us. And I knew that there was one place I could go to see everything that breeders and growers had done to flowers in their attempts to give us what we want. I was on my way to the famous Dutch flower auction.

CHAPTER 8

The Dutch Auction

I woke up at 5 a.m. and stared at the ceiling of my Amsterdam hotel room. Outside, the canal boats, which were rented to rowdy, hard-drinking college students, had just gone quiet. This was a city of late risers. I got dressed and walked gingerly through the lobby, not wanting to wake the innkeeper who slept on the ground floor, and stepped into the dark, empty streets. The coffee shops I passed on my way to the bus stop were not due to open for a few more hours, and as much as I craved a cup of coffee I appreciated their position on not starting the day before dawn. But the fact is that if you want to go see someone in the flower trade, this is the hour at which you must rise. Even then, when you finally show up at 6 or 7 a.m., blinking in the sudden daylight and trying to remember why you scheduled the meeting in the first place, the person you've gone to meet will look impatient, as though half the day is wasted already.

I was on my way to Aalsmeer to see the famous Dutch flower auction. It's known around the world as a remarkably high-tech, high-speed way to sell flowers, but it had modest beginnings: in a café outside of Amsterdam in 1911 some growers came up with the idea of holding an auction to give them more control over how their flowers were priced and sold. They called their auction Bloemenlust. It was not long before a competing auction sprang up nearby—the history of flower markets everywhere is that as soon as there is one, there are two—and each day as the auctions ended, flowers were piled onto bicycles and boats to be delivered along Holland's narrow canals and even narrower streets. Street vendors came in by train and took their merchandise back with them on the train. When trucks were finally introduced, they were, in the Dutch tradition of egalitarianism, owned cooperatively by the two auctions. This arrangement continued until 1968, the two auctions thriving nearly side by side, until they finally merged and became what is known today as Bloemenveiling Aalsmeer, the largest of a handful of major flower auctions going on year-round in the Netherlands.

The bus to Aalsmeer took me through the shuttered streets of Amsterdam and headed south, past the airport. The world seemed to be coming to life at last, and on the road we passed dozens of trucks—some of them plastered with the same grower and whole-saler logos you'd see in Miami—carrying flowers to and from the auction. This next phase of a flower's life, after it leaves the grower and before it settles into a vase on someone's hall table, is remark-able for both its duration and its complexity. A flower can spend a week making its way through a maze of warehouses, airports, auctions, and wholesale markets, and it will emerge from this ex-hausting journey looking almost as fresh as the day it was picked.

The existence of this auction highlights one major difference be-tween flowers destined for the European market and those sold in the United States. The flowers that I saw arriving in Miami were headed in every direction at once: they were going by truck, rail, and plane to wholesale markets, distribution centers, bouquet makers, retailers, and even directly to customers. There is not a single, cen-tralized market for flowers in the United States. But the flowers that come into Schiphol Airport outside of Amsterdam, the major port of entry for European flowers, are almost all going to Aalsmeer. This is the very center of the flower trade, handling most of the flowers sold on the European market and some of the goods going to Russia, China, Japan, and even the United States. (Only about 250 million flowers, or 5 percent of the flowers sold through the Dutch auction, go to the United States, where they represent just over six percent of flowers purchased.) The flowers going up for auction come from Kenya, Zimbabwe, Israel, Colombia, Ecuador, and European countries, making this a sort of global stopping-off point for most of the industry. Every flower market around the world watches the Dutch auction, which acts as a sort of engine for the trade, setting prices and standards worldwide. If you want to follow a flower to market, you'll end up here eventually.

By the time the bus pulled into the large circular driveway at the public entrance to the auction, the day really was half over. Flowers and plants had been arriving since midnight, and bidding started before dawn. I stepped off the bus into a kind of floral rush hour: trucks roaring past, people racing from one end of the complex to another, the morning sun glaring down. This place is a behemoth in the small town of Aalsmeer. It employs ten thousand people in a town of just twenty thousand and occupies almost 450 acres, an area larger than Walt Disney World's Magic Kingdom and Epcot theme parks combined. In fact, the auction is like a city in itself, one that runs twenty-four hours a day. The facility serves not just as an auction house but as a kind of regional distribution center as well. All the major growers and wholesalers keep an office, and maybe a warehouse and a loading dock, at Aalsmeer. A full 20 percent of the cut flowers in the world are sold at this very spot, and about half of the world's cut-flower supply moves through the Dutch auction system.

NATASCHA VAN DE POLDER had agreed to show me around and introduce me to some bidders and vendors. She met me in the bright, flower-filled lobby and took me to a network of catwalks high above the warehouse floor, where flowers on carts lined up for their turn at auction. It would be impossible to lead someone through the auction on ground level: carts of flowers zip around so fast that a run-in with a pallet of tulips would be inevitable, especially with a hundred thousand tourists a year turning up to watch the spectacle. Instead, we'd see it mostly from above. Even the glassed-in auction rooms are designed to keep people off the warehouse floor: they are built like college lecture halls, with an entrance for the flowers at ground level and a separate entrance for the bidders from the catwalk. The rooms slope down to the level of the warehouse floor, and bidders enter at the highest point, in the back of the room, and take their seats at rows of desks that allow them to look down at the flowers they'll be bidding on.

It's hard to describe the sheer size of the place. I could look down and make out individual carts of flowers—typically there were nine boxes of flowers on a shelf and three shelves to a cart—but off in the distance the flowers just blurred together in a mass of red or pink. It was like watching an airline terminal from above. Everything's moving very fast, according to some organizational scheme that is at first hard to see. There are constant arrivals and departures. Some make their connections; others don't. It is a more sophisticated—and puzzling—system for selling flowers than I could have imagined. Nineteen million flowers move through it every day.

I stood on the catwalk with Natascha and watched the carts move into the auction rooms, and then snake back out again and head to loading docks where the flowers would be sorted and packed. Unlike the flowers coming into Miami, which remain in their boxes until they reach their destination, these had been taken off their pallets, pulled out of boxes, and placed in water in sturdy, square white buckets with the auction logo. Every petal and leaf was on display. It made the flowers seem more vulnerable and less like ordinary freight. I could almost imagine the individual fates of these flowers. Here were millions of stems representing festivity and well wishes, the possibilities of romance, even apologies and regrets. What would these flowers be called upon to do when they finally went home with somebody? What mistakes would they have to fix? Who would they have to cheer up or seduce?

Natascha was entirely blasé about the sea of flowers in constant motion below us. "Do you mind if I smoke?" she asked me in a heavy Dutch accent as she reached in the pocket of her blazer for a lighter.

"Won't it bother the flowers?" I asked. Directly below us, thousands of yellow and orange sunflowers waited for their turn in front of the auction clock. It hardly seemed like a place for secondhand smoke.

She laughed. Silly American. "Well, the flowers don't have noses," she said. "So it is no problem."

The moment had come for the sunflowers. The carts — each of them holding about three hundred stems in buckets or boxes — jerked along their tracks and moved toward the nearest auction room, where a crowd of wholesalers waited to bid on them. This was the last sunflower lot of the day. I looked out over the warehouse floor, which spanned about six and a half acres. Off in the distance, a bluish haze hung in the air. I realized that since I'd arrived at Aalsmeer, I had not once smelled a flower. If the place could be said to have any scent at all, it was a faint warehouse smell: cement floor, cardboard box, truck exhaust, and — yes, there it was — cigarette smoke.

"Go ahead," I told Natascha. "Light up."

NATASCHA HAS WORKED at the auction for about a decade. She's performed quality control inspections and worked a desk job in the administrative office, and for the last year or two she'd been handling public relations for this, the world's largest flower shop. It seemed like an extraordinary job, one that would be impossible to leave at the end of the day. As we strolled along the catwalk, I asked her if she took flowers home much.

"No," she said.

That was it. Her English was good, but not perfect, and I spoke no Dutch at all, so I thought that maybe she didn't understand the question. "Really?" I said. "You don't bring a bouquet of flowers home for your family sometimes?"

"No," she repeated. "My ex-husband is a buyer on the auction clock here. When we were together, he would bring me so many flowers! Everything that is too old, he can take home."

"And you got tired of getting flowers?" I asked.

"It was too much. The house was filled with flowers. It was unbelievable."

I was trying to be sympathetic to this point of view, that a husband could bring a wife too many flowers. "I guess if he's just bringing you flowers he got for free, it's not the same," I said.

"*Ja,*" she said. "It was terrible. It was just not nice anymore."

Natascha didn't volunteer any information about why she got divorced, and I didn't ask, but I couldn't help but wonder if I'd stumbled across the first recorded case of flowers actually wrecking a marriage instead of improving it. She led me over to a display cabinet where a grower was exhibiting new varieties of alstroemeria in the widest range of colors I'd ever seen, from cream and lemon to salmon, scarlet, tangerine, and purple. It looked like a flock of tropical butterflies had landed in the case. This was not too far from the truth — alstroemerias are a South American flower that grow wild in the cool mountain ranges of Peru and Chile. They made their way into cultivation when the Swedish naturalist Baron Claus Alstroemer, a pupil of Carl Linnaeus, found them in the 1700s in

Spain, where they had been imported from South America. They're a member of the lily family (alstroemerias are also called Peruvian lilies), and the flowers look like miniature lilies.

Alstroemerias are, in many ways, the quintessential cut flower: brought from Latin America to the greenhouses of Holland, where they have been bred for the industry. Growers love their long, straight stems, which are easy to handle and snap out of the ground by hand. They also like the fact that the flowers can be picked closed so they will open later. Florists and consumers appreciate the long vase life (after two weeks, alstroemerias are often the only flowers remaining in a mixed bouquet) and the brilliant colors. If you had to name a flower that worked perfectly at every stage of the process, alstroemeria might be it.

I stood, riveted, in front of the glass. "These are my favorite," she said.

"But you don't even like these very much," I said.

"No," she said. "I prefer houseplants."

THE AALSMEER AUCTION sells houseplants, too. Nine million ivy plants a year. Thirteen million ficus trees. They also sell bulbs, greenery, and nursery plants like violets and petunias. And every one of those plants, along with about five billion cut flowers a year, are wheeled in front of bidders for their turn on the auction clock. I could understand how, for someone working here, flowers would lose their charm eventually. They are just a commodity, something to be taken off a truck, put up for auction, and loaded onto another truck for the next leg of the journey. Even the 'Star Gazer' lily, with its intriguing history and its worldwide popularity, seems small and insignificant here. In 2004, 13.8 million stems of 'Star Gazer' were sold at Aalsmeer, a number that seems enormous until you realize that such a quantity would represent less than one day's activity at the auction.

I stood in the back of the room and watched as one lot of flowers after another went before the bidders. Each auction room holds two to four clocks, which means that more than one auction can take place simultaneously in each room. There's a rose room that trades in nothing but roses all day, another that deals only in flowering potted plants and houseplants for the florist and gift market, and one that is dedicated to garden plants that will be sold at nurseries. Two other rooms handle a mixture of cut flowers: lilies, tulips, gerberas, carnations, alstroemerias, all wheeling in and out of the auction room on their carts, each barely pausing in front of the bidders before they are sold. You can't get close to the flowers when they come up for auction: a cart holding several hundred flowers rolls into the room on a track, an auction employee pulls out a stem or a small bunch and holds it up, and the bidding takes place a second later. If you want to examine the flowers up close, you've got to track them down early in the morning, while they're still lined up on the warehouse floor waiting for the auction to begin. Otherwise, you've just got to squint at the flowers as they are waved in the air and make your decision.

Here's how the Dutch clock auction, also called a descending bid auction, works. An enormous clock face in the front of the room is marked not with hours and minutes but with prices in euros. For a typical flower auction, where bidding is based on the price per stem, midnight on the clock face is zero; half past is fifty eurocents; and one minute before midnight is ninety-nine euro cents. There are no actual hands on the clock—this is really a digital version of a clock's shape—so instead of hands, a ring of red lights moves around the clock face the way hands would, and additional rows of yellow lights are used as a kind of second hand when the bid prices exceed one euro.

These digital hands on the clock run backward, counterclockwise, starting at a price that is considered too high for the item and dropping until someone bids. For instance, a rose might start at ninety eurocents per stem, a price far too high for the flower, and drop until someone bids at, say, thirty-five cents a stem. The bidder knows what price he or she would like to pay; the trick is to wait until the bidding drops to your price, without letting someone else jump in and buy it first for a slightly higher amount.

This tension — this pressure to jump in and bid before anyone else does — is the opposite of the kind of waiting game that happens at English auctions, also called ascending bid auctions, where the remaining bidders gradually push the price higher until only the highest bidder remains. Instead, a Dutch clock auction is a race to the bottom, a game of speed that's all about getting the merchandise at the right price before someone else does.

Although this sounds like a peculiar way to bid on flowers, it's actually not too different from the way a shopper makes decisions in a department store. Think about a coat that arrives in stores in the fall. You could pay full price for it immediately, or you could wait for it to go on sale. However, you run the risk that there won't be any left in your size by the time the sale takes place. And if you wait for an end-of-season clearance — maybe 40 percent off the already-reduced price — it is quite likely that the coat you want will already be sold. The more you want the coat, the earlier in the season you'll buy it and the higher the price you'll pay. This is exactly how buyers bidding on the clock behave, except that they do it in a split second, not over the course of several months.

When a lot of flowers comes up for bid, small screens on the clock face display other relevant information about the flowers, including the name of the grower, the type of flower, and variety. (The bidders also wear headphones and listen to an auctioneer, who is stationed in a glass booth in the front of the room, describe each lot.) The flowers' quality rating, which is determined by inspectors working for the auction, flashes across the screen. If the grower has gone through the Dutch flower certification process, the environmental and social responsibility rating bestowed by the MPS program appears as well. You can also see how many boxes of a particular variety are for sale and the number of stems per box. If a bidder doesn't want the entire lot, he can bid on fewer boxes, and the auctioneer will reset the clock and auction off the rest of the lot until it is gone. (And I use "he" on purpose: on the day I visited, the bidders were all men. Natascha told me that they are often responsible for helping to sort and pack the orders after the auction, and all this heavy lifting, not to mention the difficulty of breaking into a male-dominated work environment, has kept women away.)

Because the clock moves so fast, it can handle over a dozen transactions in a single minute. Natascha stood beside me and narrated as we watched the lily clock—a particular kind of flower is always sold on the same clock so buyers know where to go each day—and the bidding went by faster than she could describe it. "Thirty cents," she said as a cart of orange lilies went up for auction. "You can buy eighteen boxes. Fifteen boxes are left. Now ten boxes. Seven boxes. Four boxes. The price is down to twenty-five eurocents. And now they are gone." Another cart slid along the track in the front of the room to take its place, and it, too, was sold so quickly that I couldn't even jot down the prices as they went by.

This system is all about speed. With five auction rooms running a total of thirteen clocks among them, and nineteen million flowers and plants moving through the auction in a typical morning, it's hard to believe that by the end of the day, almost everything will be sold. The lower-quality flowers and the odd lots usually go to Dutch street vendors who will sell them at bargain-basement prices. Less than one-half of 1 percent of the flowers don't find a buyer at all; that doesn't sound like much until you realize that this represents just under a hundred thousand stems a day, enough flowers for a hundred weddings. These misfits are shredded and sent off to a company that makes them into compost, a cost that is borne by the unlucky grower.

The auction ends when all the flowers for the day have had their turn in front of the clock. Bidding usually begins at 6:30 a.m. and is over by 10 or 11 a.m. By noon, the place is a ghost town. The trucks have all left, and the people who work for the growers, importers, and wholesalers have retreated to their offices around the edge of the auction buildings to do some paperwork and finish up their day's work.

ANYONE WHO VISITS Aalsmeer will be struck at first by the absurdity of the arrangement. Why go to all the trouble to put something as perishable as a daisy on an airplane, fly it to another country so it can sit on the auction floor, and then put it back on a plane and fly it to its final destination? Most flowers sell for less than a dollar per stem at auction. On an individual basis, we're not talking about valuable goods here. So why do they have to show up in Holland at all?

During the time I spent at the auction, I asked this question to growers, buyers, importers, and auction staff over and over. They seemed unable to understand what I was so confused about. I kept trying to draw comparisons with other products.

"I mean, there's no soup auction," I would say. "Billions of cans of soup get sold every year and they don't have to go to an auction or a market first. There's no lettuce auction. There's no sock auction. Why does there have to be a flower auction?"

The best answer I could get was, "Flowers are not cans of soup. They are different every day. You have to see them up close and check them. People don't want to buy something they haven't seen."

Well, okay. Maybe. But take a rose like 'Grand Prix', the beefy red rose that sells by the millions and dominates Valentine's Day. If you were a buyer, you'd want to make sure that the rose looks good, that the stem is the right length, and that the blossom is large enough. Bad weather or a pest infestation could affect the size of the rose or even the color brilliance of the petals. A mistake in transit—let's say the refrigerator on the truck breaks down—could cause the flowers to wilt prematurely. But is it really necessary to see them in person to be sure that you know what you're getting? Couldn't you just make sure you're buying them from a reputable wholesaler? Is it really worth the fuss and expense of an enormous auction building and the staff that goes along with it to see the flowers yourself? What about the extra days that the flowers must spend packed in boxes, out of water, traveling from airport to airport?

But buyers and growers are adamant about the need to bring flowers together, somewhere in the world, so that they can be displayed, judged, picked over, and purchased. Even though it's difficult for bidders sitting in the auction room to get a good look at the flowers they're buying, the carts are paraded in front of them anyway. When an auction employee pulled a single stem off each cart and held it up high for the bidders to see, I wondered what kind of information they could possibly be getting from that little gesture. From the back of the room, those individual lilies or tulips, each waving in the air for just a second before the cart moves on, look so small and oddly insignificant in a place that has much more in common with Wall Street than a flower shop.

In an effort to cut costs and to keep the flowers under refrigeration longer, the Aalsmeer auction tried switching to a new system in which the carts would not actually roll into the room while the bidding took place. Instead, a photograph of the flower supplied by the grower was projected onto an enormous screen for the bidders to see, and the flowers themselves would stay in the cooler. The clock face was replaced with a computer image of a clock that was projected onto the wall. The bidding still happened in real time, but the auction clock had basically become an interactive Web site that people gathered around in a room and watched together. The auction's managers prefer this arrangement because of the savings in staff costs: right now, thirteen employees are needed to staff each clock and move the flowers for that clock around the auction floor, but if the flowers stay in the cooler, almost all of their work is eliminated.

The buyers I met at Aalsmeer reacted to this change with contempt or, at best, skepticism. They claimed that not having the flowers in the room slowed them down: instead of looking at the cart and knowing, at one glance, the color and variety, the number of stems on the cart, and who the grower was, they now had to stop and read the text on the screen. When an auction is designed to be a race, you can't afford to lose even a fraction of a second figuring out what's for sale. Still, it seemed obvious that an Internet-based system would simplify things. Sure, the flowers would still need to come together in some kind of distribution center—a grower might have a hundred thousand red roses to sell, but each buyer might want just a few boxes of roses, a few lilies, a few gerberas, so someone would still have to gather them together to sort and pack the orders—but the actual bidding and ordering wouldn't have to happen in the same building where the flowers are. Both buyers and sellers appreciate the ease of having the auction handle the money, but that could continue regardless of where the flowers are actually stored. So why does this puzzling—and glorious—institution still run the way it does?

When I asked one importer this question, he just shrugged and said, "Why are there still brokers on Wall Street? They want to be there to feel the ambience and the spirit. It's the character of the business. Before somebody buys a hundred thousand red roses, they want to see them and touch them. A picture will not help."

This belief is so entrenched among the buyers that no matter how hard I tried, I couldn't get anyone to go along with the idea that technology could eliminate the need for the flowers to have to put in a personal appearance at the auction or that the convenience would outweigh any potential downsides. "Just imagine," I said to a couple of stocky Dutch guys in polo shirts and khaki pants when bidding was suspended for a midmorning coffee break, "If you're just looking at the flower on a screen, you could be anywhere. You could go back to your office and bid online. You could be out of the country. You wouldn't have to come here at all."

They looked at me, and then looked at each other, as if I had just suggested that they get a divorce. "No, no," one of them said, perhaps thinking that I had failed, as an outsider, to understand the situation. "We come here every *day*." I realized that what he meant was, this *is* our office. And: we're Dutch. We've been doing this for one hundred years. This is our system.

ONE REASON PEOPLE in the trade are so reluctant to let go of this system has to do with the quality control inspections that take place when the flowers arrive. Natascha used to work as an inspector at Aalsmeer; she was assigned primarily to lilies. Unlike the flowers coming into Miami, shipments to the Schiphol Airport are not inspected for pests or diseases until they get to the auction. It had been Natascha's job to serve both as agricultural inspector and quality control inspector.

"I would look to see if the flowers are clean, with no diseases," she said, "or if they were damaged or too old. We're looking to see if it's a good product." Each clock has its own team of inspectors—four or five per clock—and they check each other's work to make sure that their ratings are consistent. "If I say there is a bad leaf on a flower," she said, "and the next morning, my colleague sees the same product and says nothing, we've got real problems." With the exception of some pest and disease infestations, most flowers with a flaw are not destroyed but are put up for auction anyway with a lower quality rating or a note from the inspector to alert the buyer to the problems they've discovered. The goal of the inspections, then, is to provide accurate information to the buyer without unfairly criticizing a grower's product.

"We are not for the grower," Natascha said, "and we are not for the buyer. We are in the middle. You have to be very strict, very straight. The grower says, all the time, 'I have the best products.' But the buyer wants it for the lowest price. So we are always in the middle." There is no comparable system like this for flowers coming to the United States, where the government inspects only for bugs and disease and buyers must rely on quality ratings not from a neutral third party but instead from someone working for either the grower or the wholesaler.

This isn't the only way that the auction staff checks for quality; growers are also encouraged to bring new varieties to the test center, where flowers are subject to "living-room conditions," conditions that ordinary customers will subject them to when they get them home. Over twelve thousand varieties are already for sale through the auction, and the test center acts as a kind of gatekeeper to screen out those that won't perform well and to conduct random tests of flowers already being sold on the clock. This is one advantage that Dutch breeders like Terra Nigra have by keeping their breeding program here in Holland while the growing operations are moving to Africa and Latin America: Aalsmeer provides one of the only places in the world where varieties can be tested objectively and rated against the competition. Peter Boerlage told me that Terra Nigra often sends new varieties of gerberas and roses down the road to the auction to be tested and sold in small quantities on the clock, so that they can get an idea of both the quality and the potential sales price of the flower.

The testing center is in a long, narrow room that sits above the auction floor with entrances from the catwalks. There's nothing secretive about this place or about the results of the trials: the room is surrounded by windows, so that other growers, or buyers on their coffee break, can stroll by, peer in the windows, and see how the new varieties are faring. The flowers sit in identical glass vases on long tables that run the length of the room. There's a sign next to each flower indicating the variety, the grower, and the testing conditions it will be subject to. Standing out in the hall-way, looking in at the new arrivals, I was reminded of those large hospital nurseries where you could peek in at everyone's newborn babies. If your infant was particularly scrawny, red-faced, loud, or exceptionally cute, well, there it was for everyone to see. Here, if your new variety of alstroemeria has failed to hold up in the vase for even a day, there's no hiding it.

As part of the test, most flowers will first spend four days with-out water, in a box, at forty-six degrees to simulate transportation. By industry standards, these would be minimally acceptable con-ditions for this stage of the journey. Growers would prefer to cut out as many steps in the middle as possible so that their flowers get to market in two days, not four, and wholesalers are starting to adopt standards that will allow them to reject shipments of flowers that have been stored above fifty degrees during transport. (The VeriFlora standard would help with this by requiring a cold chain plan that describes how the flowers will be kept cold until they reach the customer.)

So after four days in this less-than-perfect shipping simulation, the flowers go into a vase, where they will be subject to the same sort of abuse that you or I might put them through. There will be no changing of the water every day, no recutting of the stems, and usually no food. If a flower has special needs — for instance, a gerbera daisy, which does best with just a couple inches of water in the bottom of the vase — those needs will be soundly ignored. The room is kept at a balmy sixty-eight degrees, the lights go off at night and back on during the day, and the humidity is calibrated to match that of an ordinary living room. Short of placing the flowers in a sunny window or on top of the television set (treatment so horrible that a Dutch auction employee might not even think of it), the testers do everything they can to create the sort of homey environment that spells sure death for a bouquet of flowers.

And the flowers really do not fare well in these tests. The water in the vase gets cloudy, the petals drop (and the test center staff does not sweep them up, so that the evidence of the flower's demise is abundantly clear throughout the test), the stems droop, and the whole thing is over depressingly fast. I could imagine the kind of existential crisis growers might go through if they spent too much time in this room: is it really worth working day and night to create a product that people are going to do *this* to?

I asked one of the testing center staff what it was like to tell a grower that a product failed the test. "We do not actually tell the growers that their flowers have failed," she said. "We give them the results. Some of the growers are not happy with the results, but they can use the information for something constructive, right? But sometimes a grower will abandon a new variety after our test." If it doesn't make it here, it might never take its turn at auction, much less make it to a florist anywhere in the world.

It wasn't immediately obvious, as I walked around the auction, where the flowers were going next. The buyers in the auction rooms were mostly Dutch men working for exporters and wholesalers who would put the flowers into their vast supply chain. The auction process was more anonymous than I had thought it would be. I was expecting something like the United Nations, with a little sign in front of every bidder indicating what country, or buyer, each represented. Instead, all I could do was try to work out, from ID badges or the logos on their shirts, which importers they worked for. Quite a few of them worked for Florimex, the largest importer and exporter of flowers around the world. As the bidding came to an end for the day, I said good-bye to Natascha and stepped out into the bright midday sunlight. With trucks thundering past me on their way to the airport, I walked all the way around the auction buildings to Florimex's administrative office, where Carlos Bau Santos, director of a subsidiary of Florimex called Baardse, was just winding up his afternoon. Baardse specializes in supplying retail and mass-market chains with flowers and plants. Another division, SierraFlor, is a bouquet maker, and other subsidiaries target various niches around the world. Florimex handles five hundred million euros' worth of flowers every year, which makes it no small player at an auction that handles a billion euros in sales annually.

The company buys flowers in fifty countries around the world and sells them to every imaginable market, from the giant retailer Ikea to Martha Stewart's online flower shop to the florist for Manhattan's Waldorf-Astoria hotel. Florimex's buyers are stationed on each auction clock; upstairs in the office there are salespeople working the phones, speaking a jumble of Dutch, German, English, Spanish, Russian, and Japanese, selling those flowers as fast as they come off the clock and tacking on a 15 percent commission, which represents Florimex's stake in the deal.

Carlos watches the clock prices constantly. "You have to," he told me. "When you are working on commission, 15 percent of eight cents or 15 percent of sixteen cents—that's a big difference." The seasonal fluctuations, and even the daily fluctuations, in stem prices can be maddening for an intermediary like Florimex.

"Monday is the lowest, price-wise," Carlos said, "and there's a little valley in the middle of the week, with prices going up and down, and Friday is the most expensive day. The whole world needs to buy flowers on Friday to start their week. And if the price drops on Friday, that's a sign that there were too many flowers on the clock." Summer months are especially difficult — growers are fond of saying, "When there are girls on the beach, nobody wants to look at flowers" — in spite of the fact that growers are producing some of their best flowers in abundance thanks to the long, warm days. "The stem price is very low, and supply is high. We do buy more, which makes for huge volume and no special flower-buying holidays to supply. A lot of flowers go to the bin in the summer." The industry has just five months in the year — a season that stretches from around Christmas or Valentine's Day to Easter and Mother's Day — to make up for the imbalance created by the summer's overproduction and general lack of demand.

Then there's the need to keep on top of trends around the world. One of the best-known flower trendsetters, the one that practically every wholesaler and florist mentioned to me, is Martha Stewart. Carlos was one of the first suppliers to provide flowers to Stewart's online floral service. "It was really ridiculous at first," he said. "She saw a flower somewhere in a field, she took a picture, and she sent us an order for thirty thousand stems. It doesn't work like that."

In the early days he would learn, too late, that her company had planned a special promotion of a seasonal flower like parrot tulips during a period when they weren't available. "They'd send us a program for a year and order things that weren't there. It was a terrible moment. They learned a lot, but when they started, it was difficult."

Carlos credits Martha Stewart with creating a more sophisticated customer base and driving demand for higher-quality, more interesting flowers in the United States, but he told me that he was much less impressed with the supermarket sector of the business. "You will see my tulips in Sam's Club and Wal-Mart, and in some other chains through Dole," he said, "but I'm not too fond of the level of flowers in the U.S. Here in Europe there is more value for the money in supermarkets. You can't even compare them."

I told him about the growers in California who claim that selling cheap, short-lived flowers in supermarkets could actually turn customers away from flowers by convincing them that they aren't even worth the low price they paid for them. "They are right," he said, "because the quality is poor. I've been to a lot of supermarkets in the U.S., and the flowers look terrible. They put everything together—the cheese, the fruit, the flowers—all that ethylene, it's awful. And it's bad for us and bad for the consumer. The consumer every year gets a lower-quality flower, and we are forced to sell it for an even cheaper price." (The average wholesale price of rose imports to the United States have actually declined from twenty to thirty cents a stem, depending on the type of rose, ten years ago, to just sixteen to nineteen cents a stem today.)

I offered up the comparison that some in the industry have made between flowers and wine. "There's this idea," I said, "that it's okay for a big discount club to sell a three-dollar bottle of wine. Maybe you'll get people who don't normally drink wine to start buying it more often, and then they'll move up to a five-dollar bottle, and an eight-dollar bottle, and pretty soon you've created a new group of more sophisticated wine drinkers."

"Yes," Carlos said, "but that three-dollar bottle of wine has to taste okay, or they'll go back to beer or Coca-Cola. Look at tulips. In the tulip season, if everybody wants to buy the cheapest, that means that the nicest tulips stay here. All the tulips that you see in American supermarket chains are actually the tulips that nobody in Europe wants. Tiny heads, very closed, and they mix up white, yellow, cream. Awful. You could buy thousands of tulips in season that look so much better, but you have to pay five, eight cents more."

Carlos may be dismayed by the proliferation of cheap, mass-market flowers, but he's still in awe of the business. "Even in countries where people are poor, and the economy is bad, people still buy flowers. They only have a little money to spend, but they will give someone flowers. You look at Russia — you have rich, you have poor, and nothing in between. I know people there who are so rich they change the flowers in their house every day. And on the same street, you see somebody buy just one carnation.

"Sometimes I track where an individual box of flowers goes after it leaves here," he said, leaning back in his chair and looking at a single Asiatic lily in a vase on his desk as he spoke. "Imagine — I pack a box here, and it arrives in Boston, my customer picks it up, it goes to his flower shop, he puts it in water, and then people are coming in and choosing that one particular flower because they like it. It's funny, isn't it? Suddenly, the whole world is so close to each other."

Before I left Aalsmeer, there was one more stop that I had been both anticipating and dreading. I was going to see Multi Color Flowers, a company that buys flowers at the auction, dyes them, and sells them to exporters. Its facility was just across the street from the auction, in a long row of warehouses that held a number of bouquet makers, processors, and packagers. "For the bouquet makers," Carlos had told me, "Holland is their kitchen. This is where all the ingredients are. The cook comes here to decide what he puts in his recipe. You make a bouquet of focals and fillers, and here you can buy twenty or thirty different fillers from around the world, and that changes the bouquet." In this case Multi Color Flowers was buying flowers at the auction and doing what Mother Nature could not — turning chrysanthemums emerald green, covering oak leaves with red paint or gold glitter, and creating orange or purple gypsophila, just in case someone decides he needs such a thing.

I'd come this far without once feeling as though there was any real cheating going on. Sure, cut flowers have been bred, both in the greenhouse and in the test tube, to be larger, showier, and more productive, and yes, growers could make a flower bloom in December and survive an unnaturally long time out of water, and none of that struck me as outright chicanery. But to paint a flower—to actually gild a lily—seemed both unnecessary and unwholesome. Why bother? Isn't there enough variety at this enormous marketplace? And besides, who would want an artificially dyed flower?

But dyes have been around for decades. Stem-dyed carnations were a novelty in the 1920s, when a Chicago grower hit upon the idea of marketing a carnation in a glass tube filled with green dye. The idea was to let the customer watch the flower absorb the dye rather than sell it as a finished product after the dye was absorbed; it was attached to a little cardboard easel that read, "Day by day, in every way, I grow greener and greener." Florists in those days also used an airbrush to apply dye, but the pigments rubbed off easily and women risked getting stains on their clothes when they wore corsages of dyed flowers.

The 1950s saw the introduction of a wide range of dips and dyes that allowed florists to create any color they wanted. Some of them also included a preservative that would make the flower last longer. The early sprays were so powerful that they could melt Styrofoam, which was often used to make floral sculptures. (It's a wonder the flowers survived it, but apparently they could withstand the paint, and the foam could not.) Once the dye companies turned out a spray that would leave the foam intact, florists were finally able to sell purple Easter bunnies made of carnations, football-shaped

mums in school colors for homecoming, and baby flowers dyed
pink or blue and fashioned into the shape of a bassinet. In the
sixties, the trend moved, predictably, toward metallic paints and
glitter.

Painted flowers may have fallen out of vogue since then, but
they never went away completely. I knew that if there was anything innovative to be done with flower dyes, it would be happening at Aalsmeer. That's why, as the morning came to an end and
the trucks filled with flowers roared away from the loading docks,
I made my way across the vast auction complex to Multi Color's
front door.

Peter Knelange, the company's founder and manager, met me
at his office and walked me through the facility, where his staff of
thirty employees was dyeing all the flowers they'd bought at auction that morning. He was tall, lanky, and possessed a boyish fas-
cination for this place. Once I saw it, I couldn't blame him — there
was something magical and childlike about a factory where pale
white, pink, and yellow flowers come to get their colors. Like most
Dutch operations, it was highly automated and surprisingly clean
considering how much paint gets splattered around.

Multi Color Flowers employs several methods of dyeing flowers. The first, stem dyeing, is familiar to any kid who ever turned
a carnation green in a life science class. You add food coloring
to the water, and the water-conducting vessels known as xylem,
which are essentially hollow, dead cells that act like straws, carry
the color to the very tips of the petals. (Xylem also carries water
through the veins in leaves, which is why the leaves of a stem-dyed
plant may remain green overall, while the veins turn a somewhat
darker and duller version of the dye that's in the water.) In Multi
Color's factory, empty plastic buckets moved along a conveyor belt
and disappeared into a tangle of machinery, where they would be
filled with green or orange or purple dye. When they came out

the other end, a couple of guys stood waiting to fill them with pale pompom chrysanthemums. By tomorrow morning, the stems would have absorbed the dye and the petals would be pumped full of outrageous, psychedelic colors. The flowers would go off to their buyer, the buckets would get emptied into a system that separates the water from the paint, and the paint would go back to the assembly line to be reused.

I expected to see mums and carnations subjected to this process, but I was not prepared to see what he could do with roses. "Have you seen a blue rose?" Peter asked, leading me into a cooler.

"I thought there was no such thing," I said, and he laughed, a sort of Willy Wonka–style cackle.

"Of course there is," he said. "Look."

There, in a bucket, was John Mason's holy grail: a rose the color of blueberries. Actually, it's hard to compare this blue to any color you'd find in nature. It was more of a Las Vegas blue, a sequin-and-glitter blue. A blue you'd find in nail polish or gumballs, but not in a garden. Peter had hundreds of these blue roses, wrapped in bunches of twenty, each one tucked into a sleeve with the Multi Color logo, all bound for—where? Japan was a big market. I'd seen them in flower stalls around Union Square in San Francisco. They were a novelty, a gag, a flower to sell to tourists or teenagers. Some were sprayed with silver glitter. I could see those at a Dallas Cowboys game, or on a float in a Mardi Gras parade, but it was hard to imagine a florist taking them seriously. There was no hiding the fact that they were fake. I stood in front of them, silent and puzzled, but Peter seemed not to notice.

"We can glitter anything," he said, moving cheerfully past the roses. "See? We spray over there." He pointed to a corner of the room that was entirely covered in glitter. In fact, the more I looked around, the more I realized that there were traces of glitter everywhere in the factory—on the floors, on the walls, on all the racks and buckets. "Oh yes," Peter said when I pointed it out. "It is all over, especially when we are getting ready for the holidays. I find it in my bed."

A flower that resists stem dyeing can be dipped in paint. The dipping operations are confined to one section of the warehouse, where there has been no attempt to keep the paint contained. It would be impossible. Instead, each enormous trough is entirely drenched in its designated color—pink, purple, green, red, yellow—and the person working at that trough is similarly soaked in its particular hue. A flower has to be pretty sturdy to be able to handle a dip into this paint, but they've found a number of varieties that work: in addition to the gypsophila, they'll dip brassicas (ornamental cabbages); another filler called solidago, more commonly known as goldenrod; and ferns, eucalyptus, and oak leaves. Once they're painted, they're hung on a rack and moved along another conveyor past a row of fans, where they dry almost instantly and emerge looking . . . well, surprisingly healthy, considering what they have just been through.

About fifty million flowers move through Multi Color's facility every year, and many of those are bargain flowers, whatever they can buy cheaply on the auction clock. On the day I visited, there were mostly pink chrysanthemums lined up to be stem dyed; Peter explained that today he was able to buy the pink ones for fifteen euro cents a stem instead of the twenty euro cents he would have paid for the white flowers. The pink petals respond just as well to purple dye as the white ones do, so today there would simply be more purple flowers for sale. Next time they could get a good price on white, they'd go back to turning out green, yellow, and dark blue shades. If they could get a bargain on yellow chrysanthemums, that would be a good day to make orange, red, and chartreuse flowers.

You might think that you could spot a dyed flower in a shop, and sometimes it's easy: I've pulled a bunch of purple poms from a bucket in a supermarket and watched the bluish water drip off the stems. Other times, it's not so obvious. I was surprised to see that Multi Color took white roses and made them into orange, pink, and green roses—colors that were already available from growers, although perhaps for a much higher price than the white ones. It would be hard, at first glance, to know that you were buying a dyed rose, except that the color can get strangely dark at the tips of the petals, and the veins running through the leaves might turn an odd, greenish orange or purple.

Multi Color may have developed a more sophisticated way of dyeing flowers, but these kinds of tricks are in use all over the world. Once when I was hanging around a flower shop, I asked about the cans of spray paint behind the counter. The florist smiled, pulled down a can, gave it a hard shake, and blasted some green paint into the center of a white carnation. The painted flower didn't look entirely natural, but it also didn't look like it had just been spray painted. If you had told me that the flower been bred to look like that, I probably would have believed you. "We really don't use these much anymore," he said, "but it can be a cool look."

You can do just about anything to a flower. In addition to spray paints and glitters, there are companies that manufacture spray perfumes to substitute for the missing scent in a rose. You can buy artificial petals and bright pearl-shaped beads to stick into flowers and dress them up, and you can even wire a weak-stemmed flower to a stronger, fake stem. Now there's a company in Utah called Speaking Roses that has created a new technique for embossing roses. They'll print gold-leaf messages on an outer petal of a red rose. The company suggests business messages like THANKS FOR PERFECT ATTENDANCE, WORLD'S BEST BOSS, and WE APPRECIATE YOUR BUSINESS. They'll also print I'M SORRY or, depending on the extent of the damage, I'M VERY SORRY on a rose, and of course you can get roses printed up that say, WILL YOU MARRY ME? and even feature a small black and white head shot of you and your beloved. There's an astonishing amount of artificial assistance available to a flower, and it's a trend that doesn't seem to be going away.

"I started in 1988," Peter said, "with just one room and two colors, pink and blue. I would buy the flowers at the auction and bring them back here and dye them myself. There were a lot of people doing it back then, but everyone said this would only be popular for a few years. I said no, it is here to stay. We are still growing. Next, maybe we'll go to Miami. What do you think?"

Miami. From Aalsmeer, it seemed so remote, so small. What's three or four billion flowers to the Dutch? And how do you get your hands on them, when the flowers arrive from over a thousand farms, disappear into the warehouses of a couple hundred importers or bouquet makers, and then move through hundreds of wholesalers and on to tens of thousands of retailers? If the idea of a centralized flower auction struck me as strange when I arrived, it now seemed, from the perspective of the buyer, eminently reasonable, another one of those sensible and efficient Dutch inventions. Just finding the flower you want in Miami seemed like an impossible task compared with the ease of bidding on the clock at Aalsmeer.

Still, there's probably a place for a flower-painting factory in Miami. I thought about South Beach, where I eventually did find the pink hotels and neon signs I'd been looking for. A blue rose would sell there. If it was covered in glitter, all the better. I thought, with a little sorrow, about the vast, untapped American market for flowers embossed with corporate logos, painted with school colors, even dyed, like shoes, to match a prom dress. You could call it a novelty, but I suspected that Peter was right—painted flowers were here to stay.

"I think you'll be a big hit in Miami," I told him, and took one last look around the factory. I knew I'd see these flowers again, somewhere. I said good-bye to Peter and made my way across the empty parking lot to catch a bus back to Amsterdam. Sticking out of my bag was a tightly wrapped bunch of pale peach and cream roses, straight off the auction floor, that Natascha had given me that morning. I'd had them out of water all afternoon and it hadn't once occurred to me to worry about them. Of course they'd survive. I would leave them at the hotel and they'd still be in bloom when my plane landed in California.

The bus arrived at the stop just as I did. It was late afternoon, and only a few men and women who worked for the auction were in line to board. I dropped into a seat and laid the flowers across my lap. I sat looking down at them while the bus made its way back to the city. Thousands of roses just like these left the auction today and headed for Japan, Russia, Germany, and England, where they would finally reach the end of a long journey. They were all about to go home with somebody. It was time for me to go home, too.

CHAPTER 9

Florists, Supermarkets,
and the Next Big Thing

Teresa Sabankaya has the kind of flower shop that you would dream about opening, if you are the kind of person who dreams of opening a flower shop. It's in a little green metal kiosk outside Bookshop Santa Cruz in coastal California. The flowers—all interesting, unusual, old-fashioned, ephemeral, perfumy, not-your-typical-florist kind of flowers—dance and wave from buckets crowded around the stall. Her inventory is highly seasonal: in summer you'll find larkspur and poppies, and in winter it's all heathers and holly and berries. If you've been so busy that you haven't noticed that spring has arrived, you'll stop short at the sight of the pink cherry blossom branches bursting out of her shop in early March, and it'll make you resolve to slow down and enjoy the season. Even if you don't buy a flower—and Teresa would be happy to sell you a single flower—just the sight of her little stall will lift some of the weight off your shoulders. Anyone who doubts whether flowers can change a person's emotional state has never watched the people walking by Teresa's shop.

I once lived a few blocks from this store, which is called the Bonny Doon Garden Company, and I used to paw through the flowers on Saturday morning after I'd picked up my coffee and newspaper from the bookstore. There would be odd seed pods from her garden; fragile sweet peas from a grower in Watsonville; and, for just a few short glorious weeks in May, purple and pink and white lilacs. You also could buy a potted geranium or a trio of narcissus bulbs growing in a glass bowl. On Mother's Day she'd make up old-fashioned posies with flowers that spelled out messages in the Victorian language of flowers: Canterbury bells for gratitude, geranium leaf for comfort, rue for grace.

At the time, I didn't realize how unusual a store like this was. I hadn't yet heard of a flower farm as big as Sun Valley or as remote as Nevado in Ecuador. I couldn't imagine a flower auction like Aalsmeer or a cargo jet full of flowers on the runway in Miami. The Bonny Doon Garden Company fit with my idea of how floral commerce must work—you'd grow some flowers in your garden, you'd buy some from a farmer down the road, and you'd put them in buckets and sell them to your neighbors. Maybe that's why, even now that I've moved away, I keep going back to her shop. After all this time, it still makes sense to me.

I sat on a stool outside Teresa's kiosk one chilly morning between Christmas and New Year, and in between customers we talked about the shop. She has a broad, friendly smile, a soft Texas accent, and dark brown curls that poke out from under her hat. She looks like the sort of person who would answer to "the flower lady," and she often does. "My whole thing with flowers started in the garden," she said, leaning in the doorway of her kiosk, which was just big enough for one person and a compact assortment of tools and vases. "I love to see plants going from seed to seed, you know? We have eleven acres in Bonny Doon up the coast, and I just started putting in one garden after another. A couple hundred English roses, more gorgeous flowers than I knew what to do with. I did a wedding for a friend, and then it just took off. Pretty soon I had a chance to buy this place. The idea behind the shop was to be able to utilize some of the flowers coming off my property. Now

I'm so focused on the shop that sometimes I get home and think, 'What happened to the garden?'"

Although her customers know her best for her kiosk on Pacific Avenue, she also has a cooler and a little extra work space a few blocks away. In fact, only 30 percent of her sales come from street sales, meaning people who walk up and buy on impulse. "When I bought the shop, I quickly learned that street sales wouldn't sustain us, so we expanded to weddings, corporate accounts, and restaurants," she said. "And we do deliveries. We're a full-service florist, even though we don't look like it. I'm always telling people, 'Yeah, the little green shop on the sidewalk can do all that.'"

Her business is a little larger than it appears — she can have up to nine employees depending on the season — but because of her approach to flowers, her shop has more in common with a nineteenth-century florist than it does with the other flower shops around town. She grows some of her own flowers, just like florists did a century ago. She buys from other gardeners — women who might not be too different from the fictional Maria Gilman in *My Ten-Rod Farm*. "There's a lady who comes by here," Teresa said, "and she's just some lady, you know? She'll pull up in front of the shop and say, 'Look!' and she'll have a car full of beautiful flowers. So I buy whatever she's got. And you know, I'm always looking for something new that I could use. I'll look through a patch of weeds and think, 'That's really cool. I wonder if that will last in a vase?' If I had my way, I'd just be planting constantly. The whole reason I bought this place was to bring new things from the natural world and just put them right here in front of people."

THE FLOWER SHOP has been an oasis of beauty in a crowded city since the nineteenth century. Before that, growers sold their flowers directly to the public from their nurseries, or they could be purchased from street vendors who either set up a temporary stall or went door to door. Jacques-Laurent Agasse's 1822 painting *The Flower Seller* depicts a man in a hat and topcoat offering a potted plant for sale to two children. Behind him is a wooden cart drawn by a donkey; on the cart you can see a calla lily and a rhododendron, and other flowers and greenery. In 1840 Jules Lachaume opened his famous flower shop in Paris; it still operates today at 10, rue Royale as Paris's most exclusive florist. He is widely believed to be the first florist in the modern sense of the word, and he published the first modern book on flower arranging, *Les Fleurs Naturelles,* in 1847. The evidence of florists' designs and ideas dates back even farther — scrolls depicting ikebana, the Japanese art of flower arranging, survive from the fifteenth century, and there is even an ancient depiction of an Egyptian florist's work from an Eighteenth Dynasty (1530–1307 BC) tomb painting at Thebes. But the florist's shop, as we understand it today — that place where city dwellers seek not just violets for the opera and roses for their sweethearts but also a moment of beauty and serenity, a place where time stands deliciously, fragrantly still while the rest of the city rushes by, is a nineteenth- and twentieth-century innovation.

As early as 1864, a *New York Times* article reported on the Christmas window displays in the city's shops and observed that until recently the selling of flowers was "confined to one or two peripatetic vendors of cheap trash," while now the florists on Broadway are "filled with a profusion of costly exotics." Another *Times* story from the same period declared, "Flowers serve a more needful purpose in the economy of nature than we are prone to imagine; and they produce more effect on the dullest minds than many even of the most susceptible minds would acknowledge." Anyone who has ever ducked into a Manhattan florist, stepped carefully between the buckets of tulips and gladioli, and breathed a sigh of relief as the door closed on the roar of traffic outside, knows what effect a florist can have on the denizens of its city.

A speech given at the Society of American Florists (SAF) convention in 1896 took the florist's duty to provide beauty even more seriously: "The occupation that we follow is in itself one of the most beautiful, the most interesting and ennobling that the development of man's higher nature has brought into existence. It has always seemed to me that the intimate contact with nature and her various complicated processes, that our calling makes necessary, should tend to make up better men in every way."

That the mere sight of a flower shop, much less the presence of flowers on the nightstand or the hall table, has the ability to lift one's spirits is nothing new. We've all experienced it. But when I think about the role of a flower shop in the life of a city, I remember the Eden Alternative, a nursing home project that began in 1991 when the director of a nursing home decided that the dreary, sterile environment was hurting the residents' health. He set about filling the place with flowers and plants; he arranged visits from children; and he encouraged pet birds, cats, dogs, and rabbits. Nobody expected such a drastic outcome: prescription drug bills and the presence of infections dropped by half, and mortality dropped by 25 percent. Flowers weren't alone in bringing about that change, but the approach—injecting life into a drab environment—is exactly what a flower shop does for a city.

So far, putting flowers in front of people has had precisely the effect Teresa, and generations of florists before her, had been hoping for. "I love it when people are just rushing down the street, talking on the phone," she said, "and I see them stop in their tracks, right here, and just say, 'Oh, that's so beautiful.' In our hurried lives, we just miss so much. At least I make someone stop for a minute."

LIKE MANY FLORISTS, Teresa deals, first and foremost, in the business of romance. Florists have always watched romances unfold in their shops; one nineteenth-century florist told a newspaper reporter, "Flowers go ahead of all other gifts in winning a woman's heart, and every young gallant knows that." He went on to tell the story of a young woman who used to stop in his shop to admire the flowers. A man who had noticed her from a distance asked the florist to send her a bouquet every day. The florist agreed, and after a week of floral tributes she still had no idea who had sent the flowers. One morning she was in the shop when he walked in and placed his order, asking for the flowers to be sent as usual to her address. When she heard the address, she turned around and they saw each other for the first time. "Well I never saw such an embarrassed couple in all my days," the florist said. "She had a big Jacqueminot near her face, and it would have been hard to tell which was redder, the rose or her cheek."

Although two-thirds of flower sales are made to women, flowers have never gone out of style in a courtship. Savvy florists try to make their shops accessible to men; walking into a cluttered flower shop filled with lace and figurines could be nerve-wracking for a guy. But a kiosk on the street, like Teresa's, has plenty of exit routes. "That could be what makes the difference," she said of the unusually high percentage of male customers who frequent her shop. "I had one guy come down here who wanted to buy a bouquet for his girlfriend. He wasn't really sure what she wanted, but we put something together and he was back two weeks later to get her more flowers. Now he's sort of come out of his shell and he buys flowers for himself. I think I've got more men who are saying, 'Wow. I really like what that looks like in my house, and I like how it makes me feel.' I sign them up for my frequent flower program, and pretty soon I see them all the time." She also learned the hard way to keep the shop open until eight o'clock on weekends: one night she closed early and found out the next day that a customer had stopped by before his first date with a woman and been disappointed that "his" flower shop was closed.

Still, she faces the same competition that any other florist does. There are a dozen other places to buy flowers within a mile of her shop, including several grocery stores. But none of them are quite like hers. None of them sell bleeding hearts in spring or the pale green pods of a vine called love-in-a-puff in summer. Most probably don't carry organic flowers, either. She's a specialty florist, and she makes a real effort to point that out to her customers. "People will sometimes ask me why I would bother selling organic flowers since we don't eat them," she said. "Or they'll wonder why I might charge $3.50 per stem for a particular rose when there are roses for sale down the street for a dollar a stem. You know what I tell them? A lot went into that rose. A lot of people worked to grow it. And I'm not buying roses from Ecuador—I'm buying them here in Santa Cruz County. There's a cost to that."

GETTING THAT MESSAGE across is a challenge to specialty florists all over the world. Moyes Stevens, a florist based in London's New Covent Garden Flower Market, was established in 1876 but continues to reinvent itself in the twenty-first century. John Kennedy, the company's managing director, came from the organic chocolate company Green & Black's. "I had worked quite closely with farmers from the chocolate business, so I was interested in getting involved with flowers," he said. "The really great stories about flower farms just weren't being told to customers. And you only get that by working directly with the growers, and knowing where your flowers come from."

Moyes Stevens was known as London's premier florist in the first half of the twentieth century, employing up to two hundred florists and providing the flowers for royal weddings. Today the company employs fifty florists at six shops around London, and a third of the business now consists of floral orders placed through the website and shipped around the country. About 2.5 million stems pass through its shops every year. Kennedy's job is to work on the sourcing of flowers and to help tell the story of their provenance.

"In a shop, it's a theater," he said. "You're showing your craft, your creativity. For us, it's about how people feel after the fifteen or twenty minutes they've been with you, as well as the flowers they take home with them." Kennedy's idea is that people want to leave the flower shop with a story of their own—and that story has to do with how they were treated in the shop, but also what they learned about the farm where their flowers were grown.

Almost all of Moyes Stevens's roses come from a Fairtrade farm in Ecuador, with seasonal English roses rounding out the selection. Overall, about 40 percent of the blossoms they offer are grown in Britain. "We send people home with a card that tells them about the farm where their roses came from," he said. "And when sweet peas are in season locally—fantastic! Let's talk about sweet peas. We have a culture of flower growing and gardening in this country. I want to celebrate that."

Kennedy is trying to find a way to make sure that flowers are still culturally relevant, an interesting challenge for a business that is over one hundred and thirty years old. When Moyes Stevens was founded, its flowers would have come almost entirely from English growers. Now its best hope for reinventing itself is to once again remind people of Britain's flower-growing heritage by buying locally grown flowers and talking about those farms. "Especially because we're located in a city," he said, "people are responding very well to seasonal flowers. Anytime we can connect people to the seasons, we want to do that."

FLORISTS TODAY ARE at a crossroads. They live and breathe according to the changes in society. Is your HMO keeping you in the hospital for only a day or two? Most people don't even have time to send you flowers before you're back at work. Are you getting married in a vineyard? There's no somber church that needs to be softened with bouquets and garlands. Having a dinner party? The notion of a florist delivering your centerpiece in the afternoon sounds outdated and expensive compared with picking up some flowers at the supermarket while you're doing your shopping.

If you look very long at survey and census data for this industry, you might think that small flower shops like Teresa's are in trouble. From 1993 to 2003, florists saw their market share drop from 34 percent to 22 percent during a time when the overall amount spent on cut flowers actually increased. Over the same period, supermarkets, wholesale clubs, and home improvement stores improved their market share, essentially gobbling up what the florists lost. People may spend more money on cut flowers when they buy them from a florist — the average purchase at a florist is thirty-seven dollars — but they buy a larger volume of flowers, at a lower price, from grocery stores and other outlets. These differences are particularly striking when you compare the purchases of arrangements, which usually come from a florist, to the purchases of bunches and bouquets, which are more often bought from supermarkets and other outlets. Almost half of consumer cut flower dollars are spent on arrangements, but those arrangements make up only a fifth of American flower purchases. On the other hand, bouquets and bunches represent half of all flower purchases, but they make up less than a third of the money spent on flowers. (The rest of the purchases are single stems of flowers and other floral products — wreaths, corsages, and so forth.)

So people will pay more for an arrangement, that artful combination of flowers and greens, foam and wire, ribbons and bows,

but they don't buy those as often as they buy a simple bunch of
flowers that they can take home from the market and stick in a
vase. At first, it seems like the reason for this might be that people
buy arrangements as gifts and bunches for themselves, but even
that doesn't tell the whole story. Survey data shows that about
two-thirds of flower purchases are gifts and one-third are what
florists call self-purchases. But arrangements make up only half of
all purchases. That suggests that at least some of the time, people
are also buying bunches and bouquets to give as gifts. For instance, you might send a florist's arrangement to your mother for
Mother's Day, but you'll take a bunch of grocery store roses when
you visit a friend in the hospital or go to someone's house for dinner. So mass-market outlets like supermarkets and discount clubs
are eating up not just impulse purchases and self-purchases but
gift purchases as well.

The gap between what consumers want and what florists deliver may be growing: a study by FTD showed that 23 percent of
customers want "monobotanical" bouquets, meaning bunches of
a single flower type like roses or lilies, but only 1 percent of florists
thought customers wanted them. Twenty-six percent of customers had ordered flowers through a "boxed program," meaning a
retailer (usually an Internet retailer like Organic Bouquet) that
ships flowers in a box to the customer. Florists guessed that only 2
percent had done so. (Customers also rated their experience with
these purchases much higher than florists thought they would.)
The average customer thought that thirty-five dollars was the appropriate amount to pay for a bouquet; florists guessed forty-five
dollars.

Florists are struggling to figure out what to do about these
changes. The florists I interviewed all told me that they wished
Americans bought more flowers for themselves, like Europeans
do, as if this would help their business. Buying habits vary by

country, but in general about half of the flowers sold in Europe are self-purchases, and even the gift purchases tend to be for more informal events like birthdays and hostess gifts. European buying habits are less oriented around "calendar holidays" like Valentine's Day and Mother's Day. Ironically, European florists would like their customers to buy more flowers on holidays. They may have it right: holiday orders, which often involve deliveries and more complicated arrangements, are more likely to be placed through florists, while the increase in self-purchases that American florists wish for would mostly benefit supermarkets.

How does a florist keep going in this environment? Some don't. Since 1997, almost thirty-five hundred flower shops have closed, and the number of retail florists with no payroll has increased by about thirteen hundred, suggesting that while some shops have gone out of business, others have downsized. The Society of American Florists sees a 25 percent annual turnover in its membership, owing in part to the long hours and slim margins that idealistic wannabe florists may not have considered before they bought a flower shop. And competition is fierce: there are now more mass-market outlets—supermarkets, drug stores, discount clubs, and home improvement centers—selling flowers than there are flower shops.

Florists are trying every strategy they can think of to stay afloat. Some are stocking more gifts and candy, some are experimenting with staying open longer and offering more discount-style growers' bunches, and others are picking up corporate accounts and restaurants. Segments of the flower market that have traditionally belonged to florists are also on the decline: although the average amount spent on wedding flowers is a healthy twenty-two hundred dollars, many florists I spoke to complained that as couples are getting married later and paying for their own weddings, they're spending less on flowers. (On the other hand, one florist praised Martha Stewart for being able to sell wedding flowers that he never would have even tried to sell himself. He told the story of a woman who brought in a photograph from *Martha Stewart Weddings* in which a church aisle had been lined with white roses, lilies, and lisianthus. "It was beautiful," he said, "but it was so expensive that when we wrote up our proposal, we priced it by the yard so we wouldn't give the bride a heart attack." After seeing the bid, her grandmother came into the store, demanding to know why the flowers were so expensive. The florist showed her the photograph, and she said, "Uh-oh. I made a terrible mistake. I offered to pay for the wedding flowers." In the end, the grandmother decided to foot the bill after all. "It was beautiful," the florist said. "We never could have sold that to anyone, but Martha did it for us. That poor grandmother.")

Funeral and hospital deliveries, or what florists call the sympathy business, have also taken a hit. The Society of American Florists reports that sympathy business used to make up about half of florists' sales, and today it represents only 22 percent. Articles in trade magazines as far back as 1902 assert that funerals are the "backbone of the business" and that without it "most of us would have to get out of the business." Because flowers are so intimately connected with these major life rituals — weddings, funerals, births — as the rituals change, so does the flower trade. "It used to be that no matter what happened to the economy, the floral industry still did pretty well," Peter Moran told me. "Why? Because people still die and people still get sick." But that's changed. Shorter hospital stays mean that you may be discharged before your friends even find out that you've been in the hospital. More procedures are performed on an outpatient basis. And as for funerals, they may not take place in a church, they may not include a viewing, and they may consist of nothing more than a group of friends gathering to scatter ashes.

The floral industry does try to respond to these changes. As nurses took on more professional duties in the twentieth century, hospitals complained that their staff had no time to take care of flowers and plants. In response, florists started selling small arrangements in inexpensive vases, instead of delivering a loose arrangement in a box as they might have in the past. FTD even footed the bill for nursing scholarships after World War II to address nursing shortages. Trade publications offered ideas for novelty arrangements that included candy, small wrapped gifts, and (for men) the use of beer steins, brandy snifters, and cigarettes and ashtrays as design elements. But even today hospitals and florists find themselves working at cross-purposes: in the summer of 2005 United Hospital in St. Paul, Minnesota, announced it would start charging five dollars to accept a delivery from a florist and take it to the patient's room. There was an outcry from florists and patients, and other hospitals in the area expressed surprise, saying that delivering flowers to the patients was their most coveted volunteer job. Eventually, the hospital dropped the policy, and the florists in the area agreed to coordinate delivery times, minimize extra wrapping that the staff didn't want to deal with, and help recruit volunteers for the hospital.

Hanging on to funeral work has been even trickier. Florists used to construct elaborate blankets of flowers to cover a casket and build wreaths, crosses, horseshoes, and hearts out of white blooms and greenery. These were incredibly labor-intensive arrangements that fetched high prices: in 1913 one of these fancy "set pieces" could cost anywhere from twenty-five dollars for an open Bible made of flowers to a hundred dollars for a flower-festooned empty chair, which symbolized the loss an of authority figure. Now people send simpler arrangements if they send anything at all. The four most dreaded words to a florist are "in lieu of flowers," and those words appear on the obituary pages across the country every day.

This is not a new problem: the phrase began appearing in the early 1900s, and by 1959, 14.5 percent of obituaries used it, often in conjunction with a request that funds be sent instead to a charity. The Society of American Florists and FTD joined forces in 1951 to campaign against this notion that one should not send flowers to a funeral and started running television commercials and talking to funeral directors about the importance of sympathy flowers. Even today, they advise florists to coach local obituary writers and funeral homes about alternative phrases that don't discourage flowers, such as "Memorial contributions may be made to . . ." or "Flowers are welcome; contributions may be sent to . . ." Florists and funeral homes have to work together to make sure the flowers show up on time, go to the right place, keep their tags attached so the family will know who they came from, and so on. It can be a complicated endeavor, and emotions run high, but florists try to stay in the game, even as some funeral homes have opened their own floral concessions right in the building. Fighting to keep a piece of funeral business may sound self-serving, but as Peter Moran pointed out, "If you go to a funeral and there's no flowers, it's a pretty cold event."

Florists are also struggling to keep their share of the gift market. A 2005 study by SAF showed that 92 percent of women surveyed remembered the last time they got flowers as a gift, and 97 percent of all respondents remember the last time they gave flowers as a gift. Peter Moran said that the organization conducted another survey in which they asked people whether flowers were appropriate gifts for various situations — Valentine's Day, Mother's Day, housewarming, and so on. "We were surprised that almost across the board people thought flowers were an appropriate way to recognize whatever the occasion or situation was," Peter said. "But you ask people whether they actually buy flowers in that instance, and the results fall way off. They say they just didn't think of it. So we're undermarketed compared to other products." Other surveys have shown that people don't buy flowers because they don't last long or they cost too much, a perception that florists also see as a marketing problem. Any florist can rattle off a list of common gifts that cost the same or more than a floral arrangement but don't last a week like flowers do: concert tickets, a bottle of Champagne, fine chocolates, dinner out, even a trip to a spa.

So SAF focuses its marketing efforts on two fronts: fighting negative portrayals of flowers in advertising and persuading the public that there are actual benefits to being around flowers. It turns out that there are a surprising number of advertisements for other products that put flowers down; once you start looking for them, you'll see them everywhere. In 2004 Best Buy ran a print ad that read, "Forget the flowers. We've got gifts that are sure to turn up the heat this Valentine's Day," referring to stereos and digital cameras. Hershey's ran a commercial in 2005 asking, "Who wants roses? Roses say I'm sorry." And to the great consternation of the society, the Vermont Teddy Bear Company persists in using the slogan "Send the Creative Alternative to Flowers!"

The Society of American Florists has developed a polite but firm response to these ads that suggests that the company could promote its product on its own merits without disparaging another product to make it look good. Usually the response is swift and contrite—the company apologizes, agrees that it shouldn't have to put down flowers to sell its own chocolates or electronic gadgets, and swears it won't do it again. Sometimes these attempts backfire, however. The society reports that one year Al Roker of NBC's *Today Show* suggested that viewers make their flowers out of paper instead of "blowing the bank" on real flowers. He got one of SAF's congenial letters, to which he replied, "While I understand your concerns, as I walked around Manhattan yesterday, I didn't see one florist shop being boarded up or any florists on the street corners with signs that said, 'Will Make Arrangements for Food.' SAF needs to lighten up."

In addition to making sure other companies aren't putting down flowers as a gift, SAF and other industry groups devote considerable resources to promoting the benefits of flowers and plants. A study funded by SAF and conducted by Texas A&M University tracked participants as they completed various tasks that were similar to the kind of thing you might do in an office. Some did their work in the presence of flowers and plants, some with a sculpture nearby, and some with no decoration at all around. The study showed that people were more productive, better able to solve problems, and came up with more creative ideas if they were around plants and flowers. The society uses the data every year in its promotional efforts for the holiday formerly known as National Secretaries Day, now called Administrative Professionals Day.

Florists also like to cite a Rutgers study that was published in the journal *Evolutionary Psychology* in April 2005, which observed a group of women who were given one of three gifts: a mixed bouquet of roses, lilies, and stock (chosen after consultation with SAF), a fruit basket, or a pillar candle. The idea was that the researchers would observe the women as they were given these gifts and measure their responses. In particular, they were looking for the Duchenne smile, a particular kind of facial expression that is difficult to fake and indicates genuine happiness. All of the women who got flowers flashed the Duchenne smile, as did 90 percent of the women who got a fruit basket and 77 percent of the women who got the candle. (When I heard about this study, I couldn't help but wonder if they'd stacked the deck in favor of flowers. A fruit basket? A candle? I'm amazed that any of the women responded to them at all. But the more meaningful gifts they might have offered instead were all problematic. Chocolate was too controversial — some women might be on a diet — and jewelry was too expensive.)

The women who received flowers were not only happier to get them, they were still happier than the other women a couple of days later. The conclusion one might draw from this—that flowers make people happier than fruit baskets and candles do—caused enough excitement at SAF that the society launched a new "Flower Therapy" campaign, which suggested sending a "nurturing" bouquet of creams, peaches, and yellows to make the recipient "feel safe, snug, and loved" or a "tranquil" arrangement of pale greens and misty blues to offer "a moment of calm from life's stressful situations."

I can appreciate what industry groups are trying to do—they are trying to quantify why people buy flowers and then sell flowers on that basis. But it's difficult to do that and not have the whole campaign seem like it's trying too hard. Another example is a recent billboard campaign that showed three different sizes of bouquets with the caption EXACTLY HOW MAD IS SHE? Most of the florists I met just shook their heads in bewilderment at the campaign. "Women hate it," one florist said, "because if they're mad, they probably have a legitimate reason for being mad, one that flowers alone can't fix. Plus, I don't want guys to think of my shop as the place they have to go when they're in the doghouse. What good does that do anybody?"

A FLORIST LIKE Teresa Sabankaya seems to float above these issues, or perhaps it's more accurate to say that she ducks around them, by working a small, friendly niche. She's got a group of customers who are willing to pay for the flowers she's willing to offer. Her annual sales are well below the industry average of $290,000 per year, but she's probably more content running a small shop anyway. She doesn't build her inventory around workhorses like lilies, carnations, and mums the way a typical florist would, and although she is a member of SAF, she probably gets more sales from a *Martha Stewart Living* photograph of forget-me-nots in an egg cup than she would from a society billboard.

More significantly, she's not part of any of the major wire services like FTD or Teleflora. When you order flowers through a local florist to be delivered in another city or state, they are usually handled as wire transactions through one of these services, and you're given a choice of standard arrangements designed by the wire service. Teresa told me, "I don't like to be restricted to their design standards . . . Not everybody out there wants an FTD-style arrangement, and not every florist wants to be directed by them in their design department." That's a nice way of putting it. Some of the florists I interviewed were less diplomatic, complaining that the wire services' ho-hum arrangements of roses, ferns, and baby's breath do more to harm the industry than "in lieu of flowers," cheap supermarket bouquets, and pesticide-laden imports combined. (Even this complaint is nothing new; a late-nineteenth-century florist complained about "the old time stiffness in floral work displayed today," and a 1923 book on flower design railed against the "stiffness, pomposity, and not a little insincerity" of Victorian-era flowers.)

In the context of design, Martha Stewart's name comes up again and again, because her approach to design has run through the floral industry like a locomotive. She made zinnias cool again. She cut individual blossoms of hellebore, floated them in shot glasses, and called that a centerpiece. She decapitated long-stemmed peonies and roses to crowd them into shallow bowls, and she put short-stemmed sweet peas and pansies in champagne glasses, making them tall and elegant. She created a craze for chartreuse flowers and another for monochromatic bouquets. She got people to ask their florists for ornamental amaranth and onion blossoms. She sent baby's breath and leather leaf fern into exile, granting them re-entry only when they could be used in some new and entirely unexpected way. The wire services couldn't keep up, one florist told me. They didn't even try.

WIRE SERVICES STARTED in the early twentieth century as a way to formalize an ad hoc arrangement between florists to allow customers to send flowers to someone in another city. A florist would transmit the order by telegraph and take a 20 percent cut of the price of the bouquet. Florists who wanted to trade wire orders with their colleagues could advertise in a trade publication, where pages of small box ads provided a kind of directory of wire-friendly shops around the country. To save money on telegraph fees, they developed an elaborate system of codes and abbreviation so that an entire bouquet could be described with as few words as possible. (Even after telephones came into use, telegraphs were often more economical. Instead of having a messenger take the orders to the telegraph office a couple times a day, the shop would phone them in to the local Western Union and the order would be telegraphed from there.) Although the arrangement worked fairly well, florists wanted a more formal network, and in 1910, the Florists' Telegraph Delivery Association, or FTD, came into being.

In the early days, participating florists paid dues to FTD that were used to fund advertising programs to promote holiday sales. By the 1950s other wire services had sprung up to compete with FTD, and in 1956 a judge ruled that FTD's policy of prohibiting its members from joining other services was a violation of the Sherman Anti-Trust Act. Still, the organization remained the dominant player in the wire service business, installing an electronic network in the late 1970s and rolling out the "Pick Me Up Bouquet" in the mid-1980s to great success. Today FTD has about twenty thousand members, and Teleflora, a competing service that launched in the 1930s, boasts a slightly larger membership of twenty-four thousand florists.

Lately florists have started to grumble about not just the restrictive design standards but also about the economics of the wire service arrangement. Usually the florist that takes the order keeps a 20 percent commission, the wire service takes a cut, and the florist filling the order is left with less than 75 percent of the money. The proliferation of "order takers" — third-party companies that do not sell flowers themselves but simply take wire orders through the Internet or toll-free numbers and pocket the commission — is seen as a particular problem to the industry, since they have little accountability to the customer and divert slim profits away from brick-and-mortar florists. Some of these call centers even buy space in local phone book listings under names that are similar to actual neighborhood florists. It is difficult to avoid these services: when I did an Internet search for an Albuquerque florist, most of the listings on the first couple of pages were from order gatherers with generic "Albuquerque Flower Shop" headings at the top of the page. This practice doesn't just hurt florists: the *Atlanta Journal-Constitution* reported in 2005 that florists were getting complaints from customers who'd placed orders through one of these call centers, thinking they were talking to a local flower shop. Although their credit cards were charged, the flowers never actually arrived. The Society of American Florists works to get legislation passed banning these deceptive practices, and its spokesperson was quoted as saying, "It does cause a lot of confusion, and our concern is if customers are frustrated or dissatisfied, they're going to go to another gift besides flowers."

Still, with about a quarter of florists' sales coming from wire orders, the shops need a system to send flowers long distance. I've gotten into the habit of tracking down a florist online (I eventually found one of the trendiest florists in Albuquerque, Flowers by Martha Lee, when I stumbled across a list of official sponsors for the gay rodeo. I called and talked to an actual florist who patiently described everything he had in stock so that I could order the exact bouquet I had in mind), but there are innovative alternatives to order gatherers and traditional wire services taking hold. Teresa Sabankaya belongs to one of them—an alternative wire service for specialty florists called b brooks fine flowers.

Barbera Brooks, the company's founder, is an outspoken Southerner with little patience for traditional fern-and-baby's-breath designs. Shop around on her Web site for a romantic rose arrangement and you'll get her treatise on roses: "Traditionally, florists have presented a dozen roses with baby's breath and fern foliage . . . This traditional arrangement of a dozen long-stem roses, while very affordable, is stiff and virtually franceless which to us at b brooks fine flowers is the dead opposite of romance." Her roses, on the other hand, are combined with Oriental lilies and luxurious fillers so that they are "intoxicatingly fragrant as well as large, lush and fully overflowing out of the vase."

You can choose an arrangement by size and by general style, but most customers either opt for the "designer's choice" in their price range, or they call b brooks directly and let her staff know what they're looking for. "You would call us," Barbera told me, "and say, 'I need to send flowers to my niece who is really sophisticated and who's graduating from college in Austin and she likes pastel flowers. We'll turn around, reinterpret that order for you, and probably send it to a florist there and ask for pale pink peonies with apple greens. Really full and lush and seasonal. So you don't have to call around and find the florist and explain to them about no baby's breath and no ferns. It goes without saying. You don't even have to go there. We don't have florists who do that. Just say, 'I want pink,' and it'll be fresh and seasonal and just what you want. We definitely have an aesthetic, and either our customer base buys into that, or they go elsewhere."

There are just six hundred florists in the b brooks network, and they're all hand picked. "We have a lot of florists who call us," Barbera said, "but maybe one out of ten who apply are doing the sort of work that fits this niche. I try to explain to them that our average order is over a hundred dollars, and you've got to know what to do. It's a narrow market, and it's at the high end."

She thinks that one of the factors limiting her company's growth is the high cost of specialty flowers given their short life-span. As a gift, they're still a good value, but, she said, "You're not going to call your florist and get a five-inch-cube centerpiece for your dining room table every week." In spite of the business she's in, Barbera usually buys flowers at the grocery store, not from a florist, when she's buying for herself. "I buy flowers at the grocery store every week," she said. "The three stems of 'Star Gazer' for the bathroom? Yes, if they're just for me, I pick them up there."

IT'S NOT HARD to spot a b brooks florist once you know what you're looking for. A trendy, high-end flower shop doesn't devote floor space to ceramic figurines of angels or Irish setters, ivy plants in wicker baskets, or cow-spotted dish towels. You won't see carnations unless they're used in some unexpected way: cut short and pressed, pavé-style, into a short square vase, for instance. You're likely to find flowers you can't name, and you may see botanicals that you have never thought of putting in a vase before: seed pods, reeds, even miniature beds of grass.

One such shop is Flowers of the World in Manhattan. It's owned by Peter Grontas, whose floral empire also includes Floralia Decorators at the Waldorf-Astoria. I'd come to see Peter because when I was at Aalsmeer, Carlos Bau Santos at Florimex had mentioned him as an example of a high-end client who is represented at the auction. Where do flowers go when they leave the Dutch auction? One place they go is Flowers of the World.

Peter breezed into his shop on West Fifty-fifth Street on a blustery February afternoon, brushing the snow off his suit. He's a dark-haired, good-looking guy in his midforties who exudes charm and seems to be connected with flowers in some larger sense, some intangible way that was different from anyone in the business I'd met so far. Flowers weren't a crop to him, a product to get out the door, the way they would be to a grower. They weren't a commodity to be traded like a stock the way a wholesaler would. They weren't a profit center or a loss leader the way they might be to a grocer. And they weren't anything particularly natural: where a gardener might appreciate sweet peas not just for their charm in the vase but also for the way they scramble up a fence and bloom for months in summer, Peter didn't seem to connect with them in a dirt-under-the-fingernails fashion, either.

Instead, he inhabits a world of big-city style, and flowers just happen to be the most accurate way to express that style. You could see it by looking around his shop, with its chocolate-colored walls and flowers displayed like jewelry on a single table in the center of the room. Here is where the quest for the perfect flower plays itself out. The blossoms were bunched by variety in clear glass vases: burgundy zantedeschias (callas), deep purple hyacinths, heavenly lilacs, and parrot tulips. There was no denying that these flowers were a luxury, something entirely superfluous that you'd buy as an indulgence or a status symbol. The white callas—the same flowers that at that moment were blooming in a neglected strip outside my kitchen door back home—sold here for ten dollars a stem; roses were going for eight dollars each; and even a single tangerine ranunculus might cost six bucks. The long stems on Ecuadorian roses would be wasted here—most flowers were cut down to eight inches so that the main attraction was the perfect, brilliant bloom itself.

Peter grew up in New York; his father owned a shop in Manhattan's financial district that served Wall Street companies and their employees. "He did well," Peter said, "but he wasn't happy. He didn't find it to be a noble profession, for some reason. I don't know why. He tried to open up other businesses, but this was the only thing he ever made a dollar at." Most of his father's stock came from growers on Long Island and in New Jersey. "This time of year," Peter said, "he would have had gladiolus, chrysanthemum, lilies, carnations. And the colors—it would have been white, peppermint, red, and that's it. Some greenery, of course, and roses. And those roses had small little heads that never opened."

When Peter was just starting out, he met a guy with a window display business and was all set to take over one of his routes and start opening up accounts of his own. Just then, his father asked him to take a week off and help him open a new store. "I went to work that week," he said, "and I never left." He'd helped in the store as a kid, mostly cutting blocks of floral foam and packing orders, but this was the first time he'd worked directly with the flowers, and that's what sold him on the business. He worked for his father for twelve years.

"It was difficult to get along with him," he said. "I learned many things. He was good with the flowers, but as far as getting along with customers, suppliers, employees—well, I learned a lot of things not to do." Peter took on a business partner and opened up a number of stores in New York, including Floralia Decorators at the Waldorf and a shop that he lost in the World Trade Center. Recently he took over the floral boutique at the exclusive Takashimaya department store in midtown. The boutique is not tucked into the back of the store; instead, it's a Fifth Avenue storefront that has to hold its own next to a designer Italian clothing store that sells ten thousand dollar handbags and, just a couple doors down, the De Beers flagship diamond store. He told me that creating a flower shop that can survive and turn a profit in that environment has been a real challenge. "Let's face it," he said.

"Flowers are something people don't need. They're a luxury item. It's difficult to actually keep the store profitable and not have it be a loss leader. This is expensive real estate. The standards are incredibly high. Our clients demand a lot."

Peter's signature bouquet is unmistakable. His arrangements are both simple and opulent, usually relying on just one or two kinds of flowers and a limited palette. "The eye can only see so much," he said. "I know color's very exciting, but with flowers, they shouldn't always dominate. They should accent. When we work in the ballroom at the Waldorf, and you have a hundred tables and eleven hundred people, I would not put fifteen or twenty kinds of flowers in an arrangement. I'll use thousands and thousands of stems of just one flower, one color. It's easy on the eye."

His tight, lush arrangements are very much in demand. "Everybody wants them right now," he said. "That's our look. We don't show stems. It's all about the flowers. In a glass vase, I'll wrap the stems in leaves so you won't see them. Our designs are all about the flowers themselves." Because Peter works on the high end, he's not affected by the proliferation of inexpensive, mass-market flowers. "We decided to go this way so we didn't have to be in that game," he said, "where three cents on a flower makes a difference, and you're getting flowers that were stored in Miami for a week, and maybe dealing with less than reputable wholesalers. The grocer on the corner brings awareness to flowers, but the problem is that they're very cheap and the quality is very poor. You buy two dozen roses for $15 and they last two days? Your experience wasn't all that great. Spend $50 on some roses that open up and last ten days—there's something to be said for that." He's got a point, but $50 just barely gets you "some roses" in his shop—you can expect to pay $75 dollars for a compact arrangement of tulips and roses, or you can get a vase overflowing with four dozen 'Grand Prix' roses for $450.

Peter hopes that he can convince people to pay more for a higher quality flower. In some ways, it's surprising that he'd even have to explain the difference between his flowers and the grocery store bouquet. After all, he points out, people expect more from a thirty-dollar bottle of wine than they do from a five-dollar bottle. Shouldn't the same be true of flowers? "We're dealing with different flowers," he told me. "Our clients have a different expectation. I pay more for my flowers, but this is a passion as well as a business. It's the only way I'd do it."

He paused and looked around the shop. While we talked, people came in and out, choosing individual stems from the glass vases on a table in the center of the shop. "I go to Holland a couple times a year," he said. "I like to go in August and see the new flowers. One of my favorite things to do is stand there in the middle of the auction with thousands of carts going right by me. It doesn't get any better than that. You know what amazes me? Every part of a flower is beautiful. You look at a rose today, tomorrow, the next day, and it changes. Roses used to be sold as these tight buds, but our roses open up. They actually have a beauty when they wilt."

MOST FLORISTS DON'T have the luxury of stopping in the middle of their day to contemplate the sweet decay of a rose on the decline. They're just trying to stay afloat in a tidal wave of new competition. Lately there have been some attempts to create national florist franchises and develop brand recognition for flowers. The only surprise is that it's taken so long. Try finding a hamburger that isn't made in a chain restaurant, or filling a prescription in a family-owned pharmacy. It isn't easy. But even a small town like mine boasts several locally owned, independent florists. How long will it be before 1-800-FLOWERS.COM, with $650 million in sales, thousands of affiliate shops filling orders that are placed over the phone or online, and over 100 franchise and com-

pany-owned storefronts around the country, opens a shop around
the corner from them or simply buys them out? What about the
rapidly growing floral chain KaBloom, with 120 stores and plans
to open 300 by the end of 2006?

Each of these chains has its own strategy for dominating the
retail flower market. 1-800-FLOWERS.COM has moved aggressively
into the gift market, pairing flowers with Godiva chocolates, Gund
stuffed animals, and Lenox and Waterford vases. (One Valentine's
Day promotion featured a thousand-dollar bouquet of roses,
complete with a bottle of Dom Perignon, a Waterford vase and
champagne flutes, and a diamond necklace.) KaBloom's business
model, on the other hand, is centered around getting people to
buy flowers for everyday use, not just for special occasions — quite
an ambition given the fact that mass-market retailers, not flower
shops, practically own the self-purchase side of the floral market.
(According to the company's Web site, it sees itself as the "Starbucks of flowers.") Each KaBloom stocks about two hundred varieties of flowers, most of which are out in the store where customers
can see them, touch them, and smell them — not behind glass or
in a cooler in the back room where a traditional florist might keep
them.

One of the most innovative new retail stores is Field of Flowers
in Miami. Its owner, Donn Flipse, is a third-generation florist who
opened the shop in 1990 with the goal of creating the nation's first
floral superstore. He now owns three stores in the Miami area, and
although each one is a little different the idea is the same: devote
around ten thousand square feet to flowers, and let customers have
whatever role in the selection and arranging of flowers they want.

You can call the shop and order an arrangement to be delivered, the same way you would with any retail florist; you can walk
in and choose an arrangement from the self-serve coolers or the
mixed bouquets on floor displays, or you can ask the staff to design

whatever you have in mind. The design work is all done out in the open, not in a workshop hidden from view behind the counter, giving the impression that floral design is not a mystery, but a craft that anyone could learn.

But the best part is the rows and rows of buckets of individual stems arranged by color: first a row of red, then orange, then yellow, and so on. There's an aisle of filler greens and a row of seed pods and branches. You can also choose growers' bunches that look like they came directly from the Miami airport, still wrapped in cardboard and stapled the way they were when they left the farm. And once you've gathered up your flowers, you can make your own bouquet at one of the work tables, where shears, butcher paper, and flower food are all provided. There are aisles of potted plants, vases, silk flowers, and professional floral supplies. You are encouraged to plan your wedding here, and if your bridesmaids aren't up to the task of creating forty centerpieces the day before the wedding, there's a design class just about every week to help them figure it out.

I fell hopelessly in love with this store when I was in Miami and spent an entire day driving from one Field of Flowers location to the next because I just couldn't get enough of it. Here, at last, were all the flowers I'd seen all over the world, and now I could buy just a stem of each—a single green star-of-Bethlehem, a stalk of seeded eucalyptus, a 'Limbo' rose, and a 'Star Gazer' lily. Many flowers sold for around a dollar a stem, including gorgeous red and orange Ecuadorian roses (and this was just a few days before Valentine's Day, when most florists were selling arrangements for eighty bucks), and young green hydrangea blossoms, which are impossible to find anywhere else in winter. It was like a wholesale market for ordinary retail customers, an utterly unpretentious, bare-bones, superstore setting where you could get the most gorgeous flowers from around the world. And all of the flowers came with a firm vase life guarantee: seven days for most, and five days for some short-lived specialty flowers. I was hooked. I filled my drab hotel room with odd and unusual flowers I picked up at the three shops, and left them behind for the housekeeping staff to wonder about.

Costco has also become a significant player in the flower market. The wholesale club, which is now the fifth-largest retailer in the country, has quietly developed a reputation for paying its workers well—average pay is seventeen dollars an hour, with a generous benefits package—and offering high-end products at wholesale prices. The company's CEO, Jim Sinegal, has resisted pressure from Wall Street analysts to increase profits by cutting wages or imposing a higher markup on the merchandise. The highest markup in the store is only 15 percent. Sinegal maintains that the loyalty he gets from employees and customers more than makes up for the higher wages or slim margins. Critical to Costco's model are two concepts: simplicity and luxury. A Costco store will carry just a couple brands of, say, pickles or mayonnaise, but by streamlining the selection and buying in huge quantities the savings are significant. And the availability of luxury items seeded in among the regular merchandise—"Waterford crystal, French wine, and $5000 necklaces scattered among staples like toilet paper" as *New York Times* reporter Steven Greenhouse described it—keeps affluent customers coming back to hunt for treasures.

This approach is readily apparent in Costco's cut flower program. Costco buys flowers from vendors around the country who handle purchasing and bouquet making and even care for the flowers once they're in the store. In an effort to keep flowers as simple as everything else, the store requires that vendors use just three SKUs (stock keeping units, the unique number that identifies the item and price): one for mixed bouquets, one for growers bunches, and one for roses. They are priced at around ten or fifteen bucks, and it's up to the vendor to find the right flowers for each SKU.

Watsonville wholesaler Jeff Brothers helped Costco design its cut flower program and still supplies flowers to its northern California stores. "They have very few rules," Jeff said. "One is that you never, ever, rip off the customer. They're all about value. There are a few other things — the roses always have to be in twenty-four stem bunches, but really, as long as it's a value, they don't care. I can do all kinds of crazy recipes in my bouquets and it's okay. But if you can buy it cheaper someplace else, you're dead meat. You're out." And Costco is always looking for small efficiencies that will push prices lower. Eighteen stems of roses used to sell for $14.99; now it's twenty-four stems for $12.99. "Ouch," Jeff said. "That was painful. But that's what we do."

Costco's "treasure hunt" mentality also shows up in the cut flower program, within limits. "We can't put those five-foot-long rose stems in our stores," Jeff said, "because we don't have containers set up to ship them or display them. We've got a lot of flexibility within the box we're in. But you know, sometimes Lane [DeVries] will be long on French tulips, or some of the more exotic Oriental lilies, and selling them to Costco is a way to keep them out of the wholesale system so he doesn't depress the market. Sun Valley calls and says, 'Hey, this is what we've got,' and we just blow it out there. They're in Costco the next day, and then they're gone and you don't know when you'll see them again." Although there may not be much flexibility in terms of the size of the flowers, Costco stores are well equipped to display flowers: they sit in humidity and temperature-controlled displays that keep the flowers at thirty-five degrees, even though they aren't behind glass doors. And unlike most supermarkets, the bouquets are nowhere near the produce.

It's also worth noting that Costco's vendor code of conduct includes prohibitions against child labor and minimal standards for labor and environmental issues. While the company has not specifically adopted a set of standards for cut flowers, if the VeriFlora certification is adopted as a national standard, it may be easier for large companies to adopt it as a universal standard for their suppliers, and Costco is a likely candidate. "Sinegal is the real deal," Jeff told me. "He cares about his people, and it's not just for show. He's crazy in terms of the margins he tries to run the business at, but he's really trying to do the right thing on all levels. He knows what he's doing. They take code of conduct issues seriously."

Costco customers are probably buying on impulse as they would at any other grocery store or wholesale club, but over time there may be more and more people who come to Costco specifically to get flowers. Some stores sell so many bouquets that they restock seven days a week. The low prices have also given Costco a reputation as a place where retail florists can go and buy flowers for their shop and pay less than they would through their wholesaler. And on Costco's Web site, you can get discount prices on bulk flowers: alstroemerias, for example, were recently selling for seventy-five cents a stem, and roses were just over a dollar a stem, if you bought 150 at a time. Now you can even decorate your wedding at Costco: a wedding box costs seven hundred dollars and includes bouquets, corsages and boutonnieres, and centerpieces. (In keeping with their philosophy of offering just a few choices in large quantities, only roses and hydrangeas are available as wedding flowers.) With the typical florist bill for weddings running over two thousand dollars, it's easy to see how Costco's wedding flowers might be tempting.

NOTED BRITISH FLORAL designer Jane Packer sees a benefit to flower buyers as the quality of supermarket flowers improves. "For the majority of people, it comes down to price," she said. "The supermarkets here have really made an effort to get it right.

I worked for Marks & Spencer as a consultant for about twelve years. They are really leading the way, with incredible quality and value. It's been quite damaging for florists, with more of them closing their doors. But if you look at it from a truly professional point of view, they have actually enhanced the floristry business, because they're delivering good quality flowers." She pointed out that with sell-by dates and several levels of quality control, better flowers are available to more people.

With shops in London, New York, Tokyo, South Korea, and Kuwait, Packer truly participates in the flower market on a global scale. Fans of her simple, lush designs can also order flowers through her website for delivery via courier, and she also works with 1-800-Flowers so that her designs can be available by shipment in the United States as well. Some of her favorite flowers come from Ecuador and Colombia, through a Dutch auction. "They're so wonderful," she said. "Huge-headed roses, really incredible."

Her design school trains twelve students a day in the art of floristry. Some students are gardeners and flower lovers who take just a single class for their own pleasure, but many students are there to learn a trade, spending a full month in training on design and business practices. "Some people have already bought their shop when they sign up for my course," she said, "but I would say to most people that it would be a good idea to get some practical experience within a shop before they go out on their own," she said.

People who are entering the floral trade now are learning in Packer's classes that they have to be good designers and put their hearts into their work. "You've got to care about it," she said. "People love flowers. You see people go right to them and pick them up. If they're at a good price and they look lovely, people will buy them." What florists bring—the one thing that a supermarket can't deliver—is a human touch. Florists add the final factor to the equation. They are the ones who have always had the ability to take a flower and make it speak.

Take Mother's Day, which florists practically invented. The holiday began as an occasion that would allow sons and daughters to honor their mothers by wearing a white carnation in their buttonhole; it started in 1908 when a woman named Anna Jarvis wrote letters to businesses, including the *Weekly Florists' Review*, suggesting the practice. She chose the second Sunday in May because her own mother died on the second Sunday in May. "Crowd it and push it," she urged florists. "It has Memorial Day beat by a mile, and comes when flowers are cheap and plenty." Florists did push it, and Jarvis's idea was a success, although she had a falling-out with the industry over the idea of using white carnations exclusively. Florists were in favor of a wider variety of flowers, in part because growers couldn't supply enough white carnations at once.

Over time, Mother's Day took hold as a floral holiday and people saw it as a time to send a message to one's mother that might not get said any other way. During World War II, a soldier wired flowers to his mother, and she wrote that "it seems like a miracle to get flowers when he's so far away." Today half of consumers still buy flowers for Mother's Day, and they don't just buy them for their mothers: flowers also go to daughters, wives, and grandmothers.

But weddings remain one of the floral events most closely associated with romance, and one for which a florist is indispensable. When Queen Victoria got married in 1840, her white wedding gown was trimmed with orange blossoms. Flowers had always been a part of weddings, but thanks to Queen Victoria, brides were more likely than ever before to carry bouquets of flowers that symbolized their emotions, and florists decked out cakes, chairs, altars and tabletops with flowers. Wedding flowers were the most intricate work a florist could do, with carefully wired headdresses and cascading bouquets coming into fashion. Even today, the pressure is enormous: wedding flowers have to be fresh, perfect, and exactly what the bride dreams of. It's hard to imagine a box of flowers from a warehouse living up to that dream.

And as weddings change, florists find a way for flowers to be as relevant and meaningful as they ever were. One morning in February 2004, I opened the newspaper and found out that newly elected San Francisco mayor Gavin Newsom had announced that city staff would perform marriages for gay and lesbian couples at City Hall. It was impossible not to be moved by the sight of people dashing downtown, with no advance notice at all, no time to buy rings or call their families, before they formalized their love for each other. I'll never forget the photograph of two men, each with an infant daughter in a sling on his chest, holding hands and saying their vows. It was the most romantic Valentine's Day San Francisco has ever seen.

Two coworkers in Minneapolis, Greg Scanlan and Timothy Holtz, were chatting about the scores of newlyweds rushing out of City Hall every day. They wished they could be there to play a part in this phenomenon, and Scanlan said, "If you can't be there, send flowers." That day, they contacted a florist in San Francisco and ordered a bouquet with the instructions that they be delivered to any couple standing in line to get married.

The idea got around on the Internet, and by the end of the week, the florist was getting a hundred orders a day. Most were simply addressed, "To the happy couple," but some included more personal notes like, "I'm an 87-year-old grandmother wishing you well." Florists flew in and out of their shops, doing what florists do best—responding to the very emotional and urgent needs of their customers, putting together bouquets that would somehow convey an anonymous message of love and hope from one stranger to another, and dashing out the door within a few hours of taking the order to place the flowers in someone's hands. No superstore could pull that off.

Documentary filmmaker Peter Daulton made a film about the event called *Flowers from the Heartland.* He went to Minnesota and interviewed some of the people who had sent flowers. There were gay and lesbian people, straight couples, parents and grandparents, and even church congregations, who had all decided that nothing but flowers could express what they had to say to these couples lining up to wed. When I saw the film, I was touched by how ordinary these Midwesterners seemed. They were not political activists. They weren't trying to make a statement or deliver a message to Congress. They simply wanted to send flowers. Why? Here are the reasons they gave: To make their presence felt even though they couldn't be there in person. To let the newlyweds know that someone, somewhere, wished them happiness. And most of all, because it's a wedding, and everyone knows that weddings need flowers.

EVERY DAY, AMERICANS go out and buy about ten million cut flowers. After all I've seen, that really doesn't sound like much. It works out, on a daily basis, to one flower for every twenty-five people. Another way to look at it: Every man, woman, and child gets fourteen stems a year. That's just over one flower a month. How can anybody get by on one flower a month?

During the year I spent chasing flowers around the globe, I developed a habit of stopping every time I saw an opportunity to buy flowers. Now I realize that it is impossible to get through my day without running into them somewhere: daisies and mums at the drugstore, lilies at the supermarket, roses in a bucket from a street vendor. Tulip growers are experimenting with a vacuum-pack technology, similar to the bags that keep salad mixes fresh, that would allow cut tulips to be bagged and sealed, without water, and hung on racks like potato chips. You can even buy flowers out of a vending machine in the baggage claim area at the Oakland airport. Slip a twenty into the slot and out comes a dozen red roses. (With any luck, you can take her suitcase in one hand, offer the roses with the other, and usher her out of the airport before she notices the vending machine and realizes what an afterthought the bouquet was.)

And what good does it do us? When I consider all the time and money and effort spent on building a better flower, growing it more efficiently, getting it to market faster, and keeping it alive longer, I wonder if this industry is trying to solve a problem we didn't know we had. Will we be any better off with a blue rose or a pollen-free lily or a gerbera that lives for twenty days in a vase? The Victorians, with their messy, short-lived, and wildly fragrant posies, didn't seem deprived of romance or beauty. Then again, neither do I.

Modern flowers aren't plastic. They're not fake. They're not even a scientific abomination. They're the outcome of our tinkering and manipulation, and in some cases the results are glorious. No one can deny that Leslie Woodriff's 'Star Gazer' is a showstopper. And there's nothing I'd rather have for Valentine's Day than Nevado's enormous organic 'Esperance' roses. These are sculptures, works of art. I may not be ready for a blue rose or a chocolate-scented lilac, much less a blossom with gold lettering embossed across the petals or a bouquet dispensed by a vending machine, but I believe that the floral industry will get it right more often than it gets it wrong. I'm in favor of better flowers: flowers that are more interesting, more exotic, more colorful, and, yes, more fragrant and longer-lived than ever before.

And if anyone ever does claim to have created the perfect flower, I'll be the first in line to buy a dozen.

Valentine's Day

The phone rang at Heuer's. Aus Heuer, the owner, put down the roses he'd been stripping and grabbed the phone. "No, it's not too late," he said, and listened for a minute. "Yes. With tax and delivery, eighty-seven dollars."

The line went dead. Aus—his full name is Ausbern, but everybody calls him Aus, pronounced Oz—set the phone back on its cradle. "What's that guy going to do now?" he asked. "It's noon on Valentine's Day." He shook his head in bewilderment and went back to stripping roses.

This is the thirty-fifth time Aus has opened his shop on Eureka's Fifth Street and faced the onslaught of Valentine's Day. Over the years he's developed a carefully designed, well-run system for getting through the holiday. The shop is busy, but it's also quiet and controlled. Playing Cupid to a few hundred small-town couples requires more discipline than romance.

Valentine's Day is the busiest day a flower shop will face all year. It accounts for a third of all cut flower sales, and, as Bunny Schreiber pointed out, it all has to happen on February 14. This isn't like Christmas, when a florist's business is spread out over a couple of weeks. It all comes down to this one day.

Florists take some comfort in knowing that they can anticipate what the busiest day of the year will be like. We are a predictable people on February 14. Almost a third of American adults will buy flowers or a plant at Valentine's Day. Roughly half of those people will want roses, mostly red roses. Two-thirds of the orders will come from men, and of those men 80 percent will be buying flowers for their wives or significant others. (Another 8 percent go to mothers and daughters; the remaining 12 percent go to friends or "other." There's no data on the level of excitement or confusion created within that last category, but I have my theories.) Women are most likely to buy flowers for themselves or for their mothers on Valentine's Day, but some — 18 percent of female buyers — do send flowers to their husbands or lovers.

Florists also know that these people are procrastinators — over a third of the orders will come in on February 13, and another 22 percent are called in on the holiday itself. (This is a bad idea, by the way — almost half of all flowers shops have to start turning orders away at some point on Valentine's Day. Don't put it off.) An unfortunate 1 percent of Valentine's Day customers don't order their flowers until February 15. It's unclear whether people try this strategy because they think they'll get a deal or because they're trying to get themselves out of the doghouse, but either way it's unlikely to work: both the employees and the flowers are exhausted the day after the holiday, but the price of a rose on February 15 is just as high as it was the day before. The florist paid double and you will, too. (The Society of American Florists also tries to manage the mayhem by suggesting that people send flowers on February 13 instead, with a message like "Couldn't wait another day to say I love you!" but that idea hasn't caught on, either.)

It's even possible to predict what the calendar will do to florists' sales. If Valentine's Day lands on a Wednesday or Thursday, they're in luck. Sales tend to peak if the holiday falls midweek, when people are at work and sending flowers is both easy to do and sure to get a response from coworkers. The numbers drop off later in the week, and if a Valentine's Day falls on a Saturday or Sunday, sales are sure to be dismal. People don't think of a florist as being open on the weekend, especially a Sunday, and they're not sure whether they might be home to get the flowers anyway.

THIS YEAR, VALENTINE'S DAY came on a Monday. Aus wasn't complaining—he was on track to have a busy day. "Our goal is to run out of flowers," he told me. "I think we'll make it."

The first shipment of flowers for the holiday had arrived about ten days ago. He'd ordered carnations, mums, and greens ahead of time and stored them in the cooler, where they would keep almost indefinitely. Because he owns the building (Heuer's Café is next door, and there are apartments upstairs), he has more cooler space than most florists would. In addition to a cooler downstairs, he's got two rooms upstairs that are outfitted with air conditioners so that he can store large quantities when he needs to.

Heuer's strategy is to make about two hundred arrangements on spec—meaning that they haven't been sold—well in advance of the holiday. I had stopped by the shop about a week earlier, and there were already dozens and dozens of vases filled with ferns and other greens. A few days ahead of time, the designers would pull them all out of the cooler, add the roses and carnations, and put them back. These were the flowers they'd sell to their last-minute customers. All the orders that came in early would also get filled a few days prior and grouped according to delivery route.

Because Heuer's is located downtown, it's not unusual to see delivery guys walking down the street with two or three arrangements in their arms on Valentine's Day. They might be headed to the courthouse, City Hall, the post office, the bank. Whether they go on foot or by truck, about 350 arrangements would go out the door of this small shop in a single day.

At a time like this, Aus appreciates having Sun Valley nearby.

"We get all our bulk lilies, irises, tulips, and freesia from them," he told me. Some of Sun Valley's flowers had been sitting in buckets in the hallway upstairs for a couple of days, deliberately kept out of the cooler so that they would open just a little more before they went out the door. "Sun Valley also carries a selection of other cuts," he said. "Occasionally when I get in trouble, they bail me out."

Almost all the roses in the shop were Californian. "When we've brought imports in," he said, "our customers tell us they don't last as long. So we stick to California roses." There are enough rose growers within a day's drive of Eureka that Aus can usually buy roses that were picked just a day or two ago, a trick that not every florist can pull off. Nationwide, you've got only about a one in ten shot of dispatching an American-grown rose to your sweetheart.

The phone rang again. "Heuer's Florist," Aus said. "Sure—we can try. What's her address?" He consulted a running tally of the number of premade bouquets in the cooler. He wanted to be sure to push whatever was not selling as fast. "If you don't want roses, we've got a basket of tulips, carnations, and heather. Sure, a dozen roses. Red?" Sometimes I'd hear him on the phone coaching a customer on what to say on the card. "With love? I love you? Happy Valentine's Day? Okay, Thinking of you."

Two designers worked alongside Aus. They had all worked nineteen days straight in anticipation of the holiday. A couple of temps had been hired as runners to carry buckets of flowers down from the coolers upstairs whenever someone asked for them—at one point, a designer had to stop and show one of them the difference between stock and snapdragon—and every few minutes, a delivery driver swung through to pick up another ten arrangements. They lined the floor and the hallway, and they took up every available inch of counter space. Heuer's was maxed out, but so far they were holding it together.

Aus and his designers can make a bouquet in under five minutes. They worked quickly, holding a knife in one hand to strip off leaves and thorns. The floor was covered in cut greens; a couple times an hour, somebody stopped long enough to sweep the bulk of it away. Sometimes a rose just fell apart and the petals cascaded to the floor. "There goes seven dollars and fifty cents," one of the designers would say, without even looking up.

Around noon, the postman stopped in. "Aus," he said, but Aus didn't look up from his work. "Aus. Take a deep breath." He dropped the mail and left.

ALTHOUGH VALENTINE'S DAY has its origins in third-century Rome — one legend claims that Valentine was a priest who secretly performed marriage ceremonies for soldiers and their brides during a time when soldiers were forbidden to marry — it was not until the eighteenth century that lovers started sending cards or notes to each other to mark the holiday. If anyone wanted to send a flower, they didn't have much chance of success: a *New York Times* writer in 1853 complained, "Valentine's Day is in February, and there are no violets, no roses, no green-clad forests, so we must content ourselves with pens, ink, and paper." Florists didn't notice an upswing in business until the twentieth century. By about 1910, florists were making a real effort to promote flowers as an alternative to the "frilled paper monstrosities" people exchanged at the time. It also became more of a holiday for grown-ups around then: one advertisement from the twenties shows a young man saying that he's going to let flowers do the talking for him on Valentine's Day, and his father, hearing him, says, "Son, your idea is fine. I'll let Flowers talk to your mother, too."

At first, hand-tied bouquets of sweet violets were the most popular gift. People often gave corsage bouquets — large corsages that could be pinned at the waist — of a single type of flower like sweet peas or lilies of the valley. They would be sold in a heart-shaped box and tied with a red bow. Because violets were so popular, purple was a common Valentine's Day color in the early twentieth century, but pink and red gradually took over.

Carnations and roses had cemented their lead in Valentine's Day sales by the 1940s, and over the next few decades florists started adding cherubs, teddy bears, and balloons to pump up the value of each arrangement. Today the Society of American Florists estimates that over 175 million roses are sold on Valentine's Day, with the average arrangement of a dozen roses costing just over seventy dollars. The volume is tremendous: 1-800-FLOWERS.COM takes almost a million orders on Valentine's Day, and even the upstart Organic Bouquet shipped ten thousand bouquets in 2005.

HERE'S ONE SIGN of how traditional Heuer's customer base is: some of the baskets of balloons, bears, carnations, and roses that went out the door that day didn't look too different from how they might have looked fifty years ago. I was a long way from Manhattan, where the hip gift might have been burgundy zantedeschias or a few precious stems of early lilac, and even Teresa Sabankaya's romantic touch—her handmade Victorian posies with their cryptic messages—seemed far away. I was squarely in the center of the mainstream flower trade, where Valentine's Day had to be, by necessity, an assembly line. Orders came in the front door, and all the designers had to do was add or subtract a few flowers from their standard premade bouquet to get them out again. "Make this a sixty-dollar arrangement," a cashier said, rushing to the back with a forty-dollar vase of roses and lilies he'd taken out of the cooler. One of the designers stuffed a couple of spray roses and two 'Star Gazers' into the center, and it went back out to the front. "There's a lot of cut and cram today," Aus said, "but that's how we get through it."

The phone rang constantly in the background. Other florists

have stopped taking orders, the callers told them. Aus figured out that they were one of the only florists in town who still had flowers, but he was running out of time to make deliveries. The staff started suggesting to people on the phone that they come pick their arrangements up instead of holding out for the slim possibility of a delivery. As they worked, every designer set aside the more open roses, the ones that were almost past their prime. "Those go out front," one of them told me, "for the guys who are desperate."

One table was occupied entirely by bud vases, each containing a rose, maybe a spray of heather, and some greens, with a red ribbon tied around the neck of the vase. Those were twelve-dollar arrangements that would go to offices, where the boss had bought one for each employee. And at another table, all of the chocolates, stuffed animals, and balloons got added on. One exceptionally large basket of carnations, lilies, and roses was waiting to get dressed up. A designer added a singing balloon that played "Sugar Pie, Honey Bun" and out it went.

At one o'clock, a waitress from the café next door came over and took the staff's lunch orders. Nobody was stopping for lunch today—they'd eat a club sandwich where they were standing and then go right back to work. Just then, Aus announced that they were out of red roses. From now on, they'd push the pink and yellow roses, the lilies and tulips, the carnations and stock, even snapdragons and sunflowers. They were running low on flowers up front, too, so Aus asked one of his runners to bring down another box of cash-and-carry mixed bouquets. They came shipped in upright, water-filled containers called Proconas (basically a square bucket with a cardboard collar and a plastic top, which, as long as it was transported upright, would keep the stems in water during shipment), and they were already arranged and sleeved. "We don't take our standard markup on these," Aus said. "Usually we mark up the flowers five times. That covers the arranging, the vase, everything. For these I'll just double the price. They come in the back door and go right out the front door." He kept a sidewalk display filled with these lower-priced bouquets; by the end of the day, this would be one of the only options left for the desperate and flowerless.

VALENTINE'S DAY WAS nearly over by the time I left Heuer's and walked home. When I arrived, I found my own Valentine's Day flowers waiting for me: two dozen certified orange and red bicolor 'Lipstick' roses from Organic Bouquet, along with a card from my husband. FedEx played Cupid at our house — the truck had pulled up just a few minutes before I got there.

I opened the box and there they were, straight from Nevado Ecuador, the blossoms wrapped in that now-familiar cardboard sleeve with a thin sheet of tissue between each row of flowers. I could tell the people at Nevado had been busy: the stems were barely stripped of leaves or thorns, and there was a little spot of botrytis (not much, Roberto!) on a couple of the petals. I remembered that Roberto Nevado had once said that if you submerged roses for three hours in a bathtub filled with cold water, you could get two more days out of them.

Two more days, after all they'd been through so far? I knew how far they'd come. Seven years to design a rose in a laboratory and bring it to market. Six thousand miles from a geneticist in Amsterdam to a farmer in Ecuador. Three months of careful watching and waiting while the Valentine's Day crop grows. Five days, two airplanes, and a couple of trucks to get them to my house. Now Nevado promised they'd last a week in the vase, longer if I gave them a bath first.

I stood thinking of the equatorial hoop houses they'd come from, where each of these buds towered above the heads of the workers, where Ecuadorian pop music blared from radios to keep everybody moving on the long days leading up to the holiday, where the goats grazed on weeds outside and off in the distance, the volcano was snowy and silent.

Even after everything I'd seen, I was still swept up by the romance of it all.

The Care and Feeding of Cut Flowers

Most cut flowers should last a week in the vase, and some, like Asiatic lilies, chrysanthemums, and high-quality roses, will last longer. To get the most out of your cut flowers, try these techniques:

- Buy flowers that have been kept under refrigeration. If they've been sitting out on the sidewalk or in buckets in the produce department, they've lost vase life. That doesn't mean they have to be behind glass: some retailers have special air conditioners that keep the air right around the flowers cool.

- Ask your florist for a vase life guarantee. Most florists will replace flowers that don't last at least five or seven days in the vase.

- Roses and other sturdy flowers can be rehydrated by plunging the entire flower and stem under cold water. One rose grower says that submerging roses in the bathtub for three hours will add two days' vase life.

- Before you put flowers in a vase, make sure the vase is clean and fill it with water. Use sharp scissors or a knife to strip off any leaves that will be underwater, and then recut the stems and place immediately in water.

- Commercial flower food really will extend the vase life of flowers. You can buy it at craft stores, nurseries, and flower shops, but if you don't have any use a pinch of sugar and a drop of bleach. (If you have it, you can also use a pinch of ground-up Viagra, an expensive but effective treatment that prolongs vase life by helping to open the vessels that conduct water up the stem to the flower in much the same way that—well, never mind.)

- Keep the flowers in a cool spot out of direct sunlight. In dry climates, spritzing the flowers with water may extend their life.

- Change the water and recut the stems every few days. In mixed bouquets, remove any flowers that start to wilt early; as they wilt, they may give off ethylene, which could cause other flowers to wilt early, too.

Visiting Markets and Growers

You can get a behind-the-scenes look at the cut flower industry at any of the following markets, festivals, and tourist attractions. Remember that wholesale flower markets can move, and open hours can change every year, so please call before you go.

Wholesale markets open to the public

New Covent Garden Market
London
SW8 5NX
+44 (0)20 7720 2211
www.cgma.gov.uk
Open 3 a.m. to 11 a.m. Monday through Friday and 4 a.m. to 11 a.m. Saturday. Over fifty companies sell flowers, plants, and supplies here. This is the UK's only specialty flower market.

Columbia Road Flower Market
Columbia Road,
London
E2 7RG
+44-(0)-20 7377 8963
A London street flower market open from 8 a.m. to 2 p.m. Sunday. A wide variety of flowers, plants, and bulbs are for sale, along with antiques, food, and gifts.

San Francisco Flower Mart
640-644 Brannan St.
San Francisco, CA
+1-415-392-7944
www.sfflmart.com
Open to the public 10 a.m. to 3 p.m. Monday through Saturday

Los Angeles Flower District
766 Wall St.
Los Angeles, CA
+1-213-627-3696
www.laflowerdistrict.com
Open to the public 6 a.m. to noon Tuesday, Thursday, Saturday,
and 8 a.m. to noon Monday, Wednesday, Friday

New York Flower District
Near Sixth Ave., W. 26th to 29th streets
New York, NY
Contact information and open hours vary by shop

FloraHolland
Postbus 1000, 1430 BA Aalsmeer
The Netherlands
+31 (0)297 392185
infoaalsmeer@floraholland.nl
www.floraholland.com
The famous Dutch flower auction is open to the public 7:00–11:00
a.m. Monday through Friday year round. Aalsmeer is an easy bus
ride from Amsterdam's Central Station. Get there early, because
most of the action takes place before 9 a.m.

Growers and Other Attractions

Skagit Valley Tulip Festival
100 E. Montgomery St.
Mount Vernon, WA
+1-360-428-5959
www.tulipfestival.org
Washington State's tulip and daffodil bulb-growing region is open
to visitors every April. Exact dates vary; festival activities include art
shows, farm tours, and more.

The Flower Fields
5704 Paseo Del Norte
Carlsbad, CA
+1-760-431-0352
www.theflowerfields.com
Visitors come to the Flower Fields every spring to see their ranunculus bulb fields in bloom. The season runs from mid-March through
mid-May and is open 9 a.m. to 5 p.m. seven days a week.

Sun Valley Floral Farm
3160 Upper Bay Rd.
Arcata, CA
+1-707-826-8708
www.sunvalleyfloral.com
Sun Valley does not sell directly to the public, but it does hold an
open house at the Arcata farm once a year, usually in mid-July,
where tours of the greenhouses and fields are offered and fresh cut
flowers and bulbs are for sale.

Hortus Bulborum
Zuidkerkenlaan 23A, NL-1906 AC Limmen
The Netherlands
+31 (0)251 23 12 86
www.hortus-bulborum.nl
This treasury of historic bulbs is open to visitors from April 6
to May 16 every year when the tulips are in bloom. Hours are
10 a.m. to 5 p.m. Monday through Saturday and noon to 5 p.m.
Sunday. Limmen is about 18 miles northwest of Amsterdam.

Holland Bulb Fields
Holland's bulb production fields draw tourists from all over the
world from the end of March through early May. Precise flowering
times depend on weather, but the second half of April is usually a
good bet. Most travel agencies can book a tour of Holland's bulb
fields. For more information, visit www.holland.com.

Notes

Introduction

Estimates of the overall retail value of the cut flower market worldwide are notoriously difficult to come by, as confirmed by several industry analysts whom I interviewed for this book. Import and export data are tracked, usually in wholesale dollars, for many countries but not all of them. (Data are not available from India, for example.) Statistics for flowers that are grown domestically and sold domestically are also difficult to compile, since each country tracks that information differently. Also, sales at farmers' markets and other small-scale, local outlets are not tracked in this country and many others. Finally, cut greenery and specialty flowers are often not included in floral statistics. Forty billion dollars is the most commonly used figure, and this makes sense. In the United States alone, the retail value of cut flowers is over $6 billion (see note below). Various estimates of worldwide flower consumption come to the same conclusion: The United States makes up about 20 percent of the worldwide flower market. See Tony Seidman, "Despite Globalization Traumas, Flower Industry Blooms," *World Trade Magazine* (June 1, 2004); Nancy Laws, "World Commerce in Cut Flowers and Roses," *FloraCulture International* (October 2002), www.floraculturalintl.com/archive/articles/131.asp; and N. S. P. de Groot, "Floriculture Worldwide Trade and Consumption Patterns," paper presented at the World Conference on Horticultural Research, Rome, June 1998, www.agrsci.unibo.it/wchr/wc1/degroot.html. That comes to $31.2 billion worldwide. Throw in smaller markets, countries like India for which few data are available, and a few extras like cut greenery and specialty flowers, and the $40 billion number probably hits the mark.

For insight into the history of our connections with cut flowers, see Jack Goody, *The Culture of Flowers* (Cambridge, England: Cambridge University Press, 1993), and Peter Coats, *Flowers in History* (London: Weidenfeld and Nicolson, 1970). More suggestions for general reading about the history of flowers is included in the bibliography.

For more on the history of vases, see Julie Emerson, *Porcelain Stories from China to Europe* (Seattle, WA: Seattle Art Museum, 2000), and Lorenzo Camusso and Sandro Bortone, eds., *Ceramics of the World* (New York: Harry N. Abrams, 1991).

The 2002 Economic Census Report shows that retail sales of cut flowers at traditional retail flower shops was $4,366,394,000. The Society of American Florists reports that on a dollar basis 70 percent of cut flower sales happen at retail florists. (However, retail florists have less than half the cut flower market by volume.) Therefore, the overall retail sales of cut flowers, including florists, supermarkets, and other outlets, is estimated at $6,237,705,714. This does not include potted plants, vases, and other floriculture merchandise. A slightly higher estimate comes from international data on cut flower consumption, including one from Pathfast Publishing (www.pathfastpublishing.com), which in 2002 estimated U.S. consumption of cut flowers at $7,263,000,000. The data were presented in euros, which did reach parity with the dollar at several points in 2002.

The number of stems purchased in the United States is estimated at about 4,000,000,000. The USDA's National Agricultural Statistics Service (NASS) 2005 figures for domestic production total 854,528,000, but this does not include growers with under $100 thousand in annual sales. Data for imported flowers come from the USDA's Foreign Agricultural Service trade database; the total for 2005 comes to 2,895,245,900. The total, then would be 3,749,773,900. However, the review of USDA's Animal and Plant Health Inspection Service (APHIS) data on cut flowers that were inspected and counted at the point of import suggest that the real count of imported flowers could be as high as 6,729,357,000. The discrepancies can be explained by an undercount of specialty flowers and greens sold in smaller quanities; flowers that are tallied by the bunch rather than by individual stem; and some changes to recordkeeping that occurred when the Department of

Homeland Security assumed responsibility for the data collection. Therefore, 4,000,000,000 is a reliable conservative figure.

The figures for the imported flower business in the UK come from the British and Colombian Chamber of Commerce, 2008.

According to a September 9, 1998, McDonald's press release, Americans buy six hundred million Big Macs each year.

Chapter 1: The Birds, the Bees, and a Camel Hair Brush

Most of the information about 'Star Gazer' came from interviews and court records. In particular, the following people gave generously of their time, their memories, and their archives: George Woodriff, Betty Dupee, David and Laura Dun, Eloise Kirsch, Bill Weigle, Bert Walker, Piet Koopman, Lane DeVries, Eddie McRae, and Wim Granneman.

Reconciling the disparate memories of Woodriff's and Kirsch's friends and families was not easy. They disagreed on some important issues and some minor points. Some remember Woodriff giving the name 'Star Gazer' to his famous lily and say that he knew what he had before he sold his farm to Kirsch; others think that Kirsch or someone at Sun Valley discovered and named the flower. Some remember Woodriff keeping lily pollen in a pill box, others describe a glass bottle. I tried to be true to all their memories. I spoke to two of Woodriff's children, George and Betty, both of whom are devoted to their father and feel that their father was cheated of what was rightfully his. Kirsch's daughter, Laura, son-in-law, David, and wife, Eloise, showed an equal amount of love and respect for Kirsch and felt that Kirsch had done all he could to help Woodriff. If these families met today, they would certainly have one thing in common: the 'Star Gazer' lily, which is a source of great pride and affection on both sides.

For more information on lily breeding and growing, read Edward McRae's invaluable *Lilies: A Guide for Growers and Collectors* (Portland, OR: Timber Press, 1988), and Michael Jefferson-Brown's *Lilies: A Guide to Choosing and Growing Lilies* (New York: Rizzoli, 2004). The North American Lily Society, online at www.lilies.org, is a treasure trove of information.

A. G. Morton's *History of Botanical Science* (London: Academic Press, 1981) provides a fascinating overview of early discoveries in the field of botany.

Data on sales of particular flowers through the Dutch auction system are available from the *International Cut Flower Manual*, published annually by Pathfast Publishing (www.pathfastpublishing.com). Statistics for number of stems sold are based on 2001 figures.

Information on the history of the Plant Patent Act comes from the archives of the *New York Times* and from the United States Patent and Trademark Office. To read any patent in its entirety, go to www.uspto.gov.

Chapter 2: Engineered to Perfection

Thomas Christopher's *In Search of Lost Roses* (Chicago: University of Chicago Press, 1989) provides an excellent overview of the history of rose breeding.

For more on scent, read Sharman Apt Russell, *Anatomy of a Rose* (Cambridge, MA: Perseus, 2001), and Lyall Watson, *Jacobson's Organ and the Remarkable Nature of Smell* (London: Allen Lane, 1999).

Information about Florigene and its products came from interviews with staff and the company's own published material. Visit Florigene online at www.florigene.com.

For more about the Union of Concerned Scientists, go to www.ucsusa.org.

The American Floral Endowment funds research on cut flower breeding, production, and postharvest care. Visit www.endowment.org and check the "Scientific Research" section for more information on the work of Natalia Dudareva, David Clark, and others.

Brian Capon's *Botany for Gardeners* (Portland, OR: Timber Press, 2005) and Bob Gibbons's *The Secret Life of Flowers* (London: Blandford, 1990) provide excellent introductions to botany for the layperson.

Chapter 3: Italian Violets and Japanese Chrysanthemums

For more on the history of the cut flower industry, see *The History of U.S. Floriculture* (Willoughby, OH: Greenhouse Grower, 1999), and *A Centennial History of the American Florist* (Topeka, KS: Florists' Review Enterprises, 1997).

Two excellent histories of the Japanese American growers in California are Naomi Hirahara, *A Scent of Flowers* (Pasadena, CA: Midori Books, 2004), and Gary Kawaguchi, *Living with Flowers: The California Flower Market History* (San Francisco: California Flower Market, 1993). See also

Charles J. Gould, *History of the Flower Bulb Industry in Washington State* (Mount Vernon, WA: Northwest Bulb Growers Association, 1993), for a history of that region.

The Diary of Michael J. Floy was published by Yale University Press, New Haven, CT, in 1941. *My Ten-Rod Farm; or, How I Became a Florist* was first published in 1869 by Loring in Boston under the name Maria Gilman and was published by Henry T. Coates, Philadelphia, in about 1900, with Charles Barnard credited as the author.

Peter Henderson's many books on floriculture lend insight to the history of the industry. I particularly recommend *Practical Floriculture* (New York: Orange Judd, 1911). S. S. Skidelsky's *Tales of a Traveler* (New York: A. T. de la Mare, 1916) also gives insight into the flower business around the turn of the twentieth century.

Chapter 4: Acres under Glass

Greenhouse Grower magazine ranks the top one hundred growers each year; data on Sun Valley come from its May 2004 survey results. Although the survey is voluntary and there is some possibility that it has missed some growers, the magazine's staff confirmed that based on their knowledge of the industry, the cut flower rankings are quite accurate. The USDA does not make data on individual growers available to the public, so an industry-wide survey is the best data source available. Sun Valley's own published statistics, confirmed by DeVries, put its annual production at around a 100 million stems. Domestic cut flower production, as reported by the USDA for growers with over one hundred thousand dollars in sales, reached 784 million stems in 2004. See "Floriculture and Nursery Crops Outlook" (September 2005), www.ers.usda.gov.

Statistics on domestic cut flower production come from the USDA's "Floriculture and Nursery Crops Situation and Outlook Yearbook," published annually by the agency's Economic Research Service and available online at www.ers.usda.gov. Please note that the oft-quoted statistic that 85 percent of all roses are imports is based on the dollar value of imports as opposed to domestic roses, not on per-stem production figures. In fact, based on stem count, 92 percent of all roses sold in the United States are imports. Overall, about 80 percent of all cut flowers sold in the United States are imports, but in terms of wholesale dollar value imports represent 64 percent of sales. Also note that some import statistics that track "unit" data may count a bouquet, not an individual stem, as a unit. Finally, there have been some variations in the methodology for counting imported flowers as those duties have shifted from the USDA to the Department of Homeland Security.

Other data on Sun Valley came from interviews with Lane DeVries and his staff, and from documents published by the company. To find out more about Sun Valley, visit www.sunvalleyfloral.com.

Statistics on farmworkers come from the most recently available data from the Department of Labor's National Agricultural Workers Survey, the California State Library's California Research Bureau's "Farm Workers in California" study, published in 1998; the University of California's California Policy Research Center's "Agricultural Workers of California: Health Fact Sheet," published in January 2004; and the Rural Community Assistance Corporation's "Survey about Farm Workers," published in 2000.

Chapter 5: How the Dutch Conquered the World

For accounts of the Dutch tulip craze, see Mike Dash, *Tulipomania* (New York: Crown, 2000), and Anna Pavord, *The Tulip* (New York: Bloomsbury, 1999). Leslie Leijenhorst's *Hortus Bulborum* (Wormerveer, Netherlands: Stiching Uitgeverij Noord-Holland, 2004) provides an excellent account of the attempts to preserve the old strains of tulips and other bulbs that are a part of Holland's history.

Statistics on the Dutch flower trade come from Niala Maharaj and Gaston Dorren, *The Game of the Rose* (Utrecht, Netherlands: International Books, 1995); the Royal Netherlands Embassy; and the International Flower Bulb Centre (www.bulb.com).

For more information on the global trade in roses, see Nancy Laws, "World Commerce in Cut Flowers and Roses," *FloraCulture International* (October 2002), www.floraculturalintl.com/archive/articles/131.asp. Also see "The International Markets for Cut Roses 2000," available from www .pathfastpublishing.com. Finally, the Flower Council of Holland (www .flowercouncil.org) and the "Floriculture and Nursery Crops Yearbook," published by the USDA's Economic Research Service (www.ers.usda.gov), provide statistics on flower production, import, and sales for their respective countries.

Chapter 6: Flowers on the Equator

The White House Office of National Drug Control Policy released its 2004 figures on Colombian drug eradication on March 25, 2005; see details in the "Press Release" section of www.whitehousedrugpolicy.gov.

Information about the Dole Food Company comes from its 2004 annual report.

Statistics on wages and sexual harassment in the flower industry come from Norma Mena and Silvia Proaño, "Sexual Harassment in the Workplace: The Cut Flower Industry" (April 2005). This study is available from the International Labor Rights Fund at www.laborrights.org.

For more information on pesticides, health problems, and working conditions, see Zonia Palán and Carlos Palán, "Employment and Working Conditions in the Ecuadorian Flower Industry" (August 1999), available from the International Labour Organization (ILO), www.ilo.org/public/english/dialogue/sector/papers/ecuadflo/. See also Cecilia Castelnuovo et al., "Ecuador: Child Labour in Flower Plantations: A Rapid Assessment" (April 2000), available from the ILO, www.ilo.org/public/english/standards/ipec/simpoc/ecuador/ra/flowers.pdf.

Data on health complaints of California farmworkers come from the California Endowment's November 2000 report "Suffering in Silence: A Report on the Health of California's Agricultural Workers," www.calendow.org.

See "Tainted Harvest: Child Labor and Obstacles to Organizing on Ecuador's Banana Plantations," published by Human Rights Watch in April 2002, for more on child labor issues in agriculture. It's available at www.hrw.org/reports/2002/ecuador/.

Export statistics for Ecuador and Colombia come from Expoflores, the Ecuadorian trade association, and Asocolflores, the Colombian trade association. More information is available at www.expoflores.com and www.colombianflowers.com.

Information about Ecuadorian emigration patterns is available from the Washington, DC–based Migration Policy Institute, online at www.migrationinformation.org.

Visit www.pesticideinfo.com to see the Pesticide Action Network's database of pesticides.

The research on Colombian women in floriculture comes from Greta Friedemann-Sanchez, *Assembling Flowers and Cultivating Homes: Labor and Gender in Colombia* (Lanham, MD: Lexington Books, 2006).

Chapter 7: Forbidden Flowers

Facts and figures on Miami International Airport come from Bunny Schreiber, aviation market specialist for the airport.

Statistics on Miami's flower import economy come from the Association of Floral Importers of Florida (www.afifnet.org).

The USDA's manual "Regulating the Importation of Cut Flowers and Greenery" is available online at www.aphis.usda.gov.

Information on floral certification programs comes from interviews with staff and reports published by those programs. See Germany's Flower Label Program at www.fairflowers.de, the United Kingdom's Fairtrade Foundation at www.fairtrade.org.uk, the Swiss Max Havelaar Foundation at www.maxhavelaar.ch, and the Dutch MPS program at www.my-mps.com.

Data on per capita spending and value of imports of cut flowers come from the Flower Council of Holland (www.flowercouncil.org), the United Nations COMTRADE database (www.unstats.un.org), and from Pathfast Publishing (www.pathfastpublishing.com). It is important to note that import values are usually calculated as the landed value of the product when it first arrives in the port. According to the United Nations' COMTRADE database, Germany imported cut flowers and foliage valued at $1,122,977,000 in 2004, and the United States imported $807,416,667. Consumption figures, on the other hand, are expressed as retail value. In 2002 Pathfast Publishing reported that consumers in the United States spent $7,263,000,000 on cut flowers alone, and German consumers spent $3,403,000,000. (These figures were reported in euros, which were roughly equivalent to the dollar at several points in 2002.)

For more information about Organic Bouquet and the VeriFlora program, visit www.organicbouquet.com and www.veriflora.com.

Chapter 8: The Dutch Auction

Statistics on the flowers sold through Dutch auctions can be found at the Web site of the Dutch flower auction association, Vereniging van Bloemenveilingen or VBN (www.vbn.nl). Its 2004 annual report cites sales of 11,847,084,000 cut flowers; 5,057,000,000 of those flowers are sold at Aalsmeer, according to that auction's annual statistics, available at www.vba.nl. As explained in the endnotes for the introduction, statistics on per-stem worldwide consumption are notoriously hard to come by; however, Pathfast Publishing's 2002 consumption statistics estimate the consumption of twenty-six major flower-consuming nations at 22,975,000,000. Using this estimate for worldwide consumption, one can conclude that half the world-wide flower trade occurs through the Dutch auction system.

Statistics on U.S. imports of cut flowers come from the "Floriculture and Nursery Crops Situation and Outlook Yearbook," published by the Economic Research Service of the USDA, www.ers.usda.gov.

For more information about the Aalsmeer auction, visit www.aalsmeer.com, where you can find its annual report and read the history of the auction.

Information on the number of flowers sold at Aalsmeer and headed for the United States comes from the auction's published materials, which cite statistics from the Dutch Floricultural Wholesale Board that Dutch exports to the United States were worth 101 million euros in 2004. Adrienne Lansbergen, press relations officer for the Aalsmeer auction, estimates that about half of those flowers are sold through the auction. This would represent about 5 percent of the flowers sold at auction.

Statistics on average per-stem rose prices at wholesale over time can be found in the annual "Floriculture and Nursery Crops Situation and Outlook Yearbook," available from the USDA's Economic Research Service at www.ers.usda.gov.

Information on Florimex and Multi Color Flowers comes from personal interviews and materials published by the company. See www.florimex.com and www.multicolorflowers.nl.

History of the floral industry and of dyed flowers comes from *A Centennial History of the American Florist* (Topeka, KS: Florists' Review Enterprises, 1997), as well as newspaper accounts.

Chapter 9: Florists, Supermarkets, and the Next Big Thing

Data on the flower purchasing habits of American consumers come from the American Floral Endowment, whose study on consumer trends is available at www.endowment.org. Data also come from the Society of American Florists and from the United States Census Bureau's 1997 and 2002 economic censuses. The Society of American Florists estimates, based on census data, that there are about sixty thousand mass-market outlets selling flowers, and 2002 census data show that there are 48,316 retail florists, including 25,563 that have no employees and 22,753 that do have employees.

Information on the Society of American Florists' ad campaigns, scientific studies, and so on come from published SAF materials available at www.safnow.org, and from interviews with Peter Moran. For more information on the Rutgers study, see Jeannette Haviland-Jones et al., "An Environmental Approach to Positive Emotion: Flowers," *Evolutionary Psychology* (April 2005).

History of the floral industry and of FTD comes from *A Centennial History of the American Florist* (Topeka, KS: Florists' Review Enterprises, 1997).

For more on the early history of florists, see Mary Rose Blacker, *Flora Domestica* (London: National Trust Enterprises, 2000).

Membership and other information about FTD, Teleflora, KaBloom, and 1-800-FLOWERS.COM comes from the companies' Web sites and news reports.

Jeff Brothers is the owner of CAblooms and the general manager of Nature's West Costco floral program. CAblooms is a marketing company specializing in sales to Costco and supermarkets.

Epilogue: Valentine's Day

Statistics on Valentine's Day buying patterns come from the Society of American Florists.

History of the Valentine's Day floral holiday comes from *A Centennial History of the American Florist* (Topeka, KS: Florists' Review Enterprises, 1997) and newspaper accounts.

Selected Bibliography

Aftel, Mandy. *Essence and Alchemy: A Book of Perfumes*. New York: North
    Point Press, 2002.
Amherst, Alicia. *A History of Gardening in England*. London: Bernard
    Quaritch, 1895.
Armitage, Allan. *Specialty Cut Flowers: The Production of Annuals,
    Perennials, Bulbs, and Woody Plants for Fresh and Dried Cut Flowers*.
    Portland, OR: Timber Press, 2003.
Barnard, Charles. *My Ten-Rod Farm; or, How I Became a Florist*.
    Philadelphia: Henry T. Coates, n.d., but ca. 1900.
Bernhardt, Peter. *The Rose's Kiss: A Natural History of Flowers*. Chicago:
    University of Chicago Press, 1999.
Bernhardt, Peter. *Wily Violets and Underground Orchids: Revelations of a
    Botanist*. Chicago: University of Chicago Press, 2003.
Blacker, Mary Rose. *Flora Domestica: A History of British Flower Arranging*.
    London: National Trust Enterprises, 2000.
Campbell-Culver, Maggie. *The Origin of Plants: The People and Plants
    That Have Shaped Britain's Garden History*. Cornwall, England: Eden
    Project Books, 2004.
Capon, Brian. *Botany for Gardeners: An Introduction and Guide*. Rev. ed.
    Portland, OR: Timber Press, 2005.
A Centennial History of the American Florist. Topeka, KS: Florists' Review
    Enterprises, 1997.
Christopher, Thomas. *In Search of Lost Roses*. Chicago: University of
    Chicago Press, 1989.

Coats, Alice. *Flowers and Their Histories*. London: London Hulton Press, 1956.

Coats, Peter. *Flowers in History*. London: Weidenfeld and Nicolson, 1970.

Corbin, Alain. *The Foul and the Fragrant: Odor and the French Social Imagination*. New York: Berg, 1986.

Dash, Mike. *Tulipomania*. New York: Crown, 2000.

Duthie, Ruth. *Florists' Flowers and Societies*. Haverfordwest, England: C. I. Thomas, 1988.

Eiseley, Loren. *How Flowers Changed the World*. San Francisco: Sierra Club Books, 1996.

Elliott, Brent. *Flora: An Illustrated History of the Garden Flower*. Buffalo, NY: Firefly Books, 2003.

Feldmaier, Carl. *Lilies*. London: B. T. Batsford, 1970.

Fleissner, Robert. *A Rose by Any Other Name: A Survey of Literary Flora from Shakespeare to Eco*. West Cornwall, CT: Locust Hill Press, 1989.

Floy, Michael. *The Diary of Michael J. Floy*. New Haven, CT: Yale University Press, 1941.

Gibbons, Bob. *The Secret Life of Flowers: A Guide to Plant Biology*. London: Blandford, 1990.

Goody, Jack. *The Culture of Flowers*. Cambridge, England: Cambridge University Press, 1993.

Gould, Charles J. *History of the Flower Bulb Industry in Washington State*. Mount Vernon, WA: Northwest Bulb Growers Association, 1993.

Halpin, Anne. *The Naming of Flowers*. New York: Harper and Row, 1990.

Henderson, Peter. *Practical Floriculture: A Guide to the Successful Cultivation of Florists' Plants, for the Amateur and Professional Florist*. New York: Orange Judd, 1911.

Hillier, Malcolm. *Flowers: The Book of Floral Design*. New York: Dorling Kindersley, 2001.

Hirahara, Naomi. *A Scent of Flowers: The History of the Southern California Flower Market, 1912–2004*. Pasadena, CA: Midori Books, 2004.

The History of U.S. Floriculture. Willoughby, OH: Greenhouse Grower, 1999.

Hollingsworth, E. *Flower Chronicles*. Chicago: University of Chicago Press, 2004.

Jefferson-Brown, Michael. *Lilies: A Guide to Choosing and Growing Lilies.* New York: Rizzoli, 2004.

Jerardo, Alberto. *Floriculture and Nursery Crops.* Washington, DC: United States Department of Agriculture, 2005.

Kawaguchi, Gary. *Living with Flowers: The California Flower Market History.* San Francisco: California Flower Market, 1993.

Leijenhorst, Leslie. *Hortus Bulborum: Treasury of Historical Bulbs.* Wormerveer, Netherlands: Stiching Uitgeverij Noord-Holland, 2004.

Maharaj, Niala, and Gaston Dorren. *The Game of the Rose: The Third World in the Global Flower Trade.* Utrecht, Netherlands: International Books, 1995.

Manniche, Lisa. *An Ancient Egyptian Herbal.* Austin: University of Texas Press, 1989.

McCann, Jim. *Stop and Sell the Roses: Lessons from Business and Life.* New York: Ballantine, 1998.

McRae, Edward. *Lilies: A Guide for Growers and Collectors.* Portland, OR: Timber Press, 1988.

Morris, Edwin. *Fragrance: The Story of Perfume from Cleopatra to Chanel.* New York: Charles Scribner, 1984.

Morton, A. G. *History of Botanical Science: An Account of the Development of Botany from Ancient Times to the Present Day.* London: Academic Press, 1981.

Pavord, Anna. *The Tulip: The Story of a Flower That Has Made Men Mad.* New York: Bloomsbury, 1999.

Proctor, Michael. *The Natural History of Pollination.* Portland, OR: Timber Press, 1996.

Russell, Sharman Apt. *Anatomy of a Rose: Exploring the Secret Life of Flowers.* Cambridge, MA: Perseus Publishing, 2001.

Schmidt, Leigh. *Consumer Rites: The Buying and Selling of American Holidays.* Princeton, NJ: Princeton University Press, 1995.

Skidelsky, S. S. *The Tales of a Traveler: Reminiscences and Reflections from Twenty-eight Years on the Road.* New York: A. T. de la Mare, 1916.

Ward, Bobby. *A Contemplation upon Flowers: Garden Plants in Myth and Literature.* Portland, OR: Timber Press, 1999.

Webber, Ronald. *Market Gardening: The History of Commercial Flower, Fruit and Vegetable Growing.* Devon, England: David & Charles Newton Abbot, 1972.

Wilder, Louise. *The Fragrant Garden: A Book about Sweet Scented Flowers and Leaves.* New York: Dover, 1974.